# CONTENTS

THE SHILOAH CENTER FOR MIDDLE EASTERN AND AFRICAN STUDIES
THE MONOGRAPH SERIES

# NASSERIST IDEOLOGY
## ITS EXPONENTS AND CRITICS

The Shiloah Center for Middle Eastern and African Studies
Tel Aviv University

*The Shiloah Center is, with the Department of Middle Eastern and African History, a part of the School of History at Tel Aviv University. Its main purpose is to contribute, by research and documentation, to the dissemination of knowledge and understanding of the modern history and current affairs of the Middle East and Africa. Emphasis is laid on fields where Israeli scholarship is in a position to make a special contribution and on subjects relevant to the needs of society and the teaching requirements of the University.*

## The Monograph Series

The studies published in this series are the work of the Research Associates and Visiting Research Associates at the Shiloah Center. The views expressed in these publications are entirely those of the authors.

Uriel Dann / IRAQ UNDER QASSEM
David Kimche / THE AFRO-ASIAN MOVEMENT
Itamar Rabinovich / SYRIA UNDER THE BA'TH 1963–66
Aryeh Yodfat / ARAB POLITICS IN THE SOVIET MIRROR
Benjamin Shwadran / THE MIDDLE EAST, OIL AND THE GREAT POWERS
Nissim Rejwan / NASSERIST IDEOLOGY

# NASSERIST IDEOLOGY
## ITS EXPONENTS AND CRITICS

*Nissim Rejwan*

A HALSTED PRESS BOOK

JOHN WILEY & SONS, New York · Toronto
ISRAEL UNIVERSITIES PRESS, Jerusalem

ISRAEL UNIVERSITES PRESS
is a publishing division of
KETER PUBLISHING HOUSE JERUSALEM LTD.
P.O. Box 7145, Jerusalem, Israel

Published in the Western Hemisphere and Japan by
HALSTED PRESS, a division of
JOHN WILEY & SONS, INC., NEW YORK

**Library of Congress Cataloging in Publication Data**

Rejwan, Nissim.
Nasserist ideology.

"A Halsted Press book."
1. Egypt – Politics and government – 1952–
I. Title.
DT107.83.R42 320.9'62'05 74–2116
ISBN 0–470–71628–2

Distributors for the U.K., Europe, Africa and the Middle East
JOHN WILEY & SONS, LTD., CHICHESTER

Distributed in the rest of the world by
KETER PUBLISHING HOUSE JERUSALEM LTD.
IUP cat. no. 25089
ISBN 0 7065 1406 8

PRINTED IN ISRAEL

# PREFACE

The bulk of the present work was completed in 1970, shortly before Nasser's death on September 28. The concluding chapter was written in its final form late in 1971, when Nasserism as it had been known during Nasser's own lifetime was beginning to lose ground both in Egypt and in other parts of the Arab world. When this Preface was written, very little indeed was left of this once dominant ideology of radical Arab nationalism and pan-Arabism. The slogan, "Nasserism without Nasser," which was raised by Nasser's followers immediately after his death, became largely meaningless. A process of de-Nasserization was started early in the proceedings; its first victims were the so-called "power centres" reportedly led by former Vice-President 'Ali Ṣabri and his followers in high places, who were all demoted in a swift move on May 15, 1971. While no specific ideological significance was attached to the purge, it was nevertheless given the suggestive name *thawrat at-taṣḥīḥ* (the revolution of rectification).

It is to be noted that each of the three years following Nasser's death witnessed the proclamation of a new document which, though making no specific claim to replace the *Charter* or supersede it, introduced some new concepts or reinterpretations of well-established ones. On the occasion of the 19th anniversary of the Revolution, on July 23, 1971, President Anwar as-Sādāt submitted to a special meeting of the National Congress of the Arab Socialist Union (ASU) the text of *barnāmaj al-'amal al-waṭanī* ("The Programme of National Action"), which was essentially what it purported to be – namely a programme for action. Issued in a year that came to be known as "the year of decision" – in which the Egyptian President declared repeatedly that his country would go to war with Israel unless the stalemate in the Middle East crisis were to be broken – the *Programme* concentrated on practical matters. Asserting that during the previous months the ASU had been reorganized and a new Constitution proclaimed, Sādāt said in his introductory remarks that "we [thus] . . . embark on a new phase in the history of our revolution – the phase of building the modern state and . . . the new society which we have chosen for ourselves, the society of dignity, security, tranquillity and affluence." (Text of the *Programme* is printed in *aṭ-Ṭalī'a,* Cairo, October 1971, pp. 165–177.)

The second manifesto proclaimed during Sādāt's regime was more ambitious ideologically. The document, which was approved in August 1972 by a newly formed body called the National Action Committee of the ASU, was given the title, *dalīl al-'amal as-siyāsī w'al-fikrī w'at-tanẓīmī* ("The Guide to Political, Ideological and Organizational Action"). Again, the *Guide* dealt mostly with the reorganization of the ASU, in a way that would make it more effective as a mass organization and "an expression of the alliance of the people's labouring forces." It had some rather harsh things to say about the organization as it had been until then. In the guidelines which he submitted to the Committee Sayyid Mar'ī, then ASU Secretary-General, spoke of "mental adolescence," "the preponderance of personal considerations over objective ones in appraising individuals," "confusion and lack of clarity concerning the relation between the organization and the Executive Power," and "hiding facts from the people." (Text of Mar'ī's guidelines in *aṭ-Ṭalī'a,* May 1972, pp. 12–20.) The *Guide* itself spoke of the ASU's "losing the confidence of the masses," its infiltration by "opportunist elements which . . . were able to create an atmosphere of terror in which the rule of law was weakened," and its use by these elements "to lend a semblance of sham legitimacy to many forms of corruption . . . and injustice."

Apart from these strictures, the *Guide* touched upon several issues of ideology, many of which had been the subject of endless debates since the proclamation of the *Charter* ten years previously. Part Two is devoted to a detailed definition of "Our Socialism" and its theoretical dimensions. The first of these is "the spiritual dimension," which the document finds "in religion and in belief in the divine missions which Islam perfected by its tolerance, its humane values, its ideals and its jurisdiction." Arab Socialism, in its turn, "believes in the existence of basic laws which govern the universe and regulate life," and these laws are drawn from "our heritage and our faith" rather than from "what has been formulated and introduced by socialist thought during the 19th and

20th centuries." One crucial theoretical issue which the *Guide* seeks to resolve is the equation, implicit in the *Charter,* of Arab Socialism and "scientific socialism." "The firm scientific basis of our Socialism," it asserts, "means that it tries to attain its goals of sufficiency and justice on the strength of sound scientific principles . . . . " (Text of the *Guide* is given in full in *aṭ-Ṭalī'a,* October 1972, pp. 96–105.)

President Sādāt's decision on July 8, 1972 to terminate the presence of Soviet military experts and advisors was followed by a gradual but systematic purge affecting reputed left-wingers and ex-communists, though there was no apparent consistency in the trend. However, by the summer of 1973, all the State-controlled news media were out of the hands of known Nasserists and Leftists. Men like Maḥmūd Amīn al-'Ālim Rajā' an-Naqqāsh, Aḥmad Bahā' ad-Dīn, Yūsuf Idrīs, Muḥammad 'Awda and several other political intellectuals whose works are mentioned in this book were pushed aside, their places being taken by known mediocrities, some of them belonging to the traditional Right, others to the pre-revolutionary period.

This process of de-Nasserization, however, was seldom openly conducted on the *ideological* plane. Indeed, echoes of the old controversies as to the precise implications of Nasser's opinions and utterances were heard up to the autumn of 1973, when Egyptian and Arab opinion became totally absorbed in the conflict with Israel following the October war. To give one example, as late as July 26, 1973 President Sādāt found it necessary to refer to the *Charter* as still constituting the regime's credo and ideological guide. In an address delivered before the Central Committee of the ASU on that date, Sādāt spoke of a certain "ideological paper" which he said was being prepared and would be submitted to the forthcoming National Congress of the ASU. The paper, he added, was necessary for "enabling us to interpret the *Charter* so as to avoid attempts at misrepresentation to which it has been subjected." Interpretations given to the *Charter* so far, he explained, "tended to favour one single doctrine – Marxism . . . . The aim of the [ideological] paper now in preparation is to avoid all vagueness and all doubt in this respect." "Our interpretation of the *Charter*," Sādāt concluded, "must spring from the reality of the phase through which we are passing, the reality of the various changes and ramifications which surround us at present." For this purpose, he said, "an open popular dialogue" would be launched in order that all sections of the public would participate in clarifying the issues involved. (Text of address in *al-Ahrām,* July 27, 1973.) It is interesting to note that the popular discussion promised by Sādāt and conducted throughout July, August and September scarcely touched upon any of the major ideological issues dealt with in the *Charter* or the *Guide,* discussion being devoted overwhelmingly to Egypt's position in the changing world constellation which was said to have followed the *détente* between the two superpowers. Until the date of writing, moreover, the "ideological paper" promised by Sādāt was not brought before the National Congress of the ASU.

* * *

The Appendix presented a problem. At first, the intention was to give selections from the *National Charter* dealing with the same subjects covered by the work. However, selection proved difficult owing to the style and internal organization of the document. In the end, both the Shiloah Center and the author thought it advisable to present the *Charter* in its entirety despite its disproportionate length. The official English translation of the work, which was published some time in 1962 by The Information Department, the United Arab Republic, Cairo, is rather poor in quality and contains a number of substantial errors. Although no attempt was made at a complete revision of the translation, a number of alterations were introduced after consulting the Arabic original – and this apart from changes in wording, phrasing, punctuation and paragraphing as well as corrections of printing errors. It is hoped that in its present form the *Charter* is both more readable and closer to the original. Wherever necessary, too, the Appendix has been included in the Index.

Research for the present work was carried out mainly in 1968–1969, when the author was a Research Fellow at the Shiloah Center for Middle Eastern and African Studies, Tel Aviv University. For the variety of help provided by the Center and its staff I wish to express my sincere gratitude. Professor Shimon Shamir, then Director of the Center, read the manuscript and offered many useful suggestions without which the book would have been even less adequate than it now seems. Mr. Mark Tennenboim, on the Center's research staff, was of great help with the tedious work involved in transliteration and also with getting the footnotes into acceptable shape. Mrs. Lydia Gareh, who patiently typed and retyped the manuscript, and Miss Edna Katz were both of great help. In the printing and publishing stage I drew greatly on the knowledge and patience of the staff of Keter Publishing House Jerusalem, who saw the work through to the very end and were most helpful in the compilation of the Index.

Sections of certain chapters in this book have appeared in various magazines and periodicals. For use of this material, my thanks are due to the editors and publishers, among others, of *Midstream, The Jewish Frontier* and *Judaism* of New York; *New Middle East, Jewish Observer & Middle East Review* and *Censorship* of London; *New Outlook, Keshet* and *Amot* of Tel Aviv; and *Molad* and *The Jerusalem Post* of Jerusalem.

Jerusalem, December 1973 *Nissim Rejwan*

# 1. INTRODUCTION: IDEOLOGY AND REALITY

The subject of this book is the ideology of the Egyptian Revolution led by Jamāl Abdel Nasser until his death in 1970. It surveys the various socio-political and cultural ideas which came to be known as Nasserism. To a large extent, the book focuses on the period immediately following the proclamation of the *National Charter,* in May 1962, which should be regarded as the crystallization of Nasserist ideology (see text in Appendix).[1] It was during this period that the public discussion of the ideas of Nasserism was the most vivid and fertile.

Any discussion of Nasserism as an ideology is often challenged with the arguments – quite justified in themselves – that Arab ideologies in general, and Nasserism in particular, are "vague," "not consistent" or "a far cry from the socio-political realities," and thus do not merit serious consideration. To deal with this contention it is necessary to probe briefly into the nature of ideology.

Ideology is a difficult and elusive concept not given to easy definition. Broadly viewed, the ideology of a society can be said to consist of four categories of ideas, beliefs and myths:

1. Popularly accepted ideas about the structure, internal processes and position in the world of a society.

2. Popularly accepted concepts and versions of its history.

3. Popular views and suppositions about man, society and the world which a society or culture uses in justifying and defending its values.

4. Popularly approved values and goals for the society.

It is almost in the nature of the case that the ideology of a society is rarely a perfectly defined, coherent and universally accepted or approved system of values and beliefs, and can seldom be ordered into logically consistent wholes or systems. Nor can it be easily tested against, or made to conform to, the reality it claims to describe, explain or justify. It is the "ideologists" who usually strive to formulate clear and consistent intellectual positions, especially when their ideas and doctrines are challenged or attacked. Accordingly, when dealing with the ideology of a certain regime, epoch, society or group, it is these supposedly clear, consistent and absolute formulations that one must try to adduce. To argue that the system of ideas and beliefs presented by the spokesmen of a regime or society as its ideology is in keeping with the actual state of affairs prevailing in that society or defended by that regime would be beside the point.

The point is that all ideologies deviate from both reality and what we can describe as "truth". As a matter of fact, the term ideology is still often used as a derogatory description of ideas, implying that these ideas are more or less conscious attempts at disguising the real nature of a situation. The disguises and distortions of ideologies range from conscious lies to half-conscious and unwitting ones, from calculated attempts to deceive others to sheer self-deception.

A huge gulf has always existed between political ideologies and the respective realities which they claim to depict, explain or represent. As Raymond Aron has pointed out:

> They express an outlook on the world and a will oriented towards the future. They cannot be described as literally true or false, nor do they belong to the same category as taste or colour. The ultimate philosophy and the hierarchy of preferences invite discussion rather than proof or refutation; analysis of present facts, or prognostications about facts to come, alter with the unfolding of history and the knowledge we acquire of it.[2]

Bierstedt gives a good illustration of this point when he cites the American Declaration of Independence, which states solemnly that all men are created equal. Bierstedt's comment is instructive: "This proposition is an ideology, not a scientific truth. Indeed, we know on scientific grounds that it is false."[3]

The same view is expounded by the American sociologist Harry Johnson: "Every ideology must distort social reality to some extent," even though "popular impressions are never wholly wrong."[4] The proportions in any ideology of "truth" and "error," however, may vary from one case to another. The difference between ideology and science, between an ideologist and a scientist, is that the former seeks facts (if at all) in order to "prove" a belief he has already accepted, while the latter – ideally – suspends judgement until he has deliberately looked for facts that might not be in agreement with his tentative hypotheses.

Yet, in many cases, even works of science, especially those dealing with social phenomena, can be indicative of the prevailing ideology. Indeed, as Johnson puts it, "the organized pressure for ideological conformity is sometimes strong enough to override the institutional safeguards of science, such as academic freedom." It has been known, too, that social scientists, being participating members of their societies, have temporarily and often unconsciously allowed social pressures to influence their scientific "findings."[5]

In asserting, therefore, that a wide gap existed between the ideas or the ideology of the Nasserist regime and the actual facts of life in Egypt, one does not mean to suggest that this phenomenon is in any way peculiar to Egypt or the Arab world. Moreover, even if it had been, this by itself would have had only limited import. The writer does not consider it either fair or right to try to apply Western standards and concepts to the ideologies of non-Western peoples or regimes. Whether liberal, socialist, conservative or Marxist, Western ideologies carry the legacy of a century in which Europe, though aware of the plurality of civilizations, did not doubt the universality of its own message. Even now, when it is "already succumbing to its victory and the revolt of its slaves," Europe hesitates to admit the obvious – namely, that its ideas have conquered the world but have not kept the form they used to have in the European context.[6] Obviously, we cannot delve here too deeply into the theoretical problems raised by the study of aspects of non-Western societies in the process of modernization, beyond pointing out generally that in dealing with the problems confronting these societies one must take into full account the specific circumstances which determine the realities in each country. One of the deepest ironies of the situation with which we are dealing is that the failure to examine the circumstances, of which Western theorists and observers are usually accused, has often been true of the élites themselves in these modernizing non-Western societies. This is not entirely unexpected: having themselves been brought up on Western ideas and Western political ideals, many members of these élites naturally fall into the same errors for which we tend to blame Westerners.

One of the greatest difficulties faced by Arab society, inherent in its historical circumstances, is the difficulty, not to say the impossibility, of establishing any meaningful relation between aspirations and accomplishments. In this context what Gunnar Myrdal has found about the development prospects of the countries of South East Asia applies to the Arab countries in almost every detail. Myrdal writes:

> The most probable development in South Asian countries is undoubtedly a continuation of the present course. Under the banner of a "social and economic revolution," land reform and other institutional changes of a radical character will be talked about and, occasionally, enacted into law in some form. Very little reform will actually be accomplished, and even greater inequality may result from both government policies and developments beyond governmental control.[7]

It was, then, rather natural that a gap – and a wide one at that – should emerge between the lofty ideals of the Egyptian Revolution and the grim, age-old realities of contemporary Egyptian society and culture. Nasser himself, almost ten years after assuming control, was forced to admit this discrepancy in his address to the nation a few weeks after Egypt's merger with Syria collapsed in September 1961. His conclusion was to call for a reformulation of ideas:

> The legacy inherited by the Revolution was a dark and cumbersome one, both in the machinery of government and its conditions and in the sphere of class stratification and its rules . . . We have to embark on a full-scale operation aimed at a reformulation of the values and mores of society.[8]

It was, however, far easier to speak of such a reformulation of values and mores than to do something meaningful about it. There was a time in the not too distant past when Arab intellectuals generally, and Egyptian thinkers especially, used to complain that material progress was not allowed to keep pace with the mental turmoil then becoming apparent in Arab-Islamic society, and this they blamed on sinister imperialistic machinations and the rigidity of local reactionary rulers. Since the Revolution, when their disciples became more or less free to put their ideas into practice, the complaint has been quite different; it is that the intellectual and cultural transformation is failing to keep pace with, and indeed actually delaying, the speedy process of establishing the new society to which everyone seems to aspire.

This curious paradox lies at the root of what Arab intellectuals of the left – and very few of them would today admit they are not left wing – call "the need to deepen the socialist experience." In Egypt, especially, this need is frequently stressed. The implication is that one must get rid of the inherited set of attitudes, mores and beliefs of the contemporary Muslim, which are often diametrically opposed to that essentially Western pace and frame of mind which are prerequisites for establishing a modern socialist society.

Ibrāhīm Sa'd ad-Dīn, then director of the Arab Socialist Union's Socialist Institute, once cited four attitudes which he said were prevalent amongst the Egyptian masses and which he described as being in direct contradiction to the basic values of the socialist transformation. These were: fatalism; absence of faith in science and its findings; slovenliness and refusal to submit to the requirements of organized work; and rejection of any planning or regulation of life. These attitudes, Sa'd ad-Dīn said, ought to be fought "within the ranks of the people, with a view to influencing them, giving them a socialist education, and rooting out old concepts from their minds and hearts."[9]

Sa'd ad-Dīn thus saw a great gulf between the aspirations of the Revolution, which since the middle of 1961 has been introducing drastic and farreaching measures for a genuine socio-economic transformation, and the realities of age-old attitudes and traditional ways of life.

The question as to how to deal with this state of affairs occupies men like Sa'd ad-Dīn, who consider it their duty to propagate the new socialist outlook. Broadly speaking, three guidelines are offered for achieving the intellectual transformation: combating "reactionary" trends amongst the intellectuals; reinterpreting Islam with a view to bringing out its essentially progressive, socialist content; and rewriting Arab and Egyptian history in that light.[10] To achieve the aims of the Revolution, these intellectuals demand, Egyptian society must adopt a new, "scientific" outlook on life. Aḥmad 'Abbās Ṣāliḥ, the Marxist editor of the leading cultural monthly *al-Kātib,* is of the opinion that what he terms "the science of socialism" is "very modern and quite foreign to us" – and this is the reason why it is still a closed book to the masses.[11]

The call for a scientific approach to problems was sounded by President Nasser. In the *National Charter,* candidly laying bare the practical obstacles which the drive toward modernization poses, he asserts that revolutionary action "should be scientific." Nasser continues:

> If the Revolution were to relinquish science it would become a mere emotional outburst enabling the nation to let off steam, but it would not change its state. Science is the true weapon of the revolutionary will. Here emerges the great role to be undertaken by the universities and educational centres on various levels. . . Science is the weapon with which revolutionary triumph can be achieved.[12]

The new norms and values are thus regarded as an instrument of change which is expected to close, eventually, the gap between this ideology and reality.

Before we go into details with regard to the material used, it may be useful to dwell on the actual organization of the survey as far as subject-matter is concerned. Nasserist ideology has, of course, the same characteristic elements as others; thus, the four elements mentioned in the definition of ideology given above can serve to point out the various components of Nasserism as presented in this survey.

The first component – ideas concerning the structure, internal processes, and position in the world of a society – is largely described in Chapters 8 and 9. Chapter 8, "Attitudes to Western Culture," can be said to deal with the accepted views of the society on its position in the world: the self-image of this developing society vis-à-vis the West; the question of modernization and Westernization; the choice of alternative approaches to the modern world. Because of the broad cultural framework of the subject, this chapter draws on material from other Arabic-speaking countries besides Egypt. Chapter 9, "Literature and Society," takes up what has been called "the crisis of the intellectuals" – the role of the man of letters in society and the question of commitment. The heated debates which were carried out between writers holding various opinions on this subject throw much light on a more central and wider theme – i.e., the attitude of the intellectuals towards the regime and its philosophy.

The second component of ideology – the way a society views its own history – is dealt with in Chapters 2, 3 and 4. Chapter 2, "Rewriting Egyptian History," starts with the ideological premises of the rewriting of history and then illustrates how Egypt's ancient history has been rewritten so as to substantiate the Egyptians' self-image as freedom fighters and rebels against feudalism and social injustice. Chapter 3, "The Islamic Factor," deals with the attitude of Nasserist ideology toward the Islamic era in Egypt and Islamic institutions and beliefs. In this chapter there is also a section dealing with current views on the relation of historical and doctrinal Islam to socialism. Chapter 4, "Egyptians and Arabs," deals with views on both Egypt's history and world position. In the main it is a survey of how Egypt's Arabism was seen before and after the July 23 Revolution.

The third element of ideology – the broad outlook on man, society and the world – is covered in Chapters 5, 6 and 7. Chapter 5, "In Search of a Theory," sets the stage, so to speak, for the whole subject by presenting the discussion of the need for a comprehensive philosophy, attitudes to various ideological gropings and, finally, theoretical interpretations of the nature of the July 23 Revolution. Chapter 6, "Placing Arab Socialism," asks where does Arab Socialism stand vis-à-vis communism, social democracy and other experiments in socialism – and whether it is a new, specifically "Arab" brand of socialism or just socialism being applied in Egypt. Chapter 7, "The Problem of Freedom," finally is an attempt to analyse the regime's attitude to such subjects as democracy, representative government, parliaments and personal freedom. In the main it deals with two concepts of freedom which seemed to be contending for influence on Nasserism – the traditional Western liberal view of freedom and the strictly Marxian concept of freedom as a function of economic conditions and the class struggle.

The fourth and final component of ideology – the values and goals of society – is covered, somewhat sporadically, in all the abovementioned chapters, as well as indirectly in the above discussion of the gap separating the values of society and its goals from reality. Closely connected with this aspect of ideology is the theme treated in Chapter 10, "An Autochthonous Culture? " It deals with the problem of cultural identity as reflected in the debate on the existence of an "authentic Egyptian theatre." The concluding Chapter 11 is an attempt to assess "Nasserism as an Ideology." It presents the expressions of frustration at the failure of Nasserism to fill the ideological void and supply a coherent set of values and goals for society.

The sole authoritative source for this enquiry into ideology has generally been the printed and spoken word. It has been shown above that an ideology does not have to reflect faithfully either the actions or actual practices of a regime or society for, in fact, it often contradicts these actions and practices. This is why in studying ideologies one may do without field work of almost any kind. One can, to be sure, try to find out how the tenets and assumptions of an ideology *relate* to facts, actions, truths or practices. In cases where the ideological situation is one of change and fluctuation, one can try to discover which elements and premises of the ideology are in keeping with the norms of the society – or, in other words, how much of the ideology appeals or even makes sense to the common man in that particular society. However, an enquiry on either of these lines – though perfectly legitimate and interesting in itself – would not necessarily be of direct relevance to the study of that ideology, even less to an analytical survey of it. For these reasons – and for other more obvious ones – no attempt was made in this survey to go beyond the printed and spoken word as sources. Needless to say, books, periodicals and newspapers offered the only source for both writing and speech, while radio and television were used to acquire the "feel" of things.

I would place my sources in the following order of importance:

**1. Periodicals**

Most of the ideological literature in Egypt is available in monthlies, quarterlies and a few weeklies. Important material on Egyptian ideologies is included in non-Egyptian publications as well. The main periodicals used in this survey are:

*Al-Kātib,* the theoretical organ – though never openly acknowledged – of the Arab Socialist Union.

*Aṭ-Ṭalīʿa,* published by Dār al-Ahrām and following a distinct Marxist line under the guidance of Luṭfī al-Khūlī.

*Al-Hilāl.* After 1963-4, when control of it was taken over by Aḥmad Bahā' ad-Dīn and its editorship entrusted to Kāmil Zuhayrī, this monthly acquired considerable significance as a source of ideological writing.

*Rose al-Yūsuf.* This is almost the only weekly used extensively and more or less systematically (the other weeklies, such as *Ākhir Sā'a* and *al-Mūṣawwar,* are only occasionally concerned with matters of ideology). Throughout the sixties, almost every significant name in Egypt's ideological constellation participated in this weekly. Its literary section is of particular interest.

*Al-Ādāb.* This non-Egyptian cultural monthly was used extensively in the work because, though it is edited and printed in Lebanon, it is in fact a pan-Arab periodical: Arab intellectuals and men of letters from all over the Arab world publish works in it and its philosophy is a pan-Arab one. The important thing about it is of course that, despite its name, which means "literature", it deals more with ideology and "the literature of commitment" than with detached literary subjects.

*Al-'Arabī.* Published in Kuwait, lavishly printed and generously subsidized by the Kuwait Government. This monthly is edited by Dr. Aḥmad Zakī, a veteran Egyptian scientist and man of letters. Though, like *al-Ādāb,* it is pan-Arab in character, it does not subscribe to the radical pan-Arab philosophy which the Beirut monthly advocates. However, it opens its pages to contributions by radical as well as conservative Arab thinkers, including many from Egypt.

**2. Books**

There is no dearth of books, though curiously the best of them are either compilations of various articles and studies already published in one or another of the periodicals listed above or revised and enlarged versions of such articles. Especially useful were the various series of books and booklets published by Ad-Dār al-Qawmiyya, Ad-Dār al-Miṣriyya, Dār al-Qalam and Dār al-Hilāl. The latter publishes *Kitāb al-Hilāl,* a monthly series of books started in the early thirties. This series became especially "ideological" when Aḥmad Bahā' ad-Dīn took over the general directorship of the al-Hilāl Publishing House. Other series are also well-known: *Kutub qawmiyya* ("Nationalist books"), *Kutub siyāsiyya* ("Political books"), *Ikhtarnā laka* ("We chose for you"), *Ikhtarnā l'il-'āmil w'al-fallāḥ* ("We chose for the worker and peasant"), *Ikhtarnā l'iṭ-ṭālib* ("We chose for the student"). There was also the series of books, about fifty in number, which various professors and lecturers wrote for the benefit of university students whom they had to teach what is called *al-mawād al-qawmiyya* ("nationalist subjects"), which in 1960 were made compulsory additional courses for all university students in Egypt throughout the four years of their undergraduate studies, regardless of their fields of specialization.

**3. Broadcasts**

As indicated above, radio and television broadcasts were used for "background" and in order to get an idea of the atmosphere and the "feel" of things. They were thus never used as a proper source for this study, especially since most of the important material presented on radio and television eventually found its way into print.

NOTES

1 *Mīthāq al-'amal al-waṭani* (Cairo, 1962). Official English Translation, *The Charter,* Information Department (Cairo, n.d.), see Appendix, pp. 193–266. Henceforward called the *National Charter.*

2 Raymond Aron, *The Opium of the Intellectuals* (New York, 1966), p. 236.

3 Robert Bierstedt, *The Social Order, An Introduction to Sociology* (New York, 1963), p. 172.

4 Harry Johnson, *Sociology* (London, 1966), pp. 591-592.

5 *Ibid.*

6 Aron, *op. cit.*, p. 314.

7 Gunnar Myrdal, *Asian Drama: An Inquiry into the Poverty of Nations* (3 vols., London, 1968), Prologue, pp. 5–35.

8 Nasser, in an address to the nation, 5 October 1961; *al-Ahrām,* 6 October 1961.

9 Sa'd ad-Dīn in a symposium *"dawr al-fikr fī al-mujtama' al-ishtirākī"* ["The Role of the Intellect in the Socialist Society"], *al-Kātib,* (Cairo), January 1965, pp. 7–9.

10 *Ibid.*, p. 9.

11 *Ibid.*, p. 13–15.

12 *Charter,* see Appendix, p. 254.

# 2. REWRITING EGYPTIAN HISTORY

In the autumn of 1963, after a protracted public debate which had dragged on for a few years, and in which several prominent historians and intellectuals joined forces in a bid at "rewriting Egyptian history," the Egyptian Ministry of Culture finally decided to name a special commission to plan and supervise this highly interesting operation. The commission, comprising several well-known names in the Egyptian academic world, was headed by Dr. Muḥammad Anīs, Professor of Modern History at the University of Cairo.

This was perhaps the first conscious and freely-publicised official bid at rewriting the history of any country – and as such it took some explaining. In an article published in Cairo's leading daily, *al-Ahrām,* Dr. Anīs himself set out to propound "The Socialist View of the History of our Society" and to lay bare his reasons for embarking on his ambitious project.[1]

Socialism, Dr. Anīs explained, is not merely an economic or political system; it is an all-pervading view of life, "a new ordering of our present and of our future – and also a new evaluation of our past." The socialist view of history is characterized by two main features: first, comprehensiveness, since the evolution of society does not take place in one sphere separately but embraces the political, economic, social and intellectual aspects, none of which can be studied without reference to the whole; second, the premise that historical changes occur as a result of the struggle between social forces.[2]

Viewed in this light, the "Nationalist School" of Egyptian historians has failed, said Dr. Anīs, in that it chose to deal exclusively with the political and historical side of the nationalist movement. If one reads the works of 'Abd ar-Raḥmān ar-Rāfi'ī, one finds his accounts of Muṣṭafā Kāmil and Muḥammad Farīd rather moving and full of heroic deeds – yet one fails to detect the connections between these deeds and the social forces which supported or opposed them, nor does one learn which party enjoyed the support of which social class. In this respect, the "Nationalist School" of historians is evidently less qualified than the "Socialist School". However, it is not only purely historical interpretations which this objective and comprehensive socialist view of history can contribute: it has an actual service to perform at this juncture, in that it furnishes a basis for understanding the changes which are overtaking Egyptian society today. Such an ideological basis is essential, wrote Dr. Anīs, since without it current social developments would appear rootless, rather than the natural extension they in fact are of the struggle between social forces throughout history. "This, indeed, is one of the main goals of rewriting modern Egyptian history," asserted Dr. Anīs.

It is with this end in view, he continued, that the projected study will comprise the history of the following social forces: the working class, local capitalism, foreign capitalism, feudalism, intellectual life and political thought. Since this is to be an objective, scientific study, those in charge of the project have already seen to it that a comprehensive bibliography of all published works on Egyptian history will be compiled, as well as the collection and organisation of all available historical documents.[3]

Finally, Dr. Anīs touched upon the sensitive subject of the "freedom of historical research." This freedom, he wrote, can be likened to other freedoms, such as those of political and economic activity.

> In the same way as it is impossible to grant the forces of reaction freedom to conduct their political and economic activities . . . let us confine intellectual freedom, too, to the national and socialist frameworks. If it is accepted that reaction cannot be allowed to conduct its feudalist or monopolistic-capitalistic activities unchecked, it should be equally clear that the reactionary outlook cannot be allowed to evaluate our history.[4]

Reaction to the project inside Egypt was generally favourable, but there was one weak and almost inaudible dissenting voice. Writing rather timidly, and somewhat obliquely, on the subject in the Cairo weekly *Rose al-Yūsuf* Dr. Aḥmad 'Abd ar-Raḥīm Muṣṭafā related how he had sought the opinion of Egypt's leading man of letters Tawfīq al-Ḥakīm on the subject – though what he wrote subsequently does not make it at all clear whether he was speaking for himself or quoting Ḥakīm. In the past, he wrote, "certain countries tried to write their history from their own points of view. As this naturally affected [the history of] other nations, the latter were not pleased, especially since those who did the rewriting wrote from a narrow point of view and in the pursuit of specific aims, whether it was in Nazi Germany or in Soviet Russia. Our experiment should not be made open to such charges." Dr. 'Abd ar-Raḥīm Muṣṭafā concluded by cautioning his readers that "objective reality, which springs from a deep understanding of human evolution, can serve national aims more than emotional enthusiasm."[5]

Counsel of the kind which Dr. 'Abd ar-Raḥīm Muṣṭafā was offering was not heeded. As a matter of fact, the decision to embark on the new operation was a well-considered one. Dr. Anīs and some of the "socialist historians" had been discussing the project and weighing its pros and cons for some time prior to the Ministry of Culture's decision. In an interview with a reporter from *Rose al-Yūsuf* a year previously, Anīs had put forward his view that all the histories available of the nationalist movement in Egypt and elsewhere in the Arab world were no more than a collection of lies perpetrated by the imperialists and their agents. "History," he asserted, "must be rewritten. During the coming decade I will attempt a reappraisal of the history of the national liberation movements in the Arab world in modern times." Indeed, Dr. Anīs added, he had already decided to direct his graduate students to what the *Rose al-Yūsuf* reporter called "the rectification of history." The aim of this campaign, according to the same source, was to give Egyptian history "a new look – turning it into a history of the Egyptian people rather than of the royal family."[6] We are reminded, too, that the impetus had come from President Nasser himself, who, in his *National Charter,* spoke of Egypt's history as it had been written and taught so far as "counterfeit history."

In his interview, Dr. Anīs explained that the blame for the falsification of recent Egyptian history must be laid at the feet of those who had engaged in writing it, the majority of whom were British and French. He cited a number of examples of what he considered to be wilful distortion of Egyptian history to serve the purposes of the imperialists. One of these was the assassination on February 20, 1919, of Buṭrus

Ghālī, the Coptic Prime Minister, at the hands of a Muslim fanatic called Ibrāhīm Wardānī. British historians, Dr. Anīs said, had tried to distort this episode by insisting that the murder was motivated by religious fanaticism. Their aim was a dual one: to rob the deed of its true patriotic content and to sow the seeds of strife between Muslims and Copts. The truth, Dr. Anīs argued, was that Ghālī was murdered because he was a traitor and a servant of the British, not because he was a Copt. Evidence for this could be construed from the following facts: as Foreign Minister, Ghālī's name was associated with the Treaty of 1899, "which gave the British the right to rule Sudan jointly with the Egyptians"; Ghālī's name was also associated in the minds of the Egyptians with two other national betrayals – namely, the trial of the peasants in the Danshāwī case and the attempt to extend the Suez Canal concession for forty years beyond its original termination date.[7] In marshalling his evidence Dr. Anīs refrained, however, from mentioning a few other interesting points about the Wardānī case, such as the fact that when the assassin was sentenced to death, the Grand Muftī of Egypt issued a *fatwā* (religious edict) invalidating the sentence, partly on the ground that a Muslim who slays an infidel is not liable to the death penalty.

Dr. Anīs, who also cited the cases of Muṣṭafā Kāmil and Aḥmad 'Urābī, claiming that their actions and motives were distorted by imperialist writers of history, did not even spare someone like 'Abd ar-Raḥmān ar-Rāfi'ī, whom he accused of unjustly disparaging 'Urābī and imputing false motives to him. Turning to the more general question of who precisely was to blame for this distortion of Egyptian history, Dr. Anīs told the *Rose al-Yūsuf* reporter:

> The man who is to blame for the presentation of modern [Egyptian] history in this way is King Fu'ād . . . He invited historians from everywhere – Britain, France, America, Switzerland, Spain and all the countries of Europe – to write the history of modern Egypt, and thus many books were written on the splendours of Muḥammad 'Alī's family and its historic deeds. Two of the most important of these books were *Muḥammad 'Alī: The Founder of Modern Egypt,* which was written by a British historian who was paid 500 Egyptian pounds in return, and *Modern Egypt* by Sir Evelyn Baring (Lord Cromer).[8]

These historians, Dr. Anīs went on to say, were given the specific task of glorifying Muḥammad 'Alī and depicting him and his family as heroes. They occupied themselves almost exclusively with military conquests and foreign relations, and ignored the conditions prevailing inside Egypt itself. Even when they were compelled to mention something about domestic developments, he said, they used devious methods to distort the picture.

Dr. Anīs also spoke of the difficulties facing him in his project. Foremost amongst these difficulties, he said, was the unavailability in Egypt of source material, such as proceedings of the British Parliament, the proceedings of the Mandates Commission of the League of Nations and the various journals of the learned societies dealing with Egypt. Another difficulty was the total neglect into which the state's archives had lapsed. The section housing documents in Turkish, for instance, was closed down completely following the death of its last surviving official. As to the documents pertaining to the history of revolutions and national movements, these were housed in the archives of the Presidential Palace, but these records were kept under lock and key, "because they are seething with snakes and scorpions and the authorities do not want to have accidents."[9]

One highly significant aspect of the drive to rewrite Egyptian history has been the attempt to relate the revolutionary socialist ideology of the regime to the country's Islamic legacy. Islam, it has often been argued by the regime and its spokesmen, was in no way at variance with the essence of socialism; the premises of socialism are by no means hostile to the basic precepts of the Islamic faith. What sometimes looked like hostility between the two was the result of a kind of misunderstanding that was not always unintentional: what happened was that for the past ten centuries or so, reactionary interpretations had been advanced as to the character of Islam and its social philosophy. This period started during the Umayyid dynasty, when Islam was alienated from its true egalitarian and democratic tradition of the times of the Prophet and his successors. Now was the time, it was said, to re-establish the link between Islam and socialism, between the Islamic heritage and the modern drive towards social justice and material progress.

It is from this conviction that the vogue for "reviving the heritage" sprang. The difficulty, however, has been how to revive this heritage and, still more crucial, what part of it to revive – and, finally, how to do this without the pitfall of being ensnared by the glories of the past, to the neglect of the present and the future. For the fact is that both the "reactionaries" and the "progressives" profess veneration for the heritage of the past and call for its revival. Both concentrate on what is convenient for them in this heritage and seek to emphasize that part of it which is in keeping with their teachings – and the curious thing is that both find exactly what they set out to find.

Another interesting question which emerges from discussing "the heritage" is that the socialist intellectuals who advocate reviving or maintaining past traditions, however selectively, have never quite been able to decide whether this ought to be done merely to serve as bait to attract the tradition-bound masses, or sincerely and for its own sake. This proved to be a crucial point, since it concerned the whole problem of cultural "belonging" and cultural roots. Those who take their heritage seriously and wish to revive it for its own sake, argue, rather convincingly, that the kind of cultural renaissance which the Arabs seek to bring about today cannot be created in a vacuum. As Kāmil Zuhayrī has put it, even should one wish to escape from one's cultural heritage one finds no way of doing it. Aḥmad 'Abbās Ṣāliḥ argued further that continuity is essential to maintain a nation's identity and personality. In this sense, the future always springs from the past. Ṣāliḥ cited the case of modern European civilization, which, he said, was a continuation of the Graeco-Roman one.[10]

This quest for cultural roots is, however, still rather halfhearted with many Arab intellectuals, quite a number of whom seem satisfied that the Arabs can more or less manage by aping the ways of modern European civilization and acquiring its cultural attributes. No such qualms, however, seem to exist where the rewriting of Arab and Egyptian history is concerned. This, in fact, is seen as one of the main duties of the Arab intellectual, especially in Egypt, whose history was for centuries taught and written in almost total isolation from general Arab history of which – it is now claimed – it comprises an organic part.

Another major complaint against pre-revolutionary history is that its writing and teaching were obviously used for the promotion of the regime's own ends. Rajā' an-Naqqāsh, a young Egyptian writer and literary critic, joins Anīs in accusing King Fu'ād of setting out as soon as he had ascended the Egyptian throne to rewrite Egyptian history, for which purpose "he hired a number of Western scholars known for their wide experience and brilliance – as well as relying on some leading Egyptian historians."

One of these scholars, Naqqāsh asserts, specialised in deciphering documents and twisting their contents in a way that helped to promote the King's purposes. He also specialised in writing history books for schools and colleges. The result, Naqqāsh claims, was that most of the historical information learned by heart by his generation of students was distortions or downright lies, such as the statement that 'Urābī failed in his revolutionary movement "because he rebelled against the country's legitimate ruler."[11]

Another injustice which the rewriting of Egyptian history could and should rectify, it is claimed, is the omission by pre-revolutionary historians of any research into the fortunes of the common people, and their concentration instead on kings and rulers. In this respect, even the universities now lag behind. Until this day, the history departments of Egyptian universities have ignored the part played by the working classes – labourers, peasants, and smallholders – in the liberation movements throughout the country's history. Moreover, there is not a single historical work on the rise of the Egyptian working class and its movements.

Rewriting history was, therefore, one of the ways through which Nasserist intellectuals in Egypt believed they could overcome their society's so-called "intellectual backwardness." Whether or not this particular venture could prove practical or effective was never clear, partly because many of the plans discussed and decided upon had failed to pass the verbal stage. What these plans did appear to show was that what Egypt and the Arab world sought was little short of a "rearrangement" of those forces, opposed to each other yet in a sense complementary, which had governed the Arabs' life for so long.

Examples of the kind of overall revision and "rearrangement" of forces advocated in these appeals abound in Egyptian historical writings and history textbooks during the period in which the subject was so intensively discussed. What must be one of the most glaring of these examples occurs in a history book used in Egyptian elementary schools – an example which makes historical revision appear more like historical "appropriation." In 1960, a controversy raged in the pages of a Beirut

Arab nationalist monthly on the subject "Pharaoh and Muḥammad." In the course of this debate Ibrāhim Wannūs cited a geography book used in the sixth form of elementary schools in Egypt, to the effect that the Arabs "founded flourishing civilizations in the Yemen, Mesopotamia, the Nile Valley, and on the shores of the Mediterranean." As though to strengthen this claim, and in order to leave no room for doubt as to dates, the history textbook used by the same pupils has this to say when speaking of Arab civilization: "The Babylonians in Mesopotamia, the Phoenicians in Syria and the Maghrib [North Africa] and the Ancient Egyptians *(Farā'īna)* and Copts in the Nile Valley – all those people, whom the foreigners have called Semites, are in fact nothing but Arabs."[12]

The writer who cited these passages did so approvingly. He used them, indeed, on the strength of his own arguments and even poked fun at those who wrote about the Pharaohs and the Ancient Egyptians "as though they were not Arabs, and as though they were not descendants of the Hyksos who came to the Nile Valley via the Red Sea and Sinai from the Arab Peninsula." After establishing that elementary school pupils know their history better than those doubting Thomases who question his facts, Wannūs goes on to quote "Nazi race scientists" who, he says, "found a great resemblance between the skulls of mummies of Ancient Egypt discovered in the Nile Valley and skulls excavated near the city of Zufār in the Yemen and in Petra, the ancient Arab city in Jordan – which proved that there was a real physical link between the former and the latter." Unfortunately, however, "the enemies of Nazism destroyed these books after their victory over Germany, since these theories constituted a refutation of all the rival ideologies in the world today, especially communism and capitalism and their derivatives."[13]

But there are other, less crude – if no less interesting – specimens of the rewriting of history. In the summer of 1962, Professor 'Alī Sāmī an-Nashshār, who then occupied the Chair of Islamic Philosophy at the University of Alexandria, created a great academic stir, the like of which Egypt had not experienced since the twenties, by writing a book dealing with the leaders of the Islamic modernist movement in Egypt and the intellectual roots of the Egyptian nationalist movement. In his book, Nashshār condemns in a most off-handed and unceremonious way such founding fathers of modern Islamic reform and Egyptian nationalism as

Shaykh Mūḥammad 'Abduh, Aḥmad Luṭfī as-Sayyid, former Shaykh of al-Azhar Muṣṭafā al-Marāghī, Sa'd Zaghlūl and Dr. Ṭaha Ḥusayn, as traitors both to their country and to their faith. The gist of Nashshār's thesis, which he had propounded to his students for some time in a course on the works of 'Abduh and his teacher Jamāl ad-Dīn al-Afghānī, was that 'Abduh and his followers were nothing but stooges of Lord Cromer. In his introduction, extracts of which were first published by the Cairo weekly *Ākhir Sā'a,* Nashshār contends that Cromer, when he was "absolute ruler of Egypt," sought to break the morale of the Egyptian nation and to destroy its religion, and that he found in 'Abduh the man who could perform this task for him.

How Cromer managed to do this was simple enough, it seems – namely, just by opening for 'Abduh the door to Madame Nazlī Ḥalīm's famous salon. Now this lady was Cromer's "own eye and instrument in destroying Egypt intellectually, politically and morally," and 'Abduh, by entering her salon, lost all his learning, honour and majesty: "Alas! The turban fell from his head, and he betrayed both his country and his religion. In Ḥalīm's salon 'Abduh sold everything – and how miserable were his sales and his purchases! " In this way, 'Abduh's celebrated school was set up.

> Only traitors graduated from this school, Qāsīm Amīn, Tawfīq al-Bakrī, Sa'd Zaghlūl . . . the Umma (People's) Party . . . and then Taha Ḥusayn and his school, which I would call the Modern European School. It is a very long story, which reveals a black record stained with the blood of the Egyptians and characterized by an attempt to destroy their beliefs. They have fought Islam intellectually and politically . . . This was the circle that worked with Cromer and disseminated its poisons into Islam's political and cultural history.

These are only some of Nashshār's rather unflattering views on 'Abduh and his circle, whose reputations none of the protagonists and followers of the Nasserist revolution had until then dared to touch. What is curious in Nashshār's attitude, therefore, is that he does not hesitate to lean on the Revolution: in reply to *Ākhir Sā'a's* enquiries as to the timing of his onslaughts, he said: "The Revolution came and destroyed the political idols; but the intellectual idols remain, with the great dangers they pose to our political and cultural thinking." Asked to elaborate on the other victims of his wrath, Nashshār explained that Fatḥī Zaghlūl – Sa'd's brother and a pioneer of modern Arabic translations from English and French – was a great admirer of the English, having translated such of their thinkers as Herbert Spencer and John Stuart Mill, "in order to spread atheism in Egypt at the time." As to Marāghī, "he was obviously a British agent while he worked in the Sudan; and when he was appointed Shaykh of al-Azhar he tried to implement 'Abduh's reform policy there."[15]

Similar "evidence" against others was not lacking. 'Alī 'Abd ar-Rāziq, one of the most prominent figures in modern Egyptian thought, "studied at Oxford." The British Embassy directed 'Abd ar-Rāziq to write his controversial book on the principles of Islamic government, with a view to translating it into English and Urdu "so that the British could silence the great revolution in India." 'Abduh's school, in short, produced only those who "betrayed Egypt in her thought and in her culture." Luṭfī as-Sayyid, for example, who in his old age was named the "Teacher of the Generation," was "a functionary of the Umma Party, which opposed the country's national aspirations and was financed by the British Embassy . . . He used to fight Muslim nationalism, and proclaimed that we are not Arabs and have no connection with the Arabs." He was also guilty of advocating the use of colloquial Egyptian Arabic, "with a view to eliminating any possibility of a future Arab union." The British, Nashshār declared, were behind all this. They had, he implied, a master plan to destroy the Arabs' unity, among other things by "teaching them that they are not Arabs and through promoting Pharaonic, Assyrian, and Babylonian nationalisms."[16]

Compared to the conventional view of the Islamic reform movement started by Afghānī and continued by 'Abduh, Rashīd Riḍā, 'Abd ar-Rāziq and their colleagues, Nashshār's findings seem far-reaching. The fact of the matter, however, is that the Alexandria professor was reviving what is largely an old controversy, though it must be admitted that in the Arab world at least the debate had never been articulated in quite the same terms.

Whatever Nashshār's real motivation was – sincere conviction, out-and-out debunking, a retroactive settlement of accounts, or a desire for sheer notoriety – reactions to his work were varied and rather confused. One reason for this was no doubt that the regime itself had not elaborated a clear attitude to the leaders of the modernist movement in Islam and their followers. In his *National Charter,* for instance, Nasser was somewhat non-committal. Surveying Egypt's record of patriotic deeds, he said, after mentioning 'Urābī's movement amidst prolonged cheers: "During this period, Muḥammad 'Abduh's voice was raised for religious reform. . . . Luṭfī as-Sayyid's voice proclaimed that Egypt was for the Egyptians . . . Qāsim Amīn agitated for the emancipation of women . . . and Sa'd Zaghlūl rode on the crest of the new revolutionary wave leading the stubborn popular struggle."[17]

But the rewriting of history has affected far remoter areas of the Egyptian past. That the lead in this drive was given, and the tone set, by the regime itself can be seen from the way the country's leaders treated historical events on certain occasions. A few illustrations will suffice. Louis IX, the 710th anniversary of whose defeat and capture at Manṣūra in 1250 was celebrated by the Egyptians with a good deal of pomp, was, in the words of a noted historian, "a secular saint, who formed his life on moral and religious principles and whose aim was the salvation of souls . . . . Never was a king more dearly and deservedly loved."[18] In 1244, roused by the Latins' crushing defeat in the battle of Gaza, Saint Louis embarked on preparations for his first crusade (1248–1254). His expedition was a remarkable replica of the Fifth Crusade, "pursued with the same aims and the same ignorant unwisdom"; he took Damietta (Damyāṭ) easily in 1249, but on his way to Cairo was defeated and besieged in Manṣūra, and compelled to surrender, subsequently buying his freedom with Damietta and a huge ransom.

This was a rather dismal episode in the career of a fanatical Christian King who considered the Crusade to the Holy Land to be his chief aim in external affairs. It was, however, disproportionately inflated by Nasser into an "epoch-making" historical event furnishing evidence that "nothing can stand in the way of a unified Arab nation." In the speech he made at Manṣūra on May 7, 1960, Nasser described the French King's defeat as a victory for Arab nationalism – an early page, as it were, in the history of the Egyptian regime's own pan-Arab cause.[19] For sheer inaccuracy this claim can hardly be topped. Not only is Arab nationalism less than a century old, but the whole Manṣūra affair had little, if anything, to do with Arabs. A few months before Louis IX was captured, the Sulṭān of Egypt, aṣ-Ṣāliḥ – himself of Kurdish extraction – died, and nominal power passed to his widow, a former slave-girl, while the Turkish and Circassian slaves were already assuming real control over the country. Sulṭān aṣ-Ṣāliḥ was the son of Ṣalāḥ ad-Dīn and was able, with a force of Khwarizmi Turks who had fled before Chingiz Khan, to reconquer Jerusalem and Damascus; he thus reconstituted almost the entire empire of Ṣalāḥ ad-Dīn as far as Aleppo and Mesopotamia. Nasser made much capital out of the fact that aṣ-Ṣāliḥ was lingering in Damascus, ill, when he was surprised by St. Louis' incursion into Egypt. Then as now (Nasser implied) Arab Syria came to the rescue of Arab Egypt; the Arab armies of Syria, united under a single command with the Arab armies of Egypt, managed to defeat the Western imperialist of over 700 years ago – exactly as they did in 1956, when the Anglo-French forces, direct descendants of the invaders of 1249–50, were defeated by triumphant Arab nationalism!

Going still further back, Egyptian spokesmen of the regime – professional as well as amateur historians – have extended this operation far back into Egyptian history, as far back in fact as the time of the earliest Pharaohs. A book published in 1966 by Muḥammad al-'Izb Mūsā, for instance, carries the title *The First Revolution against Feudalism.* On closer inspection it emerges that the revolution in question was none other than the violent events which took place during the time of the Twelfth Dynasty, which at first was very decentralized and has loosely been called a "feudal" state. "The tight control of the Pharaohs of the early Old Kingdom would not be regained. The centrifugal forces had been too powerful, and the spirit of the early Middle Kingdom was highly individualistic."[20] The transition from the Old to the Intermediate Kingdoms was accompanied by upheavals. The situation in the First Intermediate Kingdom is still shrouded by uncertainties. There were new movements of people in higher Asia, and the restlessness could not but affect the Egyptian Delta when the central authority collapsed. "It would be wrong," writes one historian, "to think of this in terms of an armed and unified invasion; probably there was only a constant trickle of small tribes."[21]

Obviously, it was a time of violence and great confusion, but there has not been any evidence of a "revolution." The author of *The First Revolution against Feudalism,* however, adduces "evidence" of "a colossal popular revolution which resulted in the destruction of many of the great ancient cities, and in which shrines and cemeteries were looted . . . and statues of the Pharaohs were tossed into the wells of the pyramids." Yet all the historical evidence presented by the author consists of a historical document which, he writes, "tells us in highly detailed description and fine analysis of the events of that revolution and its effects."[22]

The fact of the matter, however, is that the First Intermediate Period has left us a considerable body of literature depicting the bewilderment and despair with which the Ancient Egyptians faced the upheavel of their once stable world. These documents agree in expressing a sense of shock and grief at the sorry state of the land, and propose different antidotes for the troubled times: suicide, oblivion, indulgence, or the return of good rule. It is on two of these documents that Mūsā builds his edifice of the great anti-feudalist revolt. One was written by the prophet Ipu-wer,[23] whose weariness with life led him to suicide. The other was likewise written by a prophet, Nefer-rohu. Dismayed by the events and upheavals he witnessed in his lifetime, Nefer-rohu added his voice to that of Ipu-wer: "This land is helter-skelter, and no one knows the results . . . . I show thee the land topsy-turvey, that which never happened had happened. Men will take up weapons of warfare, so that the land lives in confusion."[24]

It is on the strength of these two documents, both probably written during the reign of the Eleventh Dynasty, that Mūsā builds up his imposing historical construction. To be sure, he admits in at least two places in the course of his account that "no one knows for certain" when and why the great revolution took place, but he insists that "Ipu-wer's statements describe the revolution at its peak," and that "we learn from these statements that it was a total revolution that brought down the country's government and destroyed the political, economic, social and intellectual foundations of the community." In Mūsā's estimate, furthermore, the revolution was "a class revolution in the full sense of the term . . . and is considered to constitute the oldest manifestation of class struggle in the whole of history."[25]

Again, according to Mūsā's reconstruction, Nefer-rohu's lamentations "depict the intellectual, political and social consequences of the revolution, which indicates that the writer had not witnessed the events himself."[26] Thus there ensue lengthy accounts of the intellectual, religious and economic effects of the revolution as well as the upheaval it brought to political life.

Mūsā's book constitutes only one of the attempts made by the Egyptian revolutionary intellectuals to rewrite and reinterpret the history of their country and of the Arabic-speaking peoples in general. One of the main aims of these attempts has been to show that, far from the passive, suffering and fatalistic people they are often taken to be by historians and observers, the Egyptians are a struggling, proud nation which has always resisted oppression and risen against tyranny. "There is," Mūsā writes, "no libel more baseless than to accuse the Egyptians of submission to oppression and enslavement – a libel disseminated by the imperialists and the enemies of the people through the ages as a sort of psychological warfare against the Egyptians." The truth belies this accusation completely, Mūsā goes on. "The Egyptians are a people who always exude vitality and dignity – and no matter how long the dark periods through which they pass and irrespective of the troubles and the crises which befall them, they never lose their distinctive personality . . . They ultimately destroy their fetters."[27]

There is, in fact, no people in the whole world that has known revolutions and was moulded by them like the Egyptian people, Mūsā concludes. To prove this he lists, in his conclusion, a number of revolutions instigated by the Egyptians against their oppressors and detractors. There was, to start with, "the first revolution against feudalism which marked the end of a whole period of Egyptian history" and which forms the subject of the book under discussion. This revolution "opened a new record distinguished for the first time (in history) by recognition of equality between men and by religious democracy." Secondly there was "the people's revolt against the Hyksos and their expulsion into the depths of the desert whence they had come." There was, thirdly, "that great intellectual and spiritual revolution which Egypt experienced during Akhnaton's reign." After this comes Basmatik's revolt against Assyrian occupation and his founding of the Twenty-Sixth Dynasty, which worked for the restoration of Egypt's glory by drawing inspiration from the culture of the ancient state. Again, during the reign of the Twenty-Seventh Dynasty, the Egyptians staged several revolts against the Persians, who conquered their land and tried to destroy their way of life. There was also the Egyptians' uprising against the Romans and their commanders in the Nile Valley. Mūsā then lauds the Copts' resistance to religious persecution; "the positive role which Muslim Egypt played in the Islamic world and the prominent cultural position that it occupied during the Middle Ages; and Egypt's leading role in breaking the waves of barbaric conquerors such as the Mongols and the Crusaders."

Turning to the period since the Turkish conquest, Mūsā enumerates the uprisings against the Mamluks and the Ottoman *wālīs*. The modern period likewise witnessed "great and proud revolutions," starting with the violent revolt against French occupation. Then came the revolution led by 'Urābī, "the commander of the peasants' army," against internal oppression and external danger; the 1919 Revolution "which witnessed the movement of the popular blocs for the sake of freedom and independence"; and finally the 1952 Revolution "which crowned the long struggle of the Egyptian people and gave it freedom and socialism."[28]

After reciting this long record of revolts and revolutions Mūsā wonders if anyone can still claim that the Egyptian people is submissive. The truth is, he writes, that the revolutionary spirit is an inseparable part of the Egyptian personality, and the flame of revolution blazes all the time under the surface – and this is one of the most important factors which contributed to the preservation of Egypt's being despite everything. For it is one of the greatest errors to argue that there is a real discontinuity between one phase of Egyptian history and another. "There is no such discontinuity between Muslim and Coptic Egypt, between Coptic Egypt and Hellenic Egypt and between Hellenic Egypt and Pharaonic Egypt. The eclipse of the civilization of the Pharaohs after the fall of the Thirty-First Dynasty does not signify an unbridgeable gap between Pharaonic Egypt and the periods which followed."[29]

According to Mūsā, Egyptian history forms an organic whole. "It is an historical error, too, to claim that Egypt lost its independence when the Persians invaded it in the fourth century B.C., and that since that time it has passed through various kinds of occupation and domination. As Dr. Ḥusayn Fawzī writes in his *Egyptian Sindbad,* "Egypt does not lose its independence even when it is ruled by foreign dynasties . . . Egypt loses its independence when it is reduced to the status of *wilāyā* and when it is then ruled by kings, patriarchs, caliphs or sulṭāns who live in capitals outside Egypt." Finally, Mūsā cites a curious set of statistics: Egyptian history goes back some 5,000 years. Of this long history, Egypt enjoyed full independence for a total of 3,500 years, during which time Egyptian dynasties ruled it for 2,500 years, while foreign ones reigned for 1,000 years. A nation that lives 5,000 years, during 3,500 of which it remains independent – i.e. some 70 per cent of its whole history – is this not a truth that must be hammered into the heads of the young? [30]

## NOTES

1 *Al-Ahrām*, 10 July 1963.

2 *Ibid.*

3 *Ibid.*

4 *Ibid.*

5 *Rose al-Yūsuf*, 8 July 1963.

6 *Ibid.*, 2 July 1962.

7 *Ibid.*

8 *Ibid.* The former book by British historian Dodwell; the latter book was written in 1907.

9 *Ibid.*

10 Kāmil Zuhayrī and Aḥmad 'Abbās Ṣāliḥ, in a symposium *"mashākil at-taḥawwul al-fikrī"* ["Problems of Mental Transformation"], *al-Kātib* (Cairo), January 1965, pp. 12–13.

11 Rajā' an-Naqqāsh, *ibid.*, pp. 13–14.

12 Ibrāhīm Wannūs, *"munāqashāt"* ["Discussions"], *al-Ādāb* (Beirut), April 1960, p. 65.

13 *Ibid.* It is curious that a rejoinder to these claims came from a citizen of what then was the Northern Region of the U.A.R. (Syria). Writing in the next issue of the same monthly, 'Alī Muḥāfaẓa, a student at the College of Education, Damascus University, points out: "If the aim of the statement quoted from the (history) school book is nationalist indoctrination, we must note that nationalist indoctrination in the teaching of history does not mean that we should distort facts. Fidelity to facts in historical surveys is of more benefit to the nation and to nationalism than forgery and misrepresentation." The claim, he adds, that the Babylonians, the Egyptians, the Phoenicians and the Copts are Arabs needs qualification and explanation. "The Arabs belong to the Semitic family, and Semitism is not a race but a linguistic group, and the languages

of the (Semitic) peoples have many things in common as far as grammar, the alphabet, verbs and derivations are concerned – in the same way as the group of Latin languages are interrelated." Besides, he goes on, "the textbook omitted to mention the Hebrews, who also belong to the Semitic group, and it ignored the great resemblance between Hebrew and other Semitic languages" (*Al-Ādāb* [Beirut], May 1960, p. 62).

14 Quoted in *Ākhir Sā'a,* 11 March 1962.

15 *Ibid.*

16 *Ibid.*

17 *Charter,* see Appendix, p. 208. Reactions to Nashshār's views from authoritative spokesmen of the regime were understandably rather unhelpful. However, these did not seem to have been unduly shocked. In fact, there has always been sharp criticism of those veteran Egyptian intellectuals, who can be considered 'Abduh's very last disciples – 'Abbās Maḥmūd al-'Aqqād, the writer, and Dr. 'Uthmān Amīn, Professor of Philosophy at Cairo University – who, incidentally, were among those who tried to incite the authorities against Nashshār and called for banning his book. Bahā' ad-Dīn, editor of *al-Akhbār,* welcomed the opening of the controversy and thought that such debates were healthy, while a writer in the monthly *al-Kātib* expressed shock at Dr. Amīn's urgent telegram to Nasser saying that Nashshār's activities ought not to be tolerated.

Under the significant title, "Those Who Burned Joan of Arc," the *al-Kātib* writer submits that 'Aqqād and Amīn were fully entitled to refute Nashshār's views by furnishing evidence to the contrary and through quiet academic discussion. "That the two venerated masters should discard this basic duty and resort to inciting the powers-that-be and invoking the law against the man who holds views opposed to their own is something which I believe has shocked all those who value the right of free expression" (*al-Kātib* [Cairo], June 1962).

18 C.W. Previte-Orton, *The Shorter Cambridge Medieval History* (Cambridge, 1955), p. 711.

19 Text of Nasser's speech, *al-Ahrām,* 8 May, 1960.

20 John A. Wilson, *The Culture of Ancient Egypt* (Chicago, 1951), p. 106.

21 *Ibid.*

22 Muḥammad al-'Izb Mūsā, *awwal thawra ḍidd al-iqṭā'* ["The First Revolution Against Feudalism"] (Cairo, 1966), pp. 13–14.

23 Wilson, *op. cit.*, pp. 106–107.
24 *Ibid.*, pp. 107–108.
25 Mūsā, *op. cit.*, 69–70.
26 *Ibid.*, p. 82.
27 *Ibid.*, p. 147.
28 *Ibid.*, pp. 147–149.
29 *Ibid.*, pp. 149, 155.
30 *Ibid.*, p. 156.

# 3. THE ISLAMIC FACTOR

Without trying to answer the question as to whether, even in the purely religious realm, there exists today, in empirical fact, an entity to which the name "Islam" can meaningfully be applied, it is apparent that no study of the dominant ideology of a Muslim country can be undertaken without reference to the Islamic factor. This is not tantamount to saying that religious faith plays a leading role in the formulation of that ideology, or even that it constitutes one of its important components. The whole subject of Islam's place in the life and political conduct of contemporary Muslim Arabs is a rather complex one and has been amply discussed by other writers. Although many Muslim-Arab thinkers have of late attempted to find out whether their faith can offer them anything by way of a coherent socio-political ideology, these attempts have, almost with no exception, been superficial, repetitive and apologetic. Believing and observant Muslim thinkers have merely kept on asserting that Islam – as a faith, a philosophy and a way of life – does not stand in opposition to socialism since it too advocates the equitable distribution of income; it also, they claim, supports Arabism since Muḥammad was himself an Arab and Arabic is the language of the Qur'ān.

It is commonly held, for instance, that the Islamic system of government is fundamentally a democratic one. 'Abbās Maḥmūd al-'Aqqād (1889-1964), one of modern Egypt's most respected Muslim thinkers, wrote that if we were to describe the system of government which the Qur'ān decrees in terms of the modern state, then that system must be described as "democratic government in its soundest form." This is because Islamic government is based on consultation *(shūrā)*, equality and the prevention of personal domination. He naturally finds no difficulty in supporting his assertion, largely by quoting Qur'ānic ordinances such as "Their [ the believers'] communal business is [to be transacted in] consultation among themselves"; or "Consult them in [all] communal business"; or "The Faithful are but brethren." The same treatment is given by 'Aqqād to the subject of equality and social justice, which he also considers as being two pillars of Islamic government.[1]

But while this has been the accepted way of generalizing the social and political principles of Islam by Muslim-Arab thinkers in recent times, there is now a somewhat more cautious approach to the subject – an approach which refrains from clearly identifying Islam with any of the accepted "-isms" of our time. Generally speaking, this reserve about equating Islam with existing socio-political philosophies has been justified on two grounds. The first is that it would be wrong to apply indiscriminately Western political terms and ideas to the entirely different concept of Islamic polity and social order. "Not infrequently," writes the Pakistani Muslim scholar Muḥammad Asad – who, by virtue of his European breeding, is at home in both Western and Muslim concepts – ' we find in the writings of modern Muslims the assertion that 'Islamic is democratic' or even that it aims at the establishment of a 'socialist' society; whereas many Western writers refer to an alleged 'totalitarianism' in Islam which must necessarily result in dictatorship." Such attempts at political definition, Asad adds, are superficial, mutually contradictory and "carry with them the danger of looking at the problems of Muslim society from the angle of Western historical experience alone and, thus, of envisaging developments [that] . . . may be wholly out of place within the world-view of Islam." Asad continues:

> One should always remember that when the European or American speaks of "democracy," "liberalism," "socialism," "theocracy," "parliamentary government," and so forth, he uses these terms within the context of Western historical experience. Within this context, such terms have not merely their legitimate place but are also easily understandable: They immediately evoke mental pictures of what has actually happened or might conceivably happen in the course of the West's historical development, and can therefore survive the changes to which the passage of time subjects all human concepts. More than that: The very fact of conceptual change – the fact that many of the political terms current today bear a meaning different from that originally given to them – is ever present in the mind of a Western thinker; and this awareness confers upon him the ability to view his political terminology as something that is in constant need

of revision and readjustment. This flexibility of thought disappears, however, as soon as a political concept is taken over ready-made by people who belong to a very different civilization and have, therefore, passed through different historical experiences. To such people the political term or institution in question appears, as a rule, to be endowed with the absolute, unchanging meaning which does not take into consideration the fact of its historical evolution and, consequently, contributes to the very rigidity of political thought which the new conceptual acquisition had sought to remove.[2]

The second ground on which Islam must not be identified with any modern socio-political " ism," we are told, is that in reality the Qur'ān does not specifically decree or recommend any particular system of government. It is true, writes Fatḥī Raḍwān, a well-known Egyptian thinker and a former Minister of National Guidance, that certain *sūras* in the Qur'ān counsel "consultation"; it is also true that the Qur'ān commands the Muslim to be guided by the principles of justice, "but apart from this the student is unable to find any body of precepts on the basis of which he can assert that the Qur'ān has laid down a specific system through which people are commanded to select their rulers. Nor has the Qur'ān laid down any rules defining relations between ruler and ruled, or specifying what is allowed and what is not allowed for each of them to do." That the Qur'ān has thus refrained from being specific about the precise system of government which Islam would favour was no coincidence, argues Raḍwān. "Islam," he explains, "is a system that is valid for all times and places, whereas systems of government are among the most mutable of human phenomena and are liable to be affected by the passage of time . . . . What is good for people in a certain period becomes intolerable in another, and what would suit them in one country may prove unworkable in another." Even more important, however, is Islam's unique system of jurisdiction. "The basis of Islamic jurisdiction is moral education," writes Raḍwān. "Instead of control by the state, with its policemen and watchmen, [Islam] sets up control through man's conscience."[3] For similar reasons Islam emphasizes the *morals* rather than the *system* of government; it is these morals that count: if they are adhered to, government becomes good; if they are neglected, then no amount of written ordinances, rifles, guns, courtrooms or jails would be of any consequence.

Islam as such, whether or not it lays down a specific system of government, has in practice never been taken by the educated, politically-conscious contemporary Muslim Arabs to entail the kind of socio-political ideology deemed necessary for the establishment and maintenance of a modern state. We thus find that, while professing whole-hearted adherence to Islam and its premises, the overwhelming majority of present-day Muslim Arab thinkers and political activists continue to toy with the leading socio-political ideologies of the day, examining the merits and demerits of these ideologies from the viewpoint of their suitability to their own situation. In addition, there have been a few supposedly native ideologies propounded by certain radical Arab groups, like the Nasserists and the Ba'th Party followers. As it will be shown, however, none of these ideologies was to be the panacea which its proponents made it out to be.

Faced thus with the apparent failure of both imported ideologies – Western-type democracy, communism, democratic socialism – and home-grown ones like Nasserist and Ba'thist Arab Socialism, some of these thinkers turned again to religion, and the more religious-oriented among them pinned their hopes on an "Islamic ideology" which they maintained would answer the modern Muslim's problems in every conceivable sphere. In a series of nine articles in the Jordan daily *al-Manār* in 1964, an anonymous writer summed up the Arabs' experience in the ideological sphere during the previous decade or so, and reached the conclusion that the Arab nation "never enjoyed a comprehensive ideology except under the State of the Prophet Muḥammad and his great Caliphs, Abū-Bakr and 'Umar."

The modern Arab's experiences in this field he finds epitomised in Iraq's experience after the 1958 revolt, where he claims both communism and Ba'thism proved to be utter failures and totally incompatible with the Arab temper. Communism, he explains, is "foreign to the Arab environment, remote from Arab traditions, contradicts the spirit of religiosity of the Arabs, incompatible with Arab morality . . . and robs man of his political freedom," and was thus doomed to failure.

The Ba'th ideology was no better. Following a period of confusion and probing, the Arabs were offered – again in Iraq – a practical illustration of that party's bankruptcy. Preaching so-called pan-Arab slogans, the Ba'th promised pan-Arab unity extending "from the Atlantic Ocean to the Persian Gulf" and offered a genuine Arab ideology emanating from the Arabs' actual condition and conforming to Arab traditions and Arab history. The Arabs were soon to discover, however, that the Ba'th was devoid of any ideology and had nothing to offer besides slogans – that Ba'thism was in fact "a distorted version of communism, adopting its principles and philosophy, its morality and political system of government, and practising the same terror." Even as communism failed, so did its "Ba'thist version."

And so again, the writer adds, "for the third or tenth time, our Arab Nation found itself facing the same ideological void." What is to be done then? Since, as was noted above, the Arabs never had anything like an all-embracing political, social and economic ideology except under Muḥammad and his caliphs, it follows that they should now return to that ideology. To be sure, the writer goes on to point out, ever since that short interlude of political bliss and stability, a host of "interested parties" managed to deal blow after blow to this ideology – right up to the emergence of Western imperialism. But the Palestine catastrophe "shattered all that," and the various political parties which emerged afterwards themselves evaporated into thin air when faced with the test of reality.

Thus, today the Arab masses again long for an ideology "that would safeguard independence and the building anew of an Arab being free from division, poverty, ignorance, unemployment and backwardness." Where can they find such an ideology? The writer's reply is straightforward: "Go back to your religion, your true element, your heritage and your history. There you will find the all-embracing ideology. Study your present condition and problems and adapt that ideology to the new circumstances and the new times." In doing so, however, the modern Arab should not for one moment desert the basic principles of this ideology, "which proved its spectacular success fifteen centuries ago."

But what of the true nature of this all-embracing ideology? The writer gives little guidance here, except by offering what he thinks the Arab masses would like to see in such an ideology: first, a philosophy offering an explanation of history and the universe and which should be derived from religion; secondly, a realistic code of morality emanating from that philosophy; thirdly, a political system based on consultation, on democracy and on respect for the rights of the individual; fourthly, an economic system that would attain social justice in its most pronounced form. Unless based on the tenets of Islam, the writer concludes, the nationalism which many Arabs now preach will be no more than "a castle built in the air."[4]

Judging by other writings in this field, the above reads like a rather well-presented articulation of the case for a return to pristine Islam. Yet it is by no means a coincidence that the writer, eloquent as he is in defending Islam's tenets and ideology, fails to offer a reply to – or even to formulate – the question as to what, in practical terms, the "all-embracing ideology" of which he speaks can actually offer.

The problem, of course, is not new. It inevitably involves a whole set of problems pertaining to Islam's place in the modern world. The history of Islam in modern times has indeed been largely that of the modern Muslim's attempts to adjust himself and his world outlook to the situation created by his encounter with Western culture and Western ways. The modernist movement in Islam, which appeared in Egypt toward the end of the last century, can be described as an expression of the necessity of an intellectual and practical response, within the religious faith, to the pressure of new circumstances and ideas as they bear upon traditional dogma and behaviour. The movement's driving force was the desire to demonstrate, in practical terms and in response to specific, concrete issues, that Islam was equal to the needs and demands of the modern world. Its protagonists and leading exponents were informed by a desire to rid Islam of a backward-looking mentality which they thought disqualified its followers from participation in a progressive, forward-looking sort of life. They sought to destroy the spirit of "obscurantism" which encouraged authoritarian loyalties to old schools of law and custom and barred the introduction of reasonable change.

Yet Islamic modernism did not intend any far-reaching theological reconstruction. The basic theological and orthodox doctrines of Islam were not, except in very rare cases, directly challenged in the debates of the modernists, whose main emphasis was on institutional adaptation and adjustment to new situations and on the liberation of the minds and ways of men from crippling restrictions imposed by *taqlīd,* i.e. slavish imitation of traditional interpretations. Though it is true that some of the achievements of the movement have had important doctrinal implications, these have tended to be only indirect and sometimes unconscious, and one can conclude with fairness that the modern reform movement in Islam, and especially in the Arab world, did not attempt any radical intellectual re-examination of Islam nor sought a revision or even a reformulation of its basic precepts.

This reluctance to deal with issues of basic doctrine was no accident. By concentrating on practical rather speculative aspects of the subject the proponents of Islamic reform managed, at least for a time, to avoid the main issue, which in reality was how to modernize Islam itself and not merely its followers. But only for a time, and this is why their work was left uncompleted and is likely to remain so for a long time to come. In Egypt, the dilemma was formulated in several ways. As Nadav Safran has put it, Egypt was heir to a system of beliefs based on Islamic doctrine, a system which served as the foundation of her political community and evolved over a period of many centuries alongside and parallel to the evolution of her material conditions. For three centuries after the beginning of the Ottoman occupation, both the system of beliefs and material conditions changed very little. Thus an increasingly widening gap developed between reality and ideology, undermining the existing political community and threatening to condemn Egyptian society to a permanent state of tension and instability. The situation called for a bridging of the gap by means of a readjustment of the traditional system of beliefs "or the formulation of a new one capable of serving as the foundation of a new political community."[5]

The extent to which neither of these eventualities has so far materialized can be fathomed from the fact that after nearly a century of endeavour the same problems continue to beset Egyptian society and culture – at least in so far as the relations between religious and secular ideologies are concerned. This is perhaps nowhere more apparent than in the ambiguity displayed by the official position of Nasserist ideology on Islam and its tenets and in the apparent discrepancy between official and non-official pronouncements on Islam in Nasser's Egypt.

The Egyptian Constitution of 1956 proclaimed Islam as Egypt's official religion. In his report to the National Congress of Popular Forces held in the summer of 1962 to consider the text of the *National Charter,* Nasser underlined the regime's adherence to Islam when he stated:

The concern which made the 1956 Constitution stipulate that the

> State's official religion is Islam, and its official language is Arabic, is the same concern that attaches all this importance and value to religion in the *Charter.* This induces us to decree that Islam is (as before) the official religion of the State. . . . This concern has made the teaching of religion compulsory in all schools for Muslim and Christian pupils.

The studied ambiguity of the last sentence is of considerable significance here. For whereas Nasserism's "concern" about Islam is said to have induced the legislator to stipulate in the Constitution that the State's religion was Islam, it is by no means obvious that the teaching of Islam in Egyptian schools, which was made compulsory by law, extended to Christian pupils either in mixed or in purely Christian schools. This ambiguity in fact runs through most references to religion in the *National Charter,* where belief in God, religious ideals, and ethical standards are dealt with in general terms and with a scrupulous avoidance of identifying them with Islam. Such references speak of the Egyptian people's "unshakable belief . . . in God and his prophets and messages"; of the validity of "the eternal moral values" which religions teach; and of the compatibility of "the essence of religion with the realities of life."

Even where specific references to Islam are made in the *National Charter,* moreover, they are invariably marginal. In the section entitled "The Roots of the Egyptian Struggle," for instance, Islam is referred to in a strictly historical context, rather than as a significant living factor. Egypt, it tells us, has always, consciously and sometimes unconsciously, influenced and was in turn influenced by her surroundings as the part interacts with the whole. This was amply demonstrated by her ancient history under the Pharaohs as well as by her development during the periods of Greek and Roman domination. "The Islamic conquest," the *National Charter* goes on to relate, "shed light on this fact and placed it in a new context of spiritual thought and feelings. In the history of Islam the Egyptian people, guided by the message of Muḥammad, assumed the main role in defending civilization and mankind." There then follows a reference to "the darkness of the Ottoman invasion" and "the colonialist and reactionary factors of weakness and disintegration imposed by the Ottoman Caliphate in the name of religion, while in fact religion is incompatible with such factors." The Muslim University of al-Azhar is depicted by the *National Charter* as "a stronghold of resistance" against the elements of weakness and disunity introduced by the Ottoman Muslim State.

The *National Charter* makes only one other reference to Islam – and this is even more marginal. In Section Ten, entitled "Foreign Policy," Nasser asserts that the Egyptian people believes in Arab unity, about which he speaks at great length in the previous section; that it believes, also, "in a close spiritual bond that ties it to the Islamic world." The measure of significance here given to the Islamic factor can be gauged by the fact that the Egyptians' belief in a spiritual bond which ties them to the Islamic world is asserted in the same breath and on the same level as their belief in pan-Africanism, Afro-Asian solidarity, and "their belonging to the United Nations and . . . loyalty to the U.N. Charter."[6]

Although these references to Islam, couched as many of them are in the general context of religion and the belief in God and his prophets, may well appear to be in the nature of mere lip-service, the fact that the official leadership of the Nasserist regime found it necessary to pay such lip-service is itself of some significance. It can be said, indeed, that though Islam cannot in any sense be considered to have been a determining factor in Egypt's official ideology in the period under discussion, it was nonetheless depicted by this ideology as being of continuous relevance in the nation's socio-cultural life.

This ambivalence in Nasserism's attitude to Islam marks the relationship between the two right from the start. For though it is apparent that, by introducing an indigenous brand of socialism, the new revolutionary regime posed a challenge to the Islamic basis of Egypt's identity, it never dared to come out openly against that basis. Even during the fierce struggle with the Muslim Brethren following the attempt on Nasser's life by one of their members in 1954, the official argument avoided a confrontation with the Islamic establishment, choosing instead to use "true" Islamic teachings as showing that the Brethren's tactics and strategy signified a deviation from rather than loyalty to the Islamic faith. Nasser and his close associates continued paying frequent visits to the shaykhs and *'ulamā* of al-Azhar University, and made a habit of attending public Friday prayer at al-Azhar mosque or some other great mosque in Cairo.

But while such surface manifestations of fidelity to Islam were being displayed, the regime went on with its reform programme. The most far-reaching measure in this direction – and the one which illustrates the Free Officers' attitude most strikingly – was the decision to abolish religious courts in Egypt as of January 1, 1956. Yet even this far-reaching challenge to the *sharī'a* system itself in a country whose official religion purported to be Islam, failed to arouse real opposition from the *'ulamā.* On the contrary, three days after the government had announced its decision to abolish religious courts, the leading daily *al-Ahrām* accompanied a picture of Shaykh al-Azhar 'Abd ar-Raḥmān Tāj shown congratulating President Nasser with this leading shaykh's thanks to the President for having taken the "liberating step" of abolishing the courts.[7]

Despite these mutual assurances of good faith, however, misgivings about the regime's drifting away from the Islamic orientation were voiced, especially outside Egypt where Muslim men of religion felt safe from the worldly power of government. The fact that the regime kept protesting that its socialist ideology was of the very essence of true Islam did not prevent the Muslim establishment from noting that Islam was being relegated to a rather marginal place as a basis of the state's policies. For while official Egypt never actually came out against the religious orientation, some of its semi-official spokesmen did question Islam's relevance to the problems confronting today's Egypt. One of these, a professor at Cairo University, said in a book called *The Foundations of Arab Socialism* that to the Islamic high ideals and aims, established for all times, society should also add what is recognised as being its aim in this age. Later on in the book the author, speaking generally of "religious communities," asserts that these communities "have dissolved," and that it is "incumbent on the Arab progressives to be free from religious prejudice."[8]

Faced with such open, if carefully phrased, challenges from the proponents of Arab Socialism, traditional Muslim opinion reacted with understandable apprehension. Yet its reaction was not uniform. If we leave aside the response of the official Muslim religious leadership in Egypt, which has in the main been one of complete conformity, we can still discern two rather contrasting traditional Muslim attitudes to the phenomenon of socialism. The most comprehensive, well-reasoned and ambitious attempt by an orthodox Muslim thinker to demonstrate Islam's compatibility with socialism has been made by a Syrian Muslim theologian who is also a leader of the Syrian branch of the Muslim

Brethren. This is Shaykh Muṣṭafā as-Sibā'ī, the late Dean of the Faculty of Islamic Jurisprudence and School of Law at the University of Damascus. In a book entitled *The Socialism of Islam,* Sibā'ī not only tries to show that Islam contains all the elements of "true socialism" but also implies that Nasser's Arab Socialism is in complete accord with Islam. The fact that the first edition of Sibā'ī's book was published in 1959, during the second year of the Egypt-Syria merger that gave birth to the United Arab Republic, is significant; but it does not seem to furnish an adequate explanation or motivation for its author's views.[9] For the fact is that to the same extent as the Arab Socialists have sought to "socialize" Islam, orthodox Muslim thinkers have been trying to Islamize socialism. Taking note of the fact that in the official ideology Islam was being gradually demoted from its position of centrality, the Islamic establishment seems to have wanted to save what could be saved by joining the bandwagon of the Arab Socialists.

All in all, Sibā'ī's treatise is disappointing and its tone is somewhat forced. To prove the socialism of Islam, he resorts to the habitual emphasis on Islamic precepts concerning "state control over social uses of wealth," the guarantee which the Islamic state gives its citizens for a life of dignity, and the fact that Islam provides for all members of society. In refuting the argument that Islam, by granting the right of private ownership in inheritance, is alien to socialism, Sibā'ī enumerates three elements which he considers the components of Islam's socialism. These are the "natural rights" which the Islamic state grants all its citizens, the laws which guarantee these rights and regulate the rules of mutual social responsibility, and ordinances ensuring the implementation of these laws.

Concerning the difficult subject of ownership, Sibā'ī conveniently begs the question by asserting that in Islam the real owner of things is God. This fundamental belief, he argues, has two advantages: firstly, it dispels vanity and arrogance from the heart of property-owning mortals; secondly, it obliges them to abide by the *sharī'a* rules of ownership. But God, though being the original and ultimate owner, has liberally and freely placed all his possessions at the disposal of human beings. Sibā'ī derives two conclusions from this Qur'ānic statement: firstly, that there is nothing in the material world which cannot be possessed by man, given the determination, intelligence and effort; secondly, that everyone is equally entitled to make use of "the good things of the earth." Once a person has taken possession of a thing through honest means, he is recognized by Islam as its rightful owner. And no means is more honest for attaining ownership than work. Consequently, ownership based on begging, injustice, deceit and harm is forbidden. But possession of a thing is not an end in itself: just as its origin should be honest work, its use should also be honest and beneficial, both individually and socially. In Islam individual ownership is a social duty.

Citing various Qur'ānic precepts and traditions, Sibā'ī then reaches the conclusion that Islam decrees the nationalization of certain categories of property. Among his authorities is a prophetic tradition to the effect that "people own three things in common: water, grass and fire" (another tradition mentions salt too). Sibā'ī argues that since these things were the basic necessities of desert life at the time of the Prophet, their enumeration should on no account be regarded as exhaustive or exclusive. Thus, in a modern context, "water" can be taken to stand for all the installations of water supply, "fire" for electricity, and "grass" and "salt" for all the indispensable requirements of contemporary life. In a word, the Prophet's saying should be interpreted as warranting the communization of any resource and material which, if allowed to remain in private hands, might lead to monopolistic exploitation of public needs. Sibā'ī argues further that the Islamic institution of *waqf* itself "consists of removing the object of an endowment from the possession of its owner, so that it ceases to be the property of only one person, and its usufruct becomes confined to those for whom the endowment is intended – and this is nationalization itself."[10]

It is significant that Sibā'ī's account of Islamic socialism meets at more than one point the version of socialism furnished by the proponents of Arab Socialism as laid down by Nasser, especially in those of its aspects where it seems to differ fundamentally from the "scientific socialism" of the Marxists (see Chapter 6). Thus, among the many general remarks he makes about Islamic socialism we find the following: Islamic socialism "establishes social equality by legislation and combats poverty, sickness, ignorance, fear and degradation"; it "takes in all citizens of the State"; it "gives people a share in the government's social security scheme by letting them look after relatives"; its principles are "flexible and applicable in every age in accordance with the evolution of society and the progress of civilization"; and it "keeps government and governors dependent on the will of the people, unlike communist socialism where people are made to depend on the will of a small group of rulers."

On this subject of the difference between Islamic socialism and the prevailing socialist ideologies of the day, Sibā'ī's views coincide with those of the advocates of Arab Socialism even more strikingly. He asserts, among other points, that Islamic socialism "harmonizes with human nature and life's necessities in allowing individual ownership, a thing which theoretical communism forbids." Moreover, whereas communism "asserts that competition is the cause of social disaster and the exploitation of the masses by the capitalists," Islamic socialism "gives a free hand to human talent in the way of constructive competition which is undoubtedly the mainspring of cultural evolution and growth." Moreover, Islamic socialism "is based on morality as an integral part of faith [and] urges man to seek perfection," while communism "does not believe in moral and emotional values such as love and mercy, nor does it believe in such social values as truth and loyalty."[11]

Sibā'ī's book is only one of numerous publications by Muslim thinkers acclaiming Islam's socialism. It is not, however, the most striking example of the remarkable flexibility and adaptability shown by the orthodox Muslim leadership vis-à-vis Nasser's Arab Socialism. In a book called *The Socialist Deception,* the Lebanese Muslim scholar and journalist Ṣalāḥ ad-Dīn al-Munajjid cites the contents of one issue of the Egyptian monthly *Minbar al-Islām* which calls itself "the organ of Islamic culture" and is published by the Higher Council for Islamic Affairs. In the magazine's issue of June 1965 he finds four articles in praise of Nasser's *National Charter* in general and of Arab Socialism in particular. The headings of these articles speak for themselves: "The Charter's Call is of [the Essence of] the Call of Islam"; "The Islamic Foundations of our Arab Socialism"; "Socialism Springs from the Depths of Our Faith"; and "The Qur'ān Created a Socialist Society".[12]

Obviously, Sibā'ī and his fellow Muslim apologists for Arab Socialism all labour under a fundamental misconception. By being overeager to justify modern socialism – which no matter how it is treated is an essentially Western ideology – in terms of the theology, philosophy, world-view and jurisprudence of Islam, they commit the common error of applying the concepts and mental framework of one culture to another. This approach errs in that it fails to take cognizance of the fact that there are many socio-political terms which, though they play a genuine and historically authentic role in Western thought, are rather equivocal with reference to Islam's outlook and its circumstances. As Asad has pointed out:

> One could . . . assert (as some modern Muslim writers do) that Islam is "socialistic" in its tendencies because it aims at a state of affairs which would ensure to all citizens equality of opportunity, economic security, and an equitable distribution of national wealth; however, one could maintain with the same degree of assurance that Islam is opposed to socialism if [this] is taken to imply . . . a rigid regimentation of all social life, the supremacy of economics over ethics, and the reduction of the individual to a mere economic factor.[13]

Asad, of course, is a fundamentalist – and as such it is natural that he should be met by his opposite number in the socialist camp more than half-way. For the fact is that in present-day Egypt both orthodox Muslims and orthodox Marxists are unhappy about the attempt – made jointly by the moderates of both camps – to identify, equate or reconcile Arab Socialism with Islam. To cite only one example, die-hard Egyptian Marxists never tire of repeating that Arab Socialism (which they claim to be identical with "scientific socialism," i.e. Marxism) entails more than just a change in the pattern of production relations. According to them, it implies the emergence of a new moral code, a new world-view, a new pattern of human behaviour. However, the emergence of such new moral and social patterns implies abandonment of the existing codes and patterns, which in Egypt are universally associated with those of Islam. In this way both "scientific socialists" and Muslim fundamentalists present the problem as a head-on confrontation between two irreconcilable ideologies. To be sure, this confrontation is seldom articulated – on the socialists' side because they are by no means sure of the regime's support, on the Muslims' side because of the religious establishment's great reluctance to antagonize the regime or bring matters to a real showdown. This is why throughout the past two decades of revolution, only one Egyptian Muslim thinker and activist has come out against the revolutionary regime and all it stands for – and why this solitary Muslim fundamentalist is now safely dead, having been condemned and executed for incitement against the regime.

Sayyid Quṭb, until his execution in September 1966, was the leader of the Muslim Brethren and its most consistent and uncompromising spokesman so far. The authenticity and deep scholarship of his Islamic outlook and its interpretation are not disputed even by those who would not agree with his conclusions. A fundamentalist and utopian, Quṭb all along refused to use what he considered an alien terminology borrowed from an alien Western context. In his book *Roadsigns on the Path,* published two years before his death, Quṭb in fact proclaims the bankruptcy of modern civilization. The real and only choice open to men today, he asserts, is that between Islam and *jāhiliyya* (the term used by Muslims to denote the paganism and ignorance of pre-Islamic times). For Quṭb, *jāhiliyya* now pervades the whole of human society, not excluding the communities which masquerade as Muslim but which in fact consistently violate the *sharī'a.* Arab Socialism, along with the whole socio-political structure of present-day Egypt, is un-Islamic and as such is to be included in the latter category.[14]

What the world needs is nothing short of a radical transformation, Quṭb argues. Human life cannot continue in its present course, and its transformation is imperative if man is to be saved from destruction. Humanity's present course is one of destroying man through the destruction of his basic characteristics and this course is now in full swing and is leading to the transformation of man into a machine on the one hand and an animal on the other. Marxism was once thought to be the right tool for the radical transformation of human life. "But this was nothing but an illusion. Marxism, with its dialectical materialist interpretation of history, represents but a phase in the present road to destruction . . . It is the apex of the materialistic trend of thought." Other ideologies are no less wanting. "They are all superficial, partial views – all artificial attempts lacking roots in human nature. The only way to salvation, to save humanity from destruction and to preserve man through the preservation of his human characteristics is to be found in the Islamic outlook, in the Islamic programme, in Islamic life and society." The establishment of the Islamic society is therefore a human necessity and an inevitable natural process. "If it does not emerge today, then it will emerge tomorrow; if it will not emerge here, it will emerge there."[15]

Quṭb spreads his net very wide indeed. The world is in a rather deplorable state, he argues; human life is itself threatened. But how have things come to such a pass? It is a tragedy, Quṭb admits, and proceeds to list "the most important elements of this tragedy." These are three in number.

Firstly, our total lack of knowledge of man, and our consequent inability to formulate for him through human reason a comprehensive system that would be in keeping with his nature and his characteristics, preserving them all in a state of renewal, growth and bloom.

Secondly, human life, being based on this ignorance, has suffered from aimlessness and lostness since it parted ways with the system laid down by its Creator.

Thirdly, the rise of a materialistic civilization unsuitable for man and disregardful of his nature, treating him in mechanistic and animalistic terms. This "mechanical-animal system" is being practised on human life in countries which have reached the apogee of materialistic civilization.[16]

The whole world, then, is in a state of total ignorance which cannot be redeemed by the achievements of modern materialistic civilization. Quṭb calls this "the new *jāhiliyya*" and asserts that it manifests itself in "an act of transgression against God's authority on earth and against the most particular of divine attributes." The only alternative to this "new *jāhiliyya*," Quṭb maintains, is Islam, which he prescribes as the only way to salvation not only, or even mainly, for the non-Islamic peoples but for the Muslims themselves, whom he sees as suffering from a worse *jāhiliyya* than that which preceded Islam. "Everything around us is *jāhiliyya*, people's beliefs and conceptions, their customs and traditions, the sources of their culture, their arts and literature, their laws and regulations. Even most of what is now regarded as Islamic culture, Islamic sources, and Islamic philosophy and thought is equally the product of this *jāhiliyya*." All political, social and economic systems based on the mechanistic and animalistic approach to man are rejected as excrescences of *jāhilī* thought. The present regime in Egypt he regards as a *jāhilī* society to which true Muslims cannot owe their loyalty, their primary mission being, on the contrary, "to transform this society . . . from its foundations" because it clashes with the Islamic way of life and the Islamic outlook.[17]

One of Sayyid Quṭb's strictures against Arab Socialism is that it is closely bound up with nationalism – another *jāhilī* creed totally foreign to the spirit of Islam. This brings us to another point at which the Islamic factor may clash with the reigning ideology in revolutionary Egypt. To be sure, the current accepted attitude to this subject is far from clear. With varying degrees of vagueness, Muslim Arabs have tended to identify Arabism with Islam, but they have been able to do this only on the strength of an erroneous and rather unhistorical understanding of both Islam and nationalism. To give one example: Ḥasan al-Bannā', who acted as the Muslim Brethren's Supreme Guide up to his assassination in the late forties, used to draw a distinction between *waṭaniyya* ("patriotism") and *qawmiyya* ("nationalism"). In his pamphlet *da'watunā* ("Our Mission"), he explains that the European interpretations of these two terms must not be accepted by Muslims, and that they should accordingly be given meanings which are in keeping with the spirit of Islam. Patriotism, according to his reading, is love of the "Islamic Fatherland," embracing all countries inhabited by Muslims; nationalism, on the other hand, is the sum total of the nationalisms of the various Islamic peoples. Bannā' does not object to these nationalisms, provided they all cooperate toward the attainment of the ultimate (Islamic) goal; for him, the essence of nationalism rests merely on following in the steps of the Muslim Fathers, believing in Jihād and devotion to work.[18]

This view furnishes a striking example of the kind of complete misunderstanding of the accepted senses in which both "patriotism" and "nationalism" are normally used. Indeed, attempts to equate Islam with Arabism, or even to reconcile Arab nationalism with the essence of the Islamic mission, have always been disputed by some Muslim Arab thinkers. For these, the main object of the Islamic mission was – in the words of 'Abd ar-Raḥmān 'Azzām, the first Secretary-General of the Arab League – "the creation of an Islamic nation and not of an Arab nation." 'Azzām argues further that the emergence of an Arab nation "was never planned or intended by the Arab Prophet or his followers." Those people whom Islam arabized "were only a by-product of Arab influence," and this "by-product nation, curiously enough, was never seriously conscious of its ethnic or cultural existence until it was aroused to the new doctrine of nationalism by its European conquerors." 'Azzām, indeed, imparts the impression that for him the fact that "the last great prophet" was an Arab was a mere accident of history. Muḥammad belonged to a great Arab tribe, it is true; yet "nothing was more distasteful to him than to glorify his tribe or race, because in Islam there was no room for discrimination whatsoever, on account of either colour, language or race."[19]

On two cardinal issues, then, Islam can safely be said to be at variance with the official ideology of the Egyptian regime. Insofar as it is a borrowing from the secular, materialistic West, Arab Socialism is an alien intrusion into the Islamic polity and society, and the attempt to present Islam now as "democracy," now as "socialism," amounts to nothing less than making a travesty of its fundamental principles. Arab nationalism – the other principal component of Nasserism – is likewise an aberration, a negation of the universal character of Islam and a manifestation of pagan *jāhiliyya.*

Thus, the part that the Islamic factor plays in Nasserist ideology is negligible. True, the average Egyptian – and this does not exclude the educated classes or even men in the highest echelons of government – still seeks the spiritual help which Islam provides. It is noteworthy, too, that Nasser's public speeches are invariably opened with recitations from the Qur'ān – and Islam is always evoked by those spokesmen of the regime who seek to expound socialism and Arabism to the masses. Yet all this seems to amount to little more than lip-service, and religious leaders in Egypt are today either themselves considerably secularized ideologically or are content to play a totally passive, subordinate, and often humiliating role as public relations men for the regime. The attitude of the regime to the religious establishment is perhaps best illustrated by the way the government effected, in June 1961, the long-contemplated reorganization of al-Azhar, the leading religious institution of Arabic Islam.[20] On June 22, 1961, the National Assembly held its last meeting of the parliamentary session, and it was in this atmosphere of urgency that it passed the bill providing for a thorough reform and reorganization of al-Azhar, and virtually eliminating the last vestiges of quasi-independence which this ancient institution had enjoyed. The shaykhs put up a show of meek and embarrassed resistance, but it was to no avail. Indeed, when some Azharites complained that the government was destroying the traditional role of al-Azhar as a place of study of the language and religious sciences, government spokesmen countered by accusing them of deviation from the institution's age-old tradition. The government, they claimed, "was now widening [al-Azhar's] role by restoring it to its traditional place as a disseminator of all sciences, not just the religious ones." "Al-Azhar," declared Ḥusayn ash-Shāfi'ī, Vice-President in charge of al-Azhar affairs, "became isolated from society and from life. In our effort now to develop al-Azhar, we are but giving expression to our determination to reinstate it in its place of honour and to strengthen the link between its past and present." Nasser went further. "Of course," he wrote in *Minbar al-Islām,* "the shaykh does not think of anything except the turkey and the food with which he fills his belly. He is no more than a stooge of reaction, feudalism and capitalism. At that time some shaykhs were trying to deceive us with *fatwas* of this nature. From the beginning, Islam was a religion of work. The Prophet used to work like everybody else. Islam was never a profession."[21]

The leading *'ulamā* quickly fell in line. *Majallat al-Azhar,* the official al-Azhar journal, contained the following statements in its January 1962 issue – the words of Maḥmūd Shaltūt, Shaykh of al-Azhar himself:

> The graduates of al-Azhar were considered only as men of religion. As a result of that, they used religion as a profession with which to earn their living. Moreover, they lived in complete isolation far away from their society, because their culture could not meet the requirements of the renaissance era, especially in the fields of work and production.
>
> The new law includes a solution for every problem, it prepares an experience for every field, it brings up preachers and guides to show humanity the straight way of its life. . . . It wants Islam to be revived, *'ulamā* to be of strong faith, living for the sake of and not by means of it.[22]

Thus, with the temporary subduing of radical Islamic opposition embodied in the Muslim Brethren, Egyptian Islam has become a willing tool of the secular regime. It is not suggested here that either the regime or the religious leadership had much of a choice in the matter. As one student of the Arab world has put it in another context, no matter how profoundly committed a Muslim statesman may be to the proposition that Islam governs both man and society, he is "bound to act in international affairs as though he were secularly oriented: he is compelled to ignore traditional Islamic theories of international relations." The only alternative to this, the writer asserts, is for the Muslim "to live and move and have his being in an unreal world, and to think in terms of obsolete theories which do not, and cannot, have the slightest bearing on the reality that envelops him."[23]

This is perhaps as true of the conduct of a Muslim country's domestic affairs as it is of its international relations. The choice, ultimately, was quite eloquently formulated by Quṭb: in the final analysis it is either true, pristine Islam or utter and unmitigated *jāhiliyya.* Along with other Muslim governments, Nasserism chose the secular way – if only because the alternative is to live, move and think in an unreal world.

## NOTES

1 'Abbās Maḥmūd al-'Aqqād, *al-falsafa al-qur'āniyya* ["Qur'ānic Philosophy"] (Cairo, 1970), pp. 36–39, 40–50.

2 Muḥammad Asad, *The Principles of State and Government in Islam* (Los Angeles, 1961), pp. 18–19.

3 Fatḥī Raḍwān, *ārā' ḥurra fī ad-dīn w'al-ḥayāt* ["Free Opinions on Religion and Life"] (Cairo, 1969), pp. 52, 56–57.

4 [Muḥammad Abū Shilbāya], *"al-farāgh al-'aqā'idī"* ["The Ideological Void"], *al-Manār* (Jerusalem), April–May 1964.

5 Nadav Safran, *Egypt in Search of Political Community* (Cambridge, Mass., 1961), pp. 1–3.

6 *Charter,* see Appendix, p. 264.

7 *Al-Ahrām,* 28 September 1955.

8 'Iṣmat Sayf ad-Dawla, *usus al-ishtirākiyya al-'arabiyya* ["The Foundations of Arab Socialism"] (Cairo, 1965), pp. 372, 412.

9 Muṣṭafā as-Sibā'ī's book *ishtirākiyyat al-islām* ["The Socialism of Islam"] is quoted extensively in Ḥamid Enayat, "Islam and Socialism in Egypt," *Middle Eastern Studies,* Vol. 4 (January 1968), No. 2, pp. 141–172. An adequate summary in English is to be found in Sami A. Hanna and George H. Gardner, *Arab Socialism: A Documentary Survey* (Leiden, 1969), in the chapter, "Islamic Socialism," by the editors, pp. 65–78.

> take as examples and whose vices we use as terms of abuse . . . The literature from which we take guidance in prosperity and adversity, which we quote, converse with and follow, whose persons we live with and whose events we witness – surely this is no other than Arabic literature.
>
> The events related in Arabic literature, whether of pre-Islamic or Islamic times, are still the objects of our attention. . . . The verse of Zuhair, Antar, Labid, etc. . . . is still the sustenance and daily bread of the Egyptian poet and man of letters. . . . Egyptians still strive to attain the ideals and noble virtues which Arab literature proclaimed. Courage, enterprise, self-respect, nobility, loyalty and generosity are still quickened by pre-Islamic poetry.[2]

But this cultural-linguistic interpretation of Egypt's Arabness, though never questioned too closely by Egyptian thinkers and writers in the past few decades, was not the one on which the Revolution was to lean. Ever since she became deeply involved in inter-Arab relations and rivalries – an involvement which started not with the establishment of the Arab League in 1943 nor with Cairo's participation in the Palestine conflict in 1948 but with the row that it had with Iraq in 1955 over the Baghdad Pact – Egypt's idea of herself as "an integral part of the Arab Nation" and as a country destined to take the lead in the drive toward Arab unity as well as in the propagation of the call for such unity has been the central theme of her national ideology. It is about this view of Egypt's Arabness that confusion has arisen, and it is with this approach that the present chapter proposes to deal.

The meaning of the word "Arab" has changed and developed in the course of time, but it is doubtful whether, with the exception perhaps of pre-Islamic days, there was ever an agreed definition of the term. Ibn-Khaldūn, for example, used the term to describe the nomads, the Bedouin. As a matter of fact, the term was used in this sense until very recently by town-dwelling "Arabs" to describe their neighbours from the desert. As has been shown by many writers on the subject, the use of the word "Arab" in its present connotation is quite recent. We have only to remember that until just before World War I, Arabic was not the administration's language in any of the countries now called "Arab." The inhabitants of these lands themselves rarely thought consciously of themselves as "Arabs." As Professor S.D. Goitein has put it, until 40–50 years ago, were you to ask any of these inhabitants about his identity he would have replied that he was from this or that tribe, such-and-such town or city, a member of this or that faith or confession – but it would hardly have occurred to him to describe himself as an Arab.[3]

Be that as it may, it is now quite common, among Arabs and non-Arabs alike, to speak of the Arab World, the Arab Nation, and Arab Nationalism. The Arab World, it is fairly generally agreed, consists of those lands where the majority of the population is Arab. If we accept this definition, the Arab World extends from the Atlantic Ocean in the West to the borders of Iran in the East, and from the Taurus mountains and the southern shores of the Mediterranean in the north to the Indian Ocean and the steppes of central Africa in the south. It includes Morocco, Algeria, Tunisia, Libya, Egypt, the Sudan, geographic Syria, Iraq and the Arabian Peninsula.

So much for the Arab World. Concerning the identity of the Arabs and the nature of the Arab Nation – two questions whose solution is essential for any serious treatment of the subject of Arab nationalism – there is no agreed answer or definition. Are the Arabs Arab because of race, religion, or language – a common culture, a shared mental make-up or common social structures? No one has succeeded in giving an answer – least of all the Arabs themselves. But it cannot be said that they have not tried.

Bernard Lewis, in *The Arabs in History,* reports that "a gathering of Arab leaders some years ago defined an Arab in these words: "Whoever lives in our country, speaks our language, is brought up in our culture, and takes pride in our glory is one of us."[4] This definition raises more questions than it manages to answer. To live in "our country" and speak "our language" are quite intelligible concepts, but when these Arab leaders start talking about "our culture" and "our glory" difficulties begin to arise: is there a uniform *Arab* culture that is different or can be taken separately from the culture of Islam? Can one think of *Arab* glory in isolation from the glory of Islam?

The problem is almost insoluble, and the more one delves into it the more perplexing it seems to become. However, one can accept provisionally the following definition, offered by Nabīh Amīn Fāris of Beirut University and Muḥammad Tawfīq Ḥusayn, in their book *The Crescent in Crisis*: "The present-day Arabs are all those who inhabit the Arab world, speak the Arabic language, take pride in Arab history, cherish the general Arab feeling, and share in the characteristics of Arab mentality, irrespective of their religious affiliations and their racial descent."[5]

Supposing, then, that we accept some such definition of the term "Arab" as valid, there remains the no less complex question as to whether the Arabs, so defined, could be said to constitute one nation, or, more specifically, one nationality. There are some Arab nationalist thinkers who date the emergence of Arab nationalism to pre-Islamic days.[6] But it would be a waste of time to deal with these theories or to take them seriously. The more moderate view, shared by most Arab thinkers today, accepts the proposition that, like all nationalist movements, Arab nationalism was a relatively recent phenomenon dating back no earlier than the second half of the 19th century. The ideas and basic postulates of this movement were formulated in a developing historical process which has been divided into five distinct stages, the first dating back to the impact of European expansion, exemplified in the occupation of Egypt and Algeria.[7]

But whatever may be said about these definitions and explanations and even if we accept them as completely valid, it was inevitable that the Arab nationalists would soon become conscious of an incongruity: there is an Arab Nation; this Nation is entitled to the rights of nationhood; Arab nationalism was neatly defined, its postulates were well-formulated and attractive; yet something was missing: a great Arab Homeland, strong, prosperous, advanced – but above all united. Instead, the Arab world was fragmented into about a dozen independent, mandated or occupied entities. The inhabitants of each of these entities possessed special characteristics of their own, they spoke widely different dialects of Arabic, had their own armies and their own vital interests and foreign policies. How were the Arab nationalists to reconcile their concept of one Arab nation with the distressing reality of its divisions into so many different nationalities? Sāṭiʿ al-Ḥuṣarī, one of the leading theoreticians of pan-Arabism, had the following explanation to offer in 1951, on the eve of the Egyptian Revolution:

> The apparent differences among the populations of the Arab states are accidental and superficial, and do not justify the assumption that

> they are members of different nationalities simply because they are citizens of different states, all of which have come into being as a result of the manoeuvres and horse-trading tactics of the Powers. . . . There are several Arab peoples, but all of them belong to one nation, the Arab nation. . . . Any member of these Arab peoples is an Arab.[8]

For Arab nationalists of the school of Ḥuṣarī the question of Egypt's cultural identity almost does not exist. In the article just quoted, Ḥuṣarī writes:

> There is no doubt whatsoever that Egypt is a part of the Arab world so long as it shares with all the other Arab countries the same language, culture and long history, to say nothing of the afflictions and dangers it has in common with them. Furthermore, it is geographically linked with them directly, thereby becoming the heartland of the extensive Arab world.[9]

It should be noted that Ḥuṣarī by placing Egypt in the heartland of the Arab world, is also *en passant* including the countries of the Arab Maghrib in the Arab world – which indeed he does as a matter of simple fact.

This view of Egypt as in some way naturally belonging to the Arab world became, in the late fifties, generally accepted as valid by Egyptians and non-Egyptians alike. Yet this was by no means a universally accepted view. Late in 1961 and at the beginning of 1962, President Nasser on several occasions found it necessary to re-assert Egypt's Arabness in face of murmurings, both in and outside Egypt, against his Arab-oriented policies – murmurings which grew considerably louder following Syria's defection from the United Arab Republic in September 1961.[10]

Here a few words will be in place on the more general subject of Egypt's cultural identity as viewed by Egyptians before and after the July 23 Revolution. This subject, however, which in the thirties and forties of the present century gave rise to debates and differences of opinion, ceased to be quite so controversial under Nasser. For the fact is that though Egypt's Arabness had always been conceded in a rather vague way, there was a time when intellectual leaders and pathfinders like Dr. Ṭāha Ḥusayn, Salāma Mūsā, Muḥammad Ḥusayn Haykal and ʿAbbās Maḥmūd al-ʿAqqād found themselves troubled by the question as to where, precisely, Egypt belongs culturally: Europe, the Mediterranean, Africa or the Arab world. However that may be, there was under Nasser something very near a consensus that Egypt belongs to the Arab world and, as he told the Egyptian National Assembly upon his re-election as President in January 1965, "is part and parcel of the Arab nation."

It must be remembered, however, that what to Nasser seemed fairly obvious did not always go unchallenged by other Egyptians. Late in 1961, as the dust was settling on the ruins of the Egypt-Syria merger, some voices began to be heard in Cairo suggesting – if only rather timidly and by implication – that the whole idea of pan-Arab union lacked a solid foundation both in history and in actual reality.

One of these was Dr. Ṭāha Ḥusayn, who in a subtly conceived newspaper article related how he first came across the idea of pan-Arab unity. It was from the Syrians, he wrote, that he heard "the talk about Arab unity" many years before, "and I never heard it for the first, the second and the third time except from the Syrians." Arab unity was the Syrians' dream when their land, their lives and their interests were in the hands of the French, and it may have been their dream before that, too, when Syria suffered under the despotic rule of the Ottoman Turks.

The Syrians hated to hear an Arab speak of the Syrian nation *(umma);* they always hastened to correct you, arguing that there was no such thing as a Syrian nation, an Iraqi nation or an Egyptian nation: there was only one nation, which is the Arab nation. They conceded, however, that there was a Syrian "people" *(shaʿb),* an Iraqi people and an Egyptian people – but they added that these peoples would inevitably unite as they used to be united in the past and merge into an Arab nation as in the past.

"I remember," Ṭāha Ḥusayn adds, "that I used to argue with them at length about this union; I used to ask them where would the capital of such a union be – in the Medīna as in the days of the first Caliphs? in Damascus as in the time of the Umayyids? or in Baghdad as in the days of the Abbasids? Eventually they accused me, in their newspapers, first of Pharaoism (*firʿawniyya*), later of *shuʿūbiyya.* Then they proceeded to accuse all, or most of, Egypt's writers of Pharaoism, which they hated exceedingly and condemned root and branch."[12]

Such "non-Arab" sentiments, expressed by Dr. Ṭāha Ḥusayn and other Egyptian thinkers following Syria's secession from the United Arab Republic, were soon to be reciprocated by certain quarters in Damascus, with the result that the regime now had to defend its belief in Egypt's Arabness on two fronts. "We have no choice," declared President Nasser in an address he gave at a mass rally on February 22, 1962. "We are Arabs, and Egypt will remain Arab because this is nature itself." Nasser was replying to unidentified persons who were making the suggestion, he said, that Egypt ought to leave the Arabs alone and start concentrating on her own affairs. Earlier, referring to Syrian charges that the Egyptians were confirmed "Pharaoists" rather than Arabs, Nasser had declared that all this talk of Egypt's *fir'awniyya* was unfounded, since it started "just because Ṭāha Ḥusayn, years ago, expressed the opinion that the Egyptians were Pharaoists."[13]

The point, of course, is that Egypt has had too many and too prolonged contacts with cultures other than the Moslem-Arab one for her to be readily identified as Arab and for her culture to be homogeneous. "Where do we stand in the world? " asked Fatḥī Ghānim, a young Egyptian writer and novelist, not long after the dismantling of the Egypt-Syria merger. "What is our attitude to the policies and the ideological, cultural and religious trends surrounding us? . . . The history of our literature in the past 25 years is a record of the attempt to answer these questions." But while in the literary field it was agreed that "we have to create a literature of our own that is not influenced by anyone," the question was harder to answer on the socio-cultural level. In fact, the writer says, the question "why should Egypt not be part of Europe and Egyptian society a part of European society? " never received a satisfactory answer from any quarter.[14]

It was this same question that Dr. Ṭāha Ḥusayn tried to answer in his well-known book *The Future of Culture in Egypt,* published in 1938. In the first part of the book, the author assesses the nature of Egyptian culture.

History, he says, will have to be our guide. From ancient times there have been two civilizations on this earth, whose very encounter was a hostile clash – i.e. that of Europe and that of the East. The question is: is the Egyptian mind Eastern or Western in terms of its concept-formation or imagination, perception, understanding and judgement?

There is but one test: is it easier for the Egyptian mind to understand a Chinese or a Frenchman or an Englishman?

The answer is obvious, Ṭāha Ḥusayn submits. There is no evidence of intellectual, political or economic ties between Egypt and the East (i.e. the Far East) in antiquity. Close ties existed solely with the Near East – Palestine, Syria, Iraq. On the other hand, there is no need to insist on the well-known connections between Egypt and the Aegean, and Egypt and the Greeks, from the very beginning of their civilization down to Alexander. In fact, Egypt resisted the Persian invader from the East with the help of the Greek volunteers and the Greek cities, until she was freed by Alexander.

Thus, the author continues, the Egyptian mind's real ties were all with the Near East and the Greeks, and in so far as it was affected by outside influences, these were Mediterranean. The Mediterranean civilizations interacted, with Egypt holding the precedence of age; but never did the Egyptian mind enter into contact with India, China and Japan. What Ṭāha Ḥusayn cannot understand, he writes, is that, despite all these well-known facts, the Egyptians will consider themselves Easterners.

Had the ready acceptance of Islam then made the Egyptians an Eastern nation? According to Ṭāha Ḥusayn, spiritual unity and political unity do not necessarily go together. The Moslems always realized that political organization and faith are two matters of a different order; they conceived of government as dedicated primarily if not exclusively to public affairs. Europe, too, is organized along the same lines, Islam and Christianity being both influenced by Greek philosophy.

The fact is that in the modern age Egypt has taken Europe for her model in all aspects of the material life. Egypt's mind, too, is purely European. To support his thesis that Egypt should aim for out-and-out Westernization, the author finally turns to the "tales" told about the "spiritualism" of the East and the "materialism" of the West. Pointing out that European civilization possessed great spiritual content, though there was a great deal of materialism in it, he argues that the Near East was the cradle of all the divine religions, those adopted by Europeans as well as those followed by Near Easterners. "Can these religions be 'spirit' in the East and 'matter' in the West? " he asks rhetorically.[15]

Ṭāha Ḥusayn was not alone in having reservations about Egypt's Arabness. Generally speaking, Egyptians have always had a somewhat low opinion of "the Arabs," and often emphasized that the Arabs had come to Egypt as conquerors, that they were as foreign to the land as were the Romans, the Tartars, the Crusaders and the Ottomans.

'Abd ar-Raḥmān 'Azzām, the Arab League's first Secretary-General and an Egyptian of note, has related how, when he once tried to discuss the subject of Arab unity with Sa'd Zaghlūl, this prominent Egyptian nationalist leader interrupted him in the middle: "If you add a zero to a zero, then to another zero, what will you get? "

'Azzām himself, when he was later faced with an increasing amount of criticism of the League and its work, and especially its Secretariat, said: "The Secretariat-General is only a mirror of the Arab states . . . . The condition which prevails in it now is nothing but the reflection in this mirror of conditions prevailing in the Arab lands."[16]

In this connection it is useful to recall a controversy started fifteen years ago by Fatḥī Raḍwān, the Egyptian writer and National Guidance Minister at the time. In a lecture which was later published in *Akhbār al-Yawm* on March 21, 1953, Raḍwān raised the question: Who are the Egyptians? "We are indeed Egyptians," he wrote. "But are these Egyptians Arab? Are they Arab by race, or are they Arab by politics? Or are they perhaps Arab by culture? " He went on to ask whether the Egyptians were Muslims, in the sense that they ought "to build our politics, education and constitution on the teachings of Islam"; or Africans in more than the geographical sense; or Mediterraneans, or Europeans. But Raḍwān refrained from giving any answers, and contented himself with inviting the politicians, the educationalists and the social scientists to answer these questions "without hesitation or delay."[17]

The results were highly interesting. The weekly *al-Muṣawwar*, on the initiative of its editor, Fikrī Abāẓa, arranged a symposium in which the participants were three ministers, the former Secretary-General of the Arab League, a former Dean of Alexandria University, the Deputy-Dean of Cairo University, and Abāẓa himself. The discussion produced no conclusive results, but what was said there was illuminating.

'Abd ar-Raḥmān 'Azzām concluded his dissertation by saying: "We are Egyptians first and foremost, then Arabs, then Moslems."

Dr. Ḥusayn Kāmil Sālim of Cairo University declared: "We are Egyptians first and last."

Abāẓa ruled: "We are ancient Egyptians and nothing else."

Dr. William Sālim Ḥanna, Municipal Affairs Minister, was rather evasive. He said: "As we speak Arabic and as our literature is Arab, we can by no means ignore the influence of that literature on our being, our life, direction, plans and everyday reactions."

Of the two other ministers, Dr. 'Abbās 'Ammār, Social Affairs Minister, dealt with many points but gave no answer at all, while Raḍwān contented himself with the role of moderator.

Finally, the former Dean of Alexandria University, Dr. Manṣūr Fahmī, complained that he had entered the hall with his head bursting with questions, but his perplexity grew after he had heard the participants speak. . . .[18]

It is important to bear in mind that all this took place after the Free Officers staged their coup d'état in July 1952, though nearly a year before Nasser had emerged triumphant from the struggle for power inside the military junta.

But it would be wrong to suppose that even in the heyday of Nasserism belief in the separateness of Egypt from the Arab world and in the uniqueness of her destiny became extinct. In a book published in Cairo, *An Egyptian Sindbad* by Dr. Ḥusayn Fawzī, the author invokes Egypt's history "as a complete whole" and says that as soon as Egypt awakens, and her eyes open on Europe's civilization,

> she will discover something strange, she who has forgotten her ancient history: she will discover that this history which she has forgotten has a place, a very important place, among the bearers of this modern civilization. She will discover that these consider the civilization of the Pharaohs the earliest awakening of man's thought, conscience and sensibility that history has ever known. It is no longer tolerable that the Egyptians should remain ignorant of the civilization of their fathers, who are forgotten solely by them.[19]

It is obvious, however, that despite all reservations and objections the idea of Egypt's Arab affiliation endures, though always in a rather vague and undefined way. This endurance seems remarkable in that the validity of the idea itself has often been put to question by the logic of events and circumstances. Yet it becomes rather understandable when we consider the broadness and all-inclusiveness of the definition which the

Arabs generally have given to Arabness and Arab nationalism. 'Abd ar-Raḥmān ar-Rāfi'ī, the historian of the Egyptian national movement, believes for example, that Arab nationalism is "a natural movement which derives its rise and existence from the factors that link the Arab peoples together." Explaining these links, Rāfi'ī enumerates language, history, beliefs, objectives, interests, common aspirations and geographical contiguity.[20]

Such definitions, loose and rather vague as they are, were however not adequate for an era in which Egypt's involvement in pan-Arab fortunes and politics was growing steadily deeper. More specific, sophisticated formulations were called for. Such formulations are to be found in the extensive literature on Arab nationalism and Arab unity written specifically for use by university students as part of the "nationalist subjects" which the Egyptian Ministry of Higher Learning made compulsory in university training. One of these subjects was called "Arab Society," and soon after its introduction in 1961, over thirty textbooks were produced on it. These books, bearing a variety of titles pertaining to Arab society and the Arab nation, dealt with such thorny problems as Arab nationalism, its emergence, its content and its objectives; systems of government in Arab countries; Arab reaction; the dominance of imperialism – as well as the geography, history and present fortunes of "the Arab Homeland." It is no wonder that so many teachers tried their hands – teachers of geography, history, law, political science, Arabic language and literature, psychology and sociology.

That the books, and accordingly the lectures themselves, could offer nothing even approaching a uniform point of view on these sensitive subjects was only to be expected. What is rather surprising is that the Ministry of Higher Learning, or whoever is in charge of these matters in Cairo, should have tolerated this state of affairs. For the books in question represent almost every possible approach: there is the Islamic approach, which dates the emergence of Arab nationalism to the rise of Islam; there is what can be termed the psychological approach, which makes nationalism a question of "feeling"; and there are those which consider religion as a component of Arab nationalism and those which disagree with this viewpoint.

Naturally enough, the confusion is at its most extreme on the subject of Arab nationalism and its emergence. For example, in a book called *A Short Study of Arab Society,* written by a number of university lecturers, we find Dr. Ḥasan Maḥmūd stating: "The events which took place in the Arab Peninsula before Islam indicated awareness of shared nationalism," whereas Dr. 'Abd al-Laṭīf Ibrāhīm – in the same book – asserts that "national consciousness in its modern meaning did not become a reality until the 18th century."[21]

A similar disparity is noticeable in the views expressed on the place of Islam in Arab nationalism. In his book *Muḥammad and Arab Nationalism,* Dr. 'Alī Ḥusnī al-Kharbūṭlī of 'Ain Shams states: "Scientific research and political events have proved that the two most important components of nationalism are language and history: language is considered the life of a nation and history its feeling." But the same author also states: "Students of nationalism agree almost unanimously that the basic components of nationalism are language and religion, in that order."[22]

A totally different view is advanced in another book on "Arab Society," this time by Dr. Suwaylim al-'Umarī, who asserts: "Nationalism does not rest on religious bases, though religion helps in bringing people together and laying the foundations for cooperation between them in accordance with the faith." Pointing out that religion has now lost its impetus as a factor in the formation of nations and states, and that modern states nowadays separate the Church from the State, Dr. 'Umarī supports his view by quoting the example of Israel: "One of the things which antagonize public opinion and is not in keeping with the political state of the world today is the insistence of fanatical Zionism to establish a state and build it up on religious foundations."[23]

One of the most novel and original of the definitions of Arab nationalism advanced in these books, however, is to be found in *Arab Society,* by Buṭrus Ghālī, 'Abdullah 'Awda and Maḥmūd Khayrī 'Isā, who have the following to say about Arabism: "We consider Arabism to be a political ideology just like democracy, communism, socialism, the movements of unity in Europe and America, and other ideologies and missions which various nations adopt and for which they fight." According to these authors, the pillars of Arabism as an ideology are three in number: liberation of the Arab world from foreign domination; unification of the Arab world within its natural borders; neutralism in the struggle between the two opposing world blocs.

These three pillars are interconnected in a very real sense, the authors assert. "For liberation cannot be realized except through unification, and will be stabilized only through disengagement from either of the two opposing blocs." As for positive neutralism, "though it is in itself one of the main pillars [of Arabism] it is also a means for the implementation of liberation and unification."[24]

But before going into these three pillars of Arabism in detail the authors take care to enumerate the elements of Arab nationalism as they collate them from the writings of leading Arab nationalist thinkers. These are four in number:

a. There is one Arab nation living in the territory extending from the Arab [Persian] Gulf to the Atlantic, and it possesses all the requisites of a nation.

b. These requisites are: the unity of language, of history and land, of culture and spiritual heritage, and of hopes and sufferings.

c. Neither religion nor race is among the foundations of the existence of the Arab nation.

d. Fragmentation and imperialism (Western, communist and Zionist) are the chief enemies of Arab nationalism.[25]

The authors then state that they will now "define and delimit the meaning of Arabism," a task which, they take care to explain, the Charter of the League of Arab States fails to perform.[26] Yet before embarking on such a definition the authors devote some space to their proposition that neither religion nor race plays a role in Arabness. "Arabism," they assert, "is not founded on Islam because not all the Arabs are Muslim, nor are all Muslims Arab. There are Arabs who are Jews, Catholic or Orthodox Christians, Druze, Bahais and others. The opposite is also true: the Turks, Afghans, Pakistanis, Iranian, Indonesians and others are nearly all Muslim but are nevertheless not Arab. Moreover, non-Muslim Arabs comprise about ten per cent of all the Arab peoples, while Muslim Arabs represent no more than about a seventh of all the Muslim peoples."

Nor is Arabism founded on race. "Had it been founded on racial traits, and were it confined to the pure Arab race, it would have been confined to the Arab Peninsula, because the Arabs who set forth from their peninsula at the beginning of the Islamic conquests mixed with other peoples, and their blood became mixed to such an extent that it became extremely difficult to tell an Arab from an Arabized person. In the Arab world today live tens of races distinguishable by the colour of their hair, their complexions, their facial features and other characteristics singled out by the sciences of race. Though we possess no accurate data on the various races of which the Arab world today is composed, it is apparent that the pure Arab race totals no more than about ten million, the rest descending from various races such as Copts, Syriacs, Berbers, Nubis, Aramaics and Phoenicians who were assimilated into the Arab nationality, thus constituting one nation whose oneness and ties are expressed in the simple statement 'We are all Arabs'."[27]

Finally, the authors assert, "Arabism is not built on a mere desire to revive old political and social systems, nor does it aim at re-establishing the Caliphate." Arabism, we are told, "is a result of contemporary international realities and ramifications which have surrounded it since the beginning of the twentieth century – rather like the realities and ramifications which confronted the Italian and German movements for unity in the previous century."

But if Arabism is founded neither on Islam nor on Arab race, nor even on a return to the past, what then is it built upon, and how do we delimit its features and enumerate its components? To this question the authors offer the somewhat surprising answer that Arabism is no more than a political creed or ideology, just like the democratic or socialist ones, or the unity movements in Europe and America "and other such creeds and drives which peoples embraced and for which they continue to strive."

Thus instead of the definition and the delimitations of the meaning and content of Arab nationalism promised by the authors we are offered only the three "pillars" on which this political doctrine is based (see above). Subsequently the authors furnish more detailed explanations as to what each of these three pillars entails, but their conclusion as to the nature of Arab nationalism remains final: "Arabism, then, is a political philosophy born in the twentieth century and whose essence is the liberation of the Arab world, its unification and its neutrality in the struggle between the two opposing blocs."[28]

The idea that Arab nationalism is a relatively new phenomenon and a recent creation, rather than the "eternal" being which the Arab nationalists attempt to make it, recurs in other works on the subject prepared for university students. In an essay entitled "The Study of Arab Nationalism from the Theoretical and Historical Aspects," Dr. Muḥammad Anīs propounds what seems to be one of the very few consistent views on the subject. Pointing out that the formation of nations is a long historical process and is not accomplished in one leap, Dr. Anīs defines the nation as a historically-formed group of people "possessing a common language, a common land, a shared economic life and psychological make-up that finds expression in a common culture." From this Dr. Anīs deduces that "Arab nationalism, like all other nationalisms, is a new historical phenomenon whose emergence does not go back to before the 19th century."

Anticipating the criticism of those who date the appearance of Arab nationalism back to the days of Muḥammad, Dr. Anīs argues that the existence of the elements of Arab nationalism in the past does not necessarily signify the emergence of this nationalism as an historical factor. He adds: "Thus the Middle Ages did not know Arab nationalism but only the Islamic mission. The defence of the Arab East, moreover, against the Tartars and the Crusaders was conducted by Ayyūbīs and Mamlūks, who are non-Arabs, while Salāḥ ad-Dīn's wars were waged not in the name of Arabism but in the name of Islam. Arabism had no existence separate from that of Islam."[29]

Though there appears to be no doubt that the dating of the Arab nationalist movement suggested by Ghālī, 'Īsā, 'Awda and Anīs is a valid one, it is indeed difficult to "place" Arab nationalism within the framework of any of the known national movements of the recent past. The terminology itself is problematic. Ghālī, 'Īsā and 'Awda consistently use the word *'urūba,* which means simply Arabism or Arabness. Anīs uses the term *al-qawmiyya al-'arabiyya,* meaning Arab nationalism. But none of them uses the term, to which all of them obviously refer – namely pan-Arabism, pan-Arab unity. One reason for this reticence is no doubt the obvious remoteness and virtual impossibility of the whole enterprise. And in this connection it is interesting to note that although the two terms are often and freely used interchangeably, "Arab nationalism" and "pan-Arabism" are not one and the same thing. Sir Hamilton Gibb drew a distinction between these two concepts 28 years ago, and despite the far-reaching developments which have taken place since then the distinction is still valid. According to this theory, "pan-Arabism" is an extremist radical effort to unite all the Arab world into a single state, as in the time of the Umayyid and 'Abbasid Caliphates; "Arab nationalism," on the other hand, merely seeks to develop the Arab personality within the states which now exist, and it recognizes the independence of these political entities. Unlike "pan-Arabs," the "Arab nationalists" would be content with a loose confederation of Arab states or some sort of spiritual and cultural union between them.

Pan-Arabism in this distinct sense has of course been associated with Nasserism, in which it is expressed by the term *qawmiyya 'arabiyya.* Nasser's first serious step in the direction of pan-Arab union was the establishment of the United Arab Republic in 1958 through the merger with Syria. Since then, however, no progress has been made in this direction; on the contrary, what with the "defection" of the revolutionary regime in Iraq, the endurance of King Hussein's regime in Jordan, and the refusal of the Lebanese to be drawn into the Nasserist orbit, it is today possible to say that "pan-Arabism" is on the retreat before the more moderate, more "pluralistic" doctrine of "Arab nationalism." Gibb's opinion that pan-Arabism is a goal not likely to be reached in the foreseeable future is as true today as it was 28 years ago.[30]

There are several decisive reasons why this is so, and many interpretations have been advanced. Quincy Wright of the University of Virginia, for example, has likened the situation to the one prevailing after the break-up of the Holy Roman Empire in Europe. In a course of lectures delivered some years ago, he pointed out that:

> there had been a quasi-political, quasi-religious union of the whole of western Europe, but that broke up after the 15th century into the national states of Europe. The great Arab Caliphates were in some respect similar to the Holy Roman Empire. We have seen in recent times the break-up of the quasi-religious, quasi-political Ottoman Empire, the last of the Caliphates, into national states. I think these states are likely to persist but will be inspired by Arab nationalism as, you may say, the states of western Europe have been inspired by Christian Nationalism.[31]

However, perhaps the chief obstacle to full Arab union, besides the local vested interests, is what may be termed the psycho-cultural barrier.

For despite a common language, a shared history and a more or less uniform cultural tradition, considerable differences persist – of temperament, of custom and of specific environment. The situation is remarkably analogous to that which confronted the pan-Slavists of a century ago. Pan-Slavism, like pan-Arabism, aspired to a union of the Slavic peoples that was based largely on the language factor. Both were movements in which – in the words of Hans Kohn describing pan-Slavism – "nationalist elements mingled with supranational and often imperialist trends." To those who have listened to General Qassem's speeches and read the literature of the "antiunionists" in Iraq, the following quotation from Karel Havliček, the great Czech intellectual who died over 100 years ago, will no doubt have a familiar ring:

> I learned to know Poland and I did not like it. With a feeling of hostility and pride I left the Sarmatian country, and in the worst cold I arrived in Moscow, being warmed mostly by the Slav feeling in my heart. The freezing temperature in Russia and other Russian aspects extinguished the last spark of Pan-Slav love in me. So I returned to Prague as a simple Czech, even with some secret sour feeling against the name Slav which a sufficient knowledge of Russia and Poland had made suspect to me. Above all, I express my firm conviction that the Slavs, that means the Russians, the Poles, the Czechs, the Illyrians, etc., are not one nation. The name Slav should forever remain a purely geographical and scientific name. Nationality is not only determined by language, but also by customs, religion, form of government, state of education, sympathies, etc.[32]

Like the present-day critics of the Egyptian and Syrian pan-Arabs, Havliček found the pan-Slavism of the Russians and Poles merely a desire on the part of these two nations to use the other Slavs for their own purposes. "I admit," he once flatly wrote, "that I prefer the Magyars, who are open enemies of the Czechs and Illyrians, to the Russians, who approach us with the Judas embrace – to put us into their pockets. We are Czechs, and we wish to remain Czechs, forever, and we do not wish to become either Germans or Magyars or Russians; and therefore we shall be cool to the Russians, if we do not wish to be hostile to them."

It would seem that the Arabs in their various lands are in need of just such local intellectual leaders as Frantisek Palacky and Karel Havliček, who, in the words of Hans Kohn, led their people "from the romantic sentimentalism of the beginning of their national rebirth to a realism which abhorred rash adventures and grandiose hopes."[33]

NOTES

1 Nasser at the National Assembly, on 20 January 1965, on being named candidate for President. Text in *al-Ahrām,* 21 January 1965.

2 'Abd al-Wahhāb 'Azzām, quoted in Charles Issawi, *Egypt in Revolution* (Oxford, 1963), p. 17.

3 S.D. Goitein, *Jews and Arabs: Their Contacts Through the Ages* (New York, 1964), p. 215.

4 Bernard Lewis, *The Arabs in History* (London, 1951), p. 9.

5 Nabīh Amīn Fāris and Muḥammad Tawfīq Ḥusayn, *The Crescent in Crisis* (London, 1955), p. 8.

6 *Ma'a al-qawmiyya al-'arabiyya* ["With Arab Nationalism"], the Federation of Kuwaiti (Student) Missions (Cairo, 1957). Quoted in Nissim Rejwan, "Arab Nationalism in Search of an Ideology," in Walter Z. Laqueur (ed.), *The Middle East in Transition* (London, 1957), p. 155.

7 Hāzim Nuseibeh, *The Ideas of Arab Nationalism* (Cornell, 1956), p. 46.

8 Sāṭi' al-Ḥuṣarī, *"usṭūrat al-kiyanāt al-'arabiyya al-munfarida"* ["Myth of the Separate Arab Entities"], *al-Ḥayāt* (Beirut), 12 August 1951.

9 *Ibid.*

10 Text in *al-Ahrām,* 23 February 1962.

11 See Note 1.

12 Ṭāha Ḥusayn, *al-Jumhūriyya* (Cairo), 7 October 1961. Shu'ūbiyya is a historical concept with roots in the eighth century. It originated in a fierce controversy that raged in the Arab world concerning the cultural orientation of the newly established and expanding Islamic culture and society. Briefly, the issue at stake then was whether this culture and this society were to become – in the words of Professor Hamilton Gibb – "a re-embodiment of the old Perso-Aramaean culture into which the Arabic and Islamic elements would be absorbed, or a culture in which the Perso-Aramaean contribution would be

subordinated to the Arab tradition and the Islamic values." Those who advocated the ascendancy of the non-Arab cultures were termed *shu'ūbiyya,* a word deriving from *shu'ūb,* plural for *sha'b* (people). Cf. Hamilton Gibb, "The Social Significance of the Shuubiya," in Hamilton H.A.R. Gibb, *Studies on the Civilization of Islam,* edited by Stanford J. Shaw and William R. Polk (London, 1962), p. 66.

13 See Note 10.

14 Fatḥī Ghānim, *"as'ila muḥayyira"* ["Perplexing Questions"], *Ṣabāḥ al-Khayr* (Cairo), 25 January 1962.

15 Ṭāha Ḥusayn, *mustaqbal ath-thaqāfa fī miṣr* ["The Future of Culture in Egypt"] (Cairo, 1938). Quoted in Nissim Rejwan, "The Intellectuals in Egyptian Islam," *New Outlook* (Tel Aviv), September 1964, pp. 40–43.

16 Abd ar-Raḥmān 'Azzām's version of the remarks made to him by Zaghlūl has been widely quoted. Among others, see article by Ṣalāḥ 'Abd al-Ṣabūr in *Rose al-Yūsuf,* 3 August 1959.

17 Fatḥī Raḍwān, *Akhbār al-Yawm,* 21 March 1953.

18 Printed in full in *al-Muṣawwar,* 17 April 1953.

19 Ḥusayn Fawzī, *sindbād misrī: jawlāt fī riḥāb at-ta'rīkh* ["An Egyptian Sindbad: Excursions in the Vistas of History"] (Cairo, 1961), p. 347.

20 'Abd ar-Raḥmān ar-Rāfi'ī, *al-qawmiyya al-'arabiyya* ["Arab Nationalism"], *al-Hilāl* (Cairo), December 1961, p. 10.

21 Ḥasan Maḥmūd, 'Abd al-Laṭīf Ibrāhīm et al., *al-wajīz fī dirāsat al-mujtama' al-'arabī* ["A Short Study of Arab Society"] (Cairo, 1963), pp. 88, 94.

22 'Alī Ḥusnī al-Kharbūṭlī, *Muḥammad w'al-qawmiyya al-'arabiyya* ["Muḥammad and Arab Nationalism"] (Cairo, 1962), pp. 12, 35.

23 Suwaylim al-'Umarī, *al-mujtama' al-'arabī* ["Arab Society"] (Cairo, 1963), pp. 36, 38.

24 Buṭrus B. Ghālī, Maḥmūd K. 'Īsā and 'Abdullah 'Awda, *al-mujtama' al-'arabī* ["Arab Society"] (Cairo, 1960), pp. 28–29.

25 *Ibid.,* p. 26.

26 *Ibid.* The authors relate that when the Arab League Charter was promulgated in 1945 one of its articles ruled that for a country to be accepted as a League member it has to be "a state, independent and Arab." When, however, one of the delegates asked that the term "Arab" should be defined, the subject was discussed and it was decided that there was no need for such a definition – though it was

agreed that the Arabism on whose foundation the League was built relies on cultural rather than religious or racial ties. This culture, it was further agreed, is formed by a feeling of a shared past and a common future. For this feeling there cannot, however, be either a gauge or a limit.

27 *Ibid.*, pp. 27–28.

28 *Ibid.*, pp. 28, 30.

29 Muḥammad Anīs, *dirāsat al-qawmiyya al-'arabiyya min an-nāḥiyatayn an-naẓariyya w'at-ta'rīkhiyya* ["The Study of Arab Nationalism from the Theoretical and Historical Aspects"] (Cairo, 1961), p. 161.

30 Hamilton Gibb, cited in Quincy Wright, "Conditions Making for Instability in the Middle East," in William Sands (ed.), *Middle East Report 1959* (Washington, 1959), p. 8.

31 Wright, *op. cit.*, pp. 8–9.

32 Quoted in Hans Kohn, *Pan-Slavism: Its History and Ideology* (New York, 1960), pp. 24–25.

33 *Ibid.*, p. 26.

# 5. IN SEARCH OF THEORY

Theory has never occupied a prominent place in Nasserist thinking. Indeed, on the few occasions when Nasser touched upon the subject of theory he invariably displayed a rather clear disinclination to "theorizing" as against action and implementation. In November 1961, when he was engaged in the formulation of the Revolution's manifesto, the *National Charter,* Nasser cautioned members of the Preparatory Committee convened for that purpose against detaching themselves from "real problems and engaging in disentangling imaginary riddles." "Such riddles," he said, "are one thing, and the problems for which solutions are required are another thing. One must rather grapple with, and seek solutions for, the real problems actually confronting the people." At another meeting of the Committee Nasser declared: "We are not here for pure theories; nor must we occupy ourselves here with pure theories. Let each of us say what he has to say; but let us all keep constantly in mind application and implementation. From our words and from implementation we can finally arrive at the theory we require. A theory is nothing but a guide to action."[1]

The truth is that Nasser could just as convincingly have said that action was a guide to theory: first act and then theorize! This, indeed, has been the declared attitude to the subject of the Revolution's spokesmen from the very beginning. In 1958 Iḥsān 'Abd al-Quddūs, one of the most prolific of these spokesmen, wondered – quoting Anwar as-Sādāt – "why do we suffer from the reluctance of intellectual scholars to interpret the July 23 [1952] Revolution, to formulate its principles and [set] its goals? " The reason, 'Abd al-Quddūs added, cannot reside in a dearth of Egyptian thinkers; it cannot lie in an insensitivity towards the Revolution or in lack of contact with it. "The reason is that the Revolution, at this particular stage, is not in need of theoretical thinking, or analysis, as much as it is in need of practical thinking, i.e. of executive study *(ad-dirāsa at-tanfīdhiyya).* The Revolution, at this stage, is no longer a mere message spread by emissaries; it is an actuality supervised by an executive power."

Every revolution, 'Abd al-Quddūs explains, goes through three stages:

1. The pre-revolutionary stage, "which is the stage of intellectual activity and doctrinal mission." This stage "is dominated by the thinkers, the philosophers, and the missionaries. In it books, manuscripts and political writing predominate."

2. The revolutionary stage. "This is the period which directly follows the revolution, and in which the revolutionaries hold power, i.e. become an executive force." In this stage, the activity of the thinkers and writers decreases in intensity, "because the revolution at this stage becomes in need of practical men – of engineers more than philosophers, of diplomats more than missionaries, of economists and soldiers more than writers."

3. The post-revolutionary stage. "After the revolution has been stabilized and its hold on power has become firm – and after it succeeds in attaining its goals – the thinkers and philosophers again assume an important role. This is to record the history of the revolution – not just its chronological development but its philosophical growth – contemplating the steps which it took and articulating outlooks and creeds that would interpret and justify these steps."[2]

Yet whereas, according to 'Abd al-Quddūs, every revolution in history has to pass through these three phases, the July 23 Revolution was unique in that "it was a Revolution not executed by a particular party with a specific ideology." It was, rather, "a Revolution carried out by a small group deriving its strength from its members, patriotism and daring, while deriving its popular power from the general dissatisfaction with the conditions then prevalent." This state of affairs, 'Abd al-Quddūs implies, puts the July 23 Revolution in need of a theory and an ideology, and he calls upon intellectuals and scholars to "philosophize" the Revolution, to set out to interpret it, to articulate its principles and to define its goals.[3]

It is noteworthy that 'Abd al-Quddūs does not speak of ideology or even of theory; he calls merely for interpreting the Revolution and formulating its goals. The most insistent calls for a "theory" have come from those who already possess one – the Marxists. The core of the theoretical problem of Arab Socialism has been the difficulty of defining and "placing" it. The *National Charter* certainly speaks of "scientific socialism" and its "inevitability"; but it also contains a good deal of other terms and concepts which tend to leave the student of ideology somewhat baffled, and in the end it transpires that when it refers to "scientific socialism" this is not the same as the "scientific socialism" which the Marxists use to denote their own brand of *Marxist* socialism. In the following chapter an attempt will be made to find out whether Arab Socialism is a new brand of socialism, an Arab application of socialism, or merely an Arab path to socialism. Here we shall try to answer the question as to whether – and to what extent – the ideology of the present regime in Egypt has occupied itself with problems of theory. Nasser himself, as we have seen, set no great store by theory, adopting a version of the learn-while-you-work philosophy.

It was natural, then, that the Marxist supporters of the regime should be the most insistent about this particular aspect of the ideology. One of the Marxist-oriented intellectuals of the regime, Muḥammad 'Awda, has been especially prolific on the subject of theory, not only in so far as it affected the July 23 Revolution but in the far wider framework of revolutionary movements in the Third World as a whole. After attaining their independence, 'Awda writes, the peoples of Asia and Africa were confronted by an acute problem: What to do with their newly-earned freedom? What guide should they have in their drive to build their new lives? To be sure, these peoples have their own intellectual and cultural heritages on which they could normally draw; but these heritages were "distorted and scattered." However, having attained their freedom in an age of mounting ideological strife, the peoples of the Third World found it difficult to participate in this strife by choosing between one or the other of the warring camps. They sought, instead, to defend their right to intellectual and ideological independence. There was, however, another objective reason for this reluctance. The ideologies of both the Capitalist and the Communist camps were products of a heritage, a mind and society that were all Western. Capitalist ideology is the ideology of the European bourgeoisie, while Marxism is the ideology of the European proletariat – and both had arisen in special, specifically Western historical, social and economic contexts. Yet, though the newly liberated peoples of the Third World had a different history, a different heritage and different socio-economic and cultural conditions, this did not mean that these peoples ought to turn their back on all Western theories and ideologies, since these comprise an integral part of the heritage of humanity as a whole – all the more so since in their basic principles these ideologies embrace part of the heritage of Asia and Africa. What it did mean is that the peoples of the Third World should study these ideologies and even be guided by them, but only through a quest for their own personalities, a search for specific solutions to their specific problems, and an attempt to create and perfect an all-embracing theory to guide them.[4]

Having said this, however, ‘Awda turns to an analysis of Marxism in which he seeks to show that it is adaptable enough to suit practically all tastes and all circumstances. Marxism, he tells us, is an all-embracing theory concerned with every facet of human existence and human society, with interpreting the world as well as changing it; yet it is not a dogma. Marx himself asserted that he was not laying the foundations of a new religion but only articulating a system of thought and a method of analysis; he even went so far as to declare that he was not a Marxist! After his death, moreover, several schools of Marxist theory emerged. There were the ultra-orthodox who advocated a sort of rigid dead-letter conformity to anything Marx wrote or said. Then there were some who, though accepting the theory and adhering to its general precepts, were able to perceive that developments in Europe in the socio-economic sphere were taking a course that was different from that delineated by Marx. A third trend went so far as to demand a revision of Marx's doctrines so as to make Marxism take cognizance of those developments which belied Marx's predictions and expectations.

Marxism thus became highly flexible, and various creative followers of the doctrine succeeded in moulding its principles and adapting them to the special circumstances in their own respective countries. Lenin did this for Russia, Tito for Yugoslavia, Mao Tse-tung for China, Gomulka for Poland, and Ho Chi Minh for Vietnam. Marxism was thus a flexible, easily adaptable philosophy that could be made to fit developed and developing, Eastern and Western countries alike.[5]

How does all this apply to the particular situation in revolutionary Egypt? ‘Awda turns to this subject in another instalment of his article. The July 23 Revolution, he asserts, has confronted "the problem of revolutionary theory" from the very beginning; it confronted it when it merged with the general Arab revolution, and it still confronts it now. In the years preceding the 1952 Revolution, 'Awda writes, four ideological trends prevailed in Egypt, each seeking to dominate the revolutionary wave and steer it in its own direction. These were the "nationalist trend," represented by the majority party, the Wafd; the "religious trend," represented by the Muslim Brethren; the "Marxist-Leninist trend," represented by the various communist groups; and the "social democratic trend," represented by the Socialist Party. The nationalist trend, which for many years gave expression to the general climate of Egyptian popular sentiment, ultimately failed because it had "no blueprint, no programme, no doctrine, and no comprehensive revolutionary theory." The religious trend failed for very much the same sort of reasons. Because it was weak ideologically and inept organizationally, it failed to comprehend, let alone lead, the people's revolution; and, instead of joining forces with the nationalist elements, it threw itself into the lap of reaction and collaborated with it against the majority party. As for the "social democratic trend," this too – although it contributed to propagating the word "socialism" and participated in the general national struggle and in disseminating the idea of a social revolution – was unable to lay down a democratic, socialist programme for resolving Egypt's national and social problems. In short, "it failed to adapt social democratic theories and principles [to the country's needs] and thus create a suitable Egyptian ideology." Finally, the communist trend, according to 'Awda, also failed, because its protagonists did not grasp Egyptian realities, neither theoretically nor on the practical level. It therefore could not adapt Marxist theory to these realities, partly because its leaders lacked the creative intellectual ability to do so. Moreover, "one of the main obstacles which separated the Egyptian masses from communist ideology was the discrepancy between Marxism's materialistic view of the world and the spiritual, mystic nature of the Egyptian people." There was, 'Awda concludes, one feature that was common to all the four pre-revolutionary trends listed above: "their theoretical weakness served as the basis of their organizational ineptness, and finally of their political ineffectuality."[6]

While all these trends failed, 'Awda reminds us, another kind of new leadership was forming and steadily growing in strength – the Free Officers' movement which developed in the ranks of the Egyptian army.

This movement, which 'Awda says was compelled, against its will and plans, to take over power in July 1952, came without any prior preparation on the ideological plane. Having early in its career had to merge with a general pan-Arab revolutionary wave, moreover, the Free Officers' movement discovered that the latter suffered from a similar ideological vacuum, and the struggle soon became one of seeking to formulate "an Arab theory of revolution." The July 23 Revolution soon realized, moreover, that "the revolutionary ideology cannot be manufactured, imposed, or borrowed, but must emerge and mature simultaneously out of theory and practice alike, and to the same degree." The Revolution also perceived that in order for the ideology genuinely to be embraced by the people it must be a continuity of that people's thought and heritage; it must not be an artificial or alien doctrine, a product of rhetoric and mere casuistry; it must be a guide for action. Finally, 'Awda concludes, the Revolution realized that the new theory must at one and the same time represent the essence of everything the people has created and produced, and the best in the thought of humanity and the intellectual endeavours of the age.[7]

The July 23 Revolution, 'Awda writes in the third and final instalment of his study, did not seek a narrow, sectarian ideology. It sought, on the contrary, to furnish "an ideological synthesis" that would serve as the basis of Arab revolutionary theory and a guide for action. The Revolution realized, he writes,

1. that the failure of the Egyptian nationalists to lead and implement the Revolution does not mean that nationalism itself ought to be rejected;

2. that the failure of the Muslim Brethren to seize the revolutionary leadership and implement the Revolution does not mean the failure of religion or its rejection;

3. that the failure of the social democrats to play the leading role in the Revolution does not imply the rejection either of socialism or democracy; and, finally,

4. that the communists' failure does not mean that Marxism should be rejected.[8]

Thus the Free Officers' Revolution of July 23, 1952, refrained from rejecting any of the ideologies prevalent in Egypt at the time; indeed, it flirted with all of them, trying to preserve something of each, without committing itself to any of them. During the first decade of the Revolution this ideological vacillation resulted in a great deal of confusion and misunderstanding, and those of the Egyptian intellectuals who tried to make a coherent whole out of the maze of fragmented doctrines, philosophical theories and political trends which seemed to have made up the official ideology got their fingers burnt very early in the proceedings. One example is that of Professor ʻAbd al-ʻAzīz ʻIzzat, Head of the Sociology Department at Cairo University. In 1960, ʻIzzat published a book entitled *Arab Ideology* in which he set out to perform the improbable feat of propounding the ideological bases of the July 23 Revolution and the Free Officers' regime. According to the poet and literary journalist Aḥmad ʻAbd al-Muʻṭī Ḥijāzī, the book presented the ideology of the Revolution as a veritable hotchpotch. The work, Ḥijāzī wrote, "combines myth with science" and, what is even more revealing, speaks "in all languages and dialects." Thus, in Professor ʻIzzat's strange book "you will hear the viewpoints of the Communists, the Black Shirts, the Capitalists, the Theologians, the Enemies of Woman . . . but will never meet with the Arab viewpoint, despite the title of the book. . . . You will never feel the depth of learning or the dignity of science, notwithstanding the author's position in the academic world."[9]

What worried Ḥijāzī most about the book was that "some foreigners may be misled into thinking that it embodies our views on the intellectual and political problems which it tackles." It transpires, moreover, that the book was originally written nearly five years previously and published under the innocuous title *Egypt and Socialist Cooperative Democracy,* and that, when union with Syria was proclaimed, the author contented himself with changing the title to "Arab Ideology." The results were disastrous.

For one thing, the author "forgot" to delete from his original book statements which clearly contradicted the Arab nationalist doctrine, such as "Egypt above all" – a sentiment which Ḥijāzī claims "never was one of our slogans neither before nor after the union." On the contrary, he explains, the United Arab Republic's greatest task is to resist the Great Powers which try to place themselves above the small states! The author's other sins include his expressions of distaste for industrialization, which Ḥijāzī counters by asking in a shocked tone whether "we should close down our cities and industries and go to the country." The author is also taken to task for opposing what he considers the un-Islamic doctrine of equality between the sexes.

But it is for his political opinions that Professor 'Izzat receives his severest chastisement. The author, for example, states that there are two dominant ideologies in the world at present, the Communist and the Capitalist, and that Arab ideology should not identify itself with either of them. This seems to be acceptable to Ḥijāzī, except for the fact that Dr. 'Izzat does not at all seem to be aware of the idea of nationalism, which his critic considers to take precedence over everything else. Loyalty to the Arab nation, he says, should transcend all other ideological loyalties. Dr. 'Izzat is also accused of the cardinal sin of defending Israel. Ḥijāzī explains:

> The most astonishing thing in the book, which purports to explain the Arab ideology to university students, is that it defends Israel . . . . True, the Professor did not intend [this], but as he is a good-natured man and blissfully unaware of what goes on in our daily life, he writes that the pessimists believe that religion in itself cannot be a pillar and a factor in nationalism and in the rise of nations. . . . He [the author] goes on: This, however, is a fallacy, something which is negated by the reality which lies under our very eyes. For the fact is that there are states which were founded on this basis, and this basis only, such as Pakistan and Israel. . . . And thus the Professor believes that the establishment of Israel on the basis of religion has nothing queer or abnormal about it . . . and believes further that Arab unity should be built on this same foundation! [10]

The confusion of which Ḥijāzī justly accuses Dr. 'Izzat is only a by-product of the confusion which continues to prevail about the precise character of the dominant ideology in Egypt. The confusion is something more than merely theoretical; it has raised difficulties not only of interpretation but also of practice and political attitude. And here too the intellectuals faced a peculiar problem – the problem of their ideological affiliation. A good deal of criticism and mutual recrimination has ensued, and the "intellectuals" have been the subject of much discussion and controversy. Whereas, however, in the early sixties this criticism was directed at the intellectuals' alleged indifference, apathy, and failure to take an active part in the "people's struggle," discussion gradually began to revolve around their political differences, the disparity between their views, and their apparent failure to agree upon one uniform meaning of socialism and the means best fitted to achieve it. This, obviously, is part and parcel of the regime's elusive search for theory.

The problem is depicted as a serious one, for it seems that despite the appearance of uniformity and conformism far-reaching differences of opinion persist among these intellectuals. 'Abd al-Quddūs has claimed that the Egyptian intellectuals are "the most disunited, scattered and mutually-hostile group in the country." He is, to be sure, quite aware that differences between intellectuals are normal and accepted all over the world, but he asserts that among Egyptian intellectuals these differences are unnatural, since they never take a clear-cut form. These differences, he writes, "refuse to come to the surface and would not define themselves frankly. They lurk beneath the surface in various undercurrents that collide with each other violently." As a result, contradictory trends appear on the surface and create political confusion and bewilderment.

'Abd al-Quddūs' analysis is revealing. The reason why these differences are never frankly aired, he writes, is that all Egyptian intellectuals, whether of the Left or of the Right, carry the banner of socialism in general and Arab Socialism in particular. What went wrong, he asserts, was that each of these intellectuals embraced Arab Socialism while continuing to maintain attitudes formed before the emergence of this socialism. Instead of revising his already formed attitudes, he contents himself with studying President Nasser's *National Charter* and looking there for justification for those attitudes that would confirm him even further in maintaining them!

Nor are these differences of opinion among the intellectuals concerned merely with ways and means; "they are basic ideological differences affecting all trends and tendencies." The surprising thing is that these differences all revolve around the *National Charter,* "so that freedom in interpreting the *Charter* has become a factor and a cause in intensifying these differences, and the primary cause of the intellectuals' disunity." The only way out of this impasse, 'Abd al-Quddūs believes, is to strive for the unity of the intellectuals. "This unity cannot be achieved unless we attain unity of doctrine. This, in turn, cannot be attained unless there is unity in interpreting the *Charter* – every line and every word of it."[11]

Be that as it may, it was obvious that a revolutionary ideology embracing so varying and rather disparate versions of socialism, democracy, and the status of religion would lead not merely to misunderstanding but also to a lot of mischief. Since the regime's opponents were not free to express their dissent, many of them took to covert opposition, a kind of ideological subversion-through-infiltration. Instead of coming out in the open in opposition to the official philosophy, they chose to exploit the general confusion by ostensibly embracing the ideology of the regime while at the same time seeking to disrupt it from within. Dr. 'Iṣmat Sayf ad-Dawla, for instance, devotes the bulk of his 400-page book, *The Foundations of Arab Socialism,* to a critique of Marxism. In the few pages which deal with the subject proper, he manages virtually to empty Arab Socialism of all really socialist content. Socialism in our country, he asserts, has "a distinctive content." He goes on to explain:

> Arab Socialism does not mean the abolition of private ownership of the means of production advocated by the Marxists. It does not mean the equitable distribution of [the national] income and job opportunities advocated by the Fabians. It does not mean the raising of the standard of living as sought by socialists in affluent lands. What it means encompasses all this and other things which spring from our circumstances and cross into our future [sic! ]. It means [Arab] unity, freedom and affluence all at once. This is what distinguishes Arab Socialism from other conceptions of socialism; this is what distinguishes Arab Socialists from other socialists, whether Marxists or non-Marxists.

It follows, therefore, that he is not an Arab Socialist who advocates and fights for the abolition of private ownership of the means of production; he is not an Arab Socialist who reconciles himself to Arab political fragmentation or accepts dictatorship (! ); and he is not an Arab Socialist who advocates and fights for an equitable distribution of the national income and job opportunities, or the raising of the standard of living. The Arab Socialist, Dr. Sayf ad-Dawla insists, is "he who advocates and fights for freedom, [Arab] unity and socialism at one and the same time."[12]

In a review of Sayf ad-Dawla's book Dr. Zakī Najīb Maḥmūd, editor of *al-Fikr al-Mu'āṣir* and one of Egypt's leading philosophers, displays similar anti-Marxist inclinations but tries to couch his sentiments in highly philosophical jargon concerning the role of will, the meaning of action, and the problem of individual freedom. ("The will itself is the action that realizes the desired objectives. Where there is no action, there is no will – and every action must represent a change in the state of things.")[13] However, such attempts at neutralizing and obscuring Arab Socialism and emptying it of all Marxist content do not normally go unchallenged. Maḥmūd Amīn al-'Alim, a known Egyptian Marxist, takes issue with both Dr. Sayf ad-Dawla and Dr. Maḥmūd. In trying to refute their claims 'Alim uses the simple but well-tested device of taking cover under the benign shade of the *National Charter,* in which Nasser speaks of the "Socialist solution" as "an historical inevitability dictated by realities."[14]

Clearly, the differences of which 'Abd al-Quddūs speaks, and of which Sayf ad-Dawla's opinions furnish a striking example, seem far too basic and significant to be resolved by offering a uniform, foolproof interpretation of the *National Charter.* There are, in fact, some who have dared to say so openly. Ghālib Halsa, for instance, believes that what the Arabs need most is "an all-embracing Arab philosophy reflecting the phase through which we are living and furnishing, at the same time, a programme to guide us in our path." Halsa submits that the most serious obstacle in the way of creating such a philosophy is the Arabs' insistence on rejecting all ideas derived from the experiences of other peoples "on the ground that they are imported ideas born in surroundings different from ours and invoking values and ideals foreign to our own." This attitude, he says, springs from "failure to distinguish between what is positive and what is negative in the human heritage." A healthier attitude toward the creation of a fertile Arab philosophy would be "to consider the positive aspects of all philosophies valid and useful for us."[15]

Halsa lays part of the blame at the door of the intellectuals. Failure to formulate such a philosophy, he claims, is nothing but "an expression of the intellectuals' despair of themselves and of their intellects." He accuses the Arab intellectual of betraying his true mission. For him, the intellectual is by definition a revolutionary, "who speaks of the future and proclaims a state of permanent protest against the present . . . . The intellectual who concentrates on praising what exists is a traitor to his mission." Halsa then demands candidly that the intellectual be permitted to play his role in full. Citing the case of Stalin's Russia, he warns that "the consequences will be grave and terrible if we fail to give the intellectuals an opportunity to perform their role properly and in a positive manner." This means, he explains, that the intellectual cannot be an official thinker serving the immediate ends of any regime. He deplores "the prevalent belief that the best way to treat the intellectual is to flood him with privileges and make of him a well-to-do man." What helps spread this belief is that many intellectuals "reach for material gains with great eagerness and are willing, for the sake of these gains, to surrender everything."[16]

Yet, despite the damning indictment, all the more striking for its frankness and candour, Halsa in the end fails to outline even in the broadest of terms the all-embracing Arab philosophy of which he says the Arabs are so direly in need. This is rather typical of most of the talk then current in Egypt and other Arab countries about the meaning of the cultural heritage and the need for an authentic and genuine Arab culture and outlook. Perhaps the most perceptive comment in this connection is the one made by Dr. Fu'ād Zakariyya, who teaches philosophy at Cairo University. Commenting on Halsa's plea that the Arabs accept the positive aspects of all philosophies as valid and useful for them, Dr. Zakariyya reflects that, though the plea sounds quite reasonable, it presupposes that the Arabs in their present condition can distinguish between what is positive and what is negative in other philosophies. Yet, in order to be able to make such distinctions one must have a basis on which to judge. In other words: "In order for the Arabs to have a philosophy, they must have a philosophy! "[17] "When and how," asks Dr. Zakī Maḥmūd in his review of Sayf ad-Dawla's book (see above), "will we have a pure Arab philosophy that can be regarded as a contribution to world and local intellectual problems – a contribution bearing our genuine mark? "[18] Yet, he too fails to provide the answer.

Far from articulating such a pure, comprehensive "Arab philosophy," the revolutionary intelligentsia of Egypt has not managed satisfactorily even to define the precise socio-economic and historical nature of the Free Officers' Revolution. The subject, indeed, has been a source of some embarrassment to the regime itself, an embarrassment which is due in large measure to that same ideological confusion inherent in the eager search for a theory. During the first two years of his regime, President Nasser advanced the theory that, while it was true that the Free Officers' coup was a purely "political revolution," it was the "social revolution" that was its true object, and that this social revolution will come in due course. The objectives of this dual revolution were finally formulated in the Preamble to the 1956 Constitution: the eradication of imperialism, feudalism and capitalist monopolies; the establishment of a strong national army; ensuring social justice; and the establishment of a democratic society.

All these and other ideological aspects of the July 23 Revolution were elaborated upon further in Nasser's *National Charter.* Yet, when "The July 23 Revolution" was introduced as a course of study in Egyptian universities and colleges as part of the compulsory "nationalist subjects," nothing approaching a clear idea was offered to the students as to the nature, historical setting and social meaning of that Revolution. Books hastily concocted by lecturers and professors holding widely divergent views on the subject were offered to the students with no apparent direction or "philosophy." However, three main approaches to the subject can be discerned in these books: the chronological, the comparative and the "scientific."

The chronological approach has been criticized on two counts: books written in this spirit confine themselves to giving liberal accounts of the events preceding and following the Revolution, with no attempt at interpretation and analysis; when such an attempt is made, however, the interpretation offered is superficial and colourless. Examples of this approach abound. In his book *The July 23 Revolution,* Dr. Muṣṭafā Ḥaddāra of Alexandria University offers a newsreel-type account of the events leading to the Officers' Revolt, while contenting himself with repeating what the *National Charter* had to say on such topics as the 'Urābī movement and the revolt of 1919.[19] Dr. Ṭu'ayma al-Jurf, author of "The July Revolution and the Principles of Government in the United Arab Republic," is only a little more helpful as far as interpretation is concerned, but his book has the drawback of ignoring the importance of outside influences and pressures in the events leading to the outbreak and failure of the 'Urābī movement, to the revolt of 1919, and to the 1952 Revolution.[20]

Errors of interpretation arising from the chronological approach and from too strict a conformity to the official text lead Dr. 'Abd al-Ḥamīd Kamāl Ḥashīsh of Cairo University's Law College to an unacceptable position in regard to the nature of the 1952 Revolution, whose dual character (political-social), he says, had marked it since its inception. The truth, however, was that up to 1961, when the famous socialist measures were announced, the Revolution remained predominantly political in character and it was only after July 1961 that its social phase was started in earnest.[21]

An even more common, and more haphazard approach is the "comparative" one, whose proponents, instead of concentrating on the subject at hand, resort to drawing doubtful comparisons between the 1952 Revolution and the great revolutions of the past – the French, American, English, Russian and Chinese. In his book *The July 23 Revolution,* Dr. Suwaylim al-'Umarī of Cairo University offers brief and rather superficial studies of each of these revolutions, and proceeds to compare each of them with the 1952 movement in Egypt. For example, after describing the English Revolution as "an extended revolution" Dr. 'Umarī finds many similarities between the two – mainly their reformist character, their avoidance of violence, and the fact that both of them are "extended." With the American Revolution he also finds affinities, since it, too, was a movement aiming at "the freedoms of the individual, equality between citizens . . . and liberation from domination, exploitation and monopoly." Between the Egyptian Revolution, on the one hand, and the Russian and Chinese ones, on the other, Dr. 'Umarī finds no room for comparison whatsoever, since in his opinion the July movement "adopted the capitalist system and respected private property" – and since it has no revolutionary aspirations outside the boundaries of the Arab world."[22]

The only instance of the third, so-called "scientific" approach to the Revolution that can be cited here is a study by Dr. Muḥammad Anīs under the title *The July 23 Revolution and its Historical Origins.* In this book Dr. Anīs, who writes in collaboration with Dr. Sayyid Kharāz, divides the 1952 Revolution into three phases:

1. "The Revolution for National Liberation," or the National

Democratic Revolution (1952–57).

2. "The Arab Nationalist Revolution," covering the period of the Egypt-Syria merger (1958–1961).

3. "The Ideological Revolution," marking the transition period between capitalist society and socialist society, and which began in 1961.[23]

The confusion was all but complete. By 1963, indeed, ideological vacillation and uncertainty became such that, partly to remedy this situation but ostensibly also in order to spread "socialist consciousness" amongst the masses, the Higher Executive Committee of the Arab Socialist Union early that year decided to set up a "Socialist Institute" whose official objective would be twofold: to conduct "comprehensive studies in socialism" and to produce "elements of leadership that are conscious ideologically." Commenting on the decision Rajā an-Naqqāsh, one of the leading intellectual spokesmen of the regime, asserted that the United Arab Republic was "in urgent need of such an institute, since the process of socialist transformation cannot be attained merely by issuing revolutionary decrees and resolutions." According to Naqqāsh, it is essential for this purpose to create "the mentality required for carrying out such decrees." For nearly 150 years, he explains, the Egyptian state engaged in training bureaucratic-minded officials who would faithfully serve and blindly obey the state. Since throughout all that period government in Egypt was in the hands of the feudalists and the British, the army of officials in that country came to assume a distinctly cynical and derisory attitude towards the common people, and this persisted even after the 1952 Revolution. Indeed, the situation is so bad that bureaucratic sloth and apathy have resulted in such revolutionary decrees as have been issued either losing much of their edge or being entirely foiled, Naqqāsh claims.

Citing the example of Government hospitals and clinics, where he says doctors and petty officials mistreat patients, boss them about and generally sneer at them, Naqqāsh asserts that this sort of old and outdated mentality neither suits the new socialist society nor gives it genuine expression.

Since this mentality is so deep-rooted, any bid at changing it will have to be a systematic and long-range operation. It may be easy to eradicate various material features of the old regime, but when it comes to habits and attitudes the effort must be long and patient. It will be one of the duties of the Socialist Institute to disseminate the new socialist attitude and mentality.

In addition to this partly practical task, the Institute will be called upon to see to it that the huge intellectual effort and output of present-day Egypt is carefully "planned." Since 1952, no original thorough studies of socialism appeared which could have a real impact on the Egyptian mind; all that was done was to publish Arabic translations of some foreign books on the subject, as well as the innumerable articles written in various magazines and newspapers. It is the Institute's duty to coordinate and plan all these diffuse efforts in a bid to produce something really effective and lasting. The fact is, Naqqāsh adds, that the *ancien régime* had its own intellectual pillars erected over a number of years. Its ideological edifice was quite impressive, and its mentality and outlook were formulated by such intellectual leaders as Aḥmad Amīn, who in the thirties and forties of this century aimed at a complete re-evaluation of Islamic and Arab history for his times; Dr. Ṭāha Ḥusayn, who, during the same period, produced re-appraisals of some aspects of Islamic history; Muḥammad Ḥusayn Haykal, 'Abbās Maḥmūd al-'Aqqād and others who engaged in similar re-appraisals.

Today's need is for the present generation of Arab Socialists to invest similar energy and effort into their own re-evaluation of Islamic, Arab and Egyptian history. So far, there has been only one such re-appraisal, i.e., the book on the Prophet Muḥammad written by the well-known Egyptian novelist 'Abd ar-Raḥmān ash-Sharqāwī.

In addition to such historical re-appraisals, Naqqāsh believes that Egyptian society in its present socialist phase has many other requirements which the new Institute can provide. There is a need for comprehensive studies of socialism and socialist theory written by Egyptians; books on socialist experiments made in the various socialist countries; studies of socialist parties everywhere, their programmes and their practices.

In conclusion, Naqqāsh expresses the hope that the new Institute will be "a turning point in our intellectual and moral life"; his hope, he says, is strengthened by the fact that the man who heads the new Institute is Kamāl Rif'at, a member of the Presidential Council and "one of the maturest socialist minds in Egypt."[24]

In this respect, however, little seems to have been accomplished by the Socialist Institute, and as the sixties came to a close the ideological problems of the revolutionary regime showed no signs of being finally resolved. (They were, to be sure, eclipsed and left lurking in the background after the defeat of June 1967; but they remained unresolved and, beneath the surface, became even more urgently relevant.) Muḥammad 'Awda's reflections on the quest for a theory, surveyed earlier in this chapter, were as valid in 1970 as in 1964, when they were published. His conclusions will furnish some perspective for this part of the Revolution's ideological endeavour. Although the Free Officers' Revolution succeeded where the four pre-revolutionary tendencies – the nationalist, religious, social democrat, and communist – failed, he argues, "this does not mean that the Revolution should remain experimental or 'pragmatic,' requiring no doctrine or theory. Nor should the resistance to the Revolution put up by all four tendencies necessarily mean that this theory and that doctrine should be sought outside these tendencies."[25]

The Revolution, 'Awda argues, was a continuation of Egyptian history and the Egyptian struggle; it was, indeed, the decisive battle of the Egyptian people and an eloquent expression of its heritage, its cultural legacy and the future to which it aspires. In order, therefore, for the theory to be authentic it must distill the essence of this heritage and integrate it into the country's new realities and the spirit of the age as a whole – it must distill this and integrate and re-create it in a way that will lay the foundations of the new theory. And this, 'Awda asserts, is what the Revolution has performed with genuine creativeness, serving this purpose in the form of the *National Charter.*

In the West, 'Awda explains, they assert that their creed and their outlook on life are a mixture of Greek philosophy, Roman law and Christian religion. In the East, they say that their creed is Marxism. Yet Marxism is itself a mixture and concoction consisting of German philosophy, English economics and French political thought. Throughout their history the Arabs' best-known intellectual characteristic was their ability to mix, synthesize and absorb – their way being to give and take, to interact and mix, to change the world and themselves to change along with the world. The Arab mind was able, within the framework of its faith and its mission, to absorb the thought of the Greeks, the Persians, the Indians and the Chinese, as well as the Western heritage of Spain, and to create something new, something distinctively Arab, thus starting a new cycle of Western civilization. The Egyptian intellect was especially suitable for this kind of mixing, synthesis, and absorption; it is as open to everything new as it is jealous of its own distinctiveness and special characteristics.

There is no reason, therefore, why political ideas and ideologies should not undertake the same kind of creative synthesizing. New creeds and theories can emerge as a result of a synthesis between, say, dialectical materialism and Christian idealism, capitalism and socialism, proletarian democracy and parliamentary democracy. What is more, this has actually been done. In India, Nehru's ideology is a synthesis of Fabianism, Marxism and Gandhism. In Indonesia, Sukarno's ideology is a synthesis of Islam, nationalism and Marxism. In Burma, they used to say: Marxists in this world, Buddhists in the next! In Africa Nkrumah described himself as a Christian Marxist, while Sékou Touré said something to the effect that he was an African Marxist leading a peaceful, religious and classless nation. Finally, Ben Bella spoke of Arab Muslim socialists – non-communists yet not anti-communists.[26]

This is why, 'Awda goes on to say, the extraction of an Arab revolutionary theory required a thorough, comprehensive study and a revolutionary re-evaluation of Egypt's heritage – a rediscovery from an Arab vantage point of the various creeds and theories. It required a re-appraisal of Islam and the Islamic religion – a re-appraisal which, conducted from the point of view of the Revolution and the age, would eliminate distortions perpetrated by the Caliphs, the rulers and their followers among the theologians. It also required a thorough study and re-appraisal of Arab history, and its rewriting as history as it was made by the people rather than history as it was manipulated and distorted by despots and imperialists. It required, too, a serious and thorough evaluation of the various ideological trends in the world as a whole and in Asia and Africa especially.

Theories, however, are not articulated in closed rooms; they emerge, grow and blossom as a result of a long process and continuous intellectual and ideological strife. The Arab revolution, as a continuous, far-reaching and wide-ranging revolution seeking no less than the re-creation of Arab life, was duty bound, in its search for a theory, to spread its net wide and conduct an extremely far-reaching process of ideological re-evaluation and re-appraisal. And this, according to 'Awda, is what the *National Charter* has largely achieved. "It furnished a basis and a blueprint for an Arab revolutionary theory in which it merged all the components of the Arab revolution and the Arab personality into the components of the age. It made clear the source on which it drew and the methodology it followed, and it has placed itself at the disposal of revolutionary thinkers and intellectuals in order that they can make it their starting point, develop it and deepen it."[27]

'Awda agrees, however, with what the *National Charter* itself asserts – namely, that the principles which the Revolution enunciated "did not comprise a comprehensive theory for revolutionary action." In the following chapters an attempt will be made to discover how adequate, coherent or consistent the socio-political and economic philosophy which the *National Charter* itself enunciates is – and the ways in which they add up to a coherent ideological whole or fail to do so.

## NOTES

1 Quoted in Fayez Sayegh, "The Theoretical Structure of Nasser's Socialism," *Middle Eastern Affairs,* St. Antony's Papers, No. 17, edited by Albert Hourani, Oxford, 1965, pp. 15–16.

2 Iḥsān 'Abd al-Quddūs, *"ayna falāsifat ath-thawra? "* ["Where are the Philosophers of the Revolution? "], *Rose al-Yūsuf,* 13 October 1958, p. 6.

3 *Ibid.*

4 Muḥammad 'Awda, *"ḥawl al-baḥth 'an naẓariyya"* ["On the Search for Theory"], *al-Kātib,* January 1964, pp. 39–42.

5 *Ibid.,* pp. 43–45.

6 Muḥammad 'Awda, *"ḥawl al-baḥth 'an naẓariyya"* ["On the Search for Theory – II"], *al-Kātib,* February 1964, pp. 25–26, 28, 30–32, 34–35. 'Awda takes pains to imply that the discrepancy between Marxism's materialist view of the world and the spiritual, mystic nature of the Egyptian people, was not authentic, but merely the result of a misunderstanding. Dialectical materialism, he explains, was partly a reaction to the role played by the Christian church in the service of feudalism and capitalism. Islam's role was different.

7 *Ibid.*, p. 40.

8 Muḥammad 'Awda, *"ḥawl al-baḥth 'an naẓariyya"* ["On the Search for Theory – III"], *al-Kātib,* March 1964, pp. 60–61.

9 Aḥmad 'Abd al-Mu'ṭī Ḥijāzī, *Rose al-Yūsuf,* 9 January 1961.

10 *Ibid.*

11 Iḥsān 'Abd al-Quddūs, *Rose al-Yūsuf,* 21 December 1964.

12 'Iṣmat Sayf ad-Dawla, *usus al-ishtirākiyya al-'arabiyya* ["The Foundations of Arab Socialism"] (Cairo, 1965), p. 379.

13 Zakī Najīb Maḥmūd, *"irādat at-taghyīr"* ["The Will to Change"], *al-Fikr al-Mu'āṣir,* July 1965. For Dr. Maḥmūd's opinions concerning Arab Socialism, see the following chapter, "Placing Arab Socialism."

14 Maḥmūd Amīn al-'Ālim, *"qaḍāyā fikriyya fī ṭarīq al-binā' al-ishtirākī"* ["Intellectual Issues on the Path of Socialist Construction"], *al-Hilāl* (Cairo), September 1964. Reprinted in his *ma'ārik fikriyya* ["Intellectual Disputations"], (Cairo, 1965).

15 Ghālib Halsa, *"al-ḥāja ilā falsafa"* ["The Need for a Philosophy"], *al-Adāb,* September 1964, pp. 18–19.

16 *Ibid.*, p. 19.

17 Fu'ād Zakariyya, *"kara'tu al-'adad al-māḍī min al-ādāb: al-abḥāth"* ["I Read the Previous Issue of al-Ādāb: Articles"], *al-Ādāb,* October 1964, p. 9. Halsa replied to Zakariyya's strictures in the following issue. See *"ḥawl naqd maqāl"* ["On Criticising an Article"], *al-Ādāb,* November 1964, pp. 65–66; a rejoinder by Zakariyya appeared in the December issue under – "I Read . . . ," see *al-Ādāb,* December 1964, pp. 17–20.

18 Zākī N. Maḥmūd, "Human Dialectics," *al-Fikr al-Mu'āṣir* (Cairo), October 1965. Quoted in Fawzī M. Najjār, "Islam and Socialism in the UAR," *Journal of Contemporary History,* Vol. 3 (July 1968), No. 3, p. 190.

19 Muṣṭafā Ḥaddāra, *thawrat thalātha wa-'ishrīn yūliu* ["The July 23 Revolution"], (Cairo, 1962), p. 23.

20 Ṭu'ayma al-Jurf, *thawrat yūliū wa-mabādi' an-niẓām as-siyāsī fī al-jumhūriyya al-'arabiyya al-muttaḥida* ["The July Revolution and the Principles of Government in the United Arab Republic"], (Cairo, 1962), p. 126.

21 'Abd al-Ḥamīd Kamāl Ḥashīsh, *thawrat thalātha wa-'ishrīn yūliū* ["The July 23 Revolution"] (Cairo, 1961), p. 200.

22 Suwaylim al-'Umarī, *thawrat thalātha wa-'ishrīn yūliū* ["The July 23 Revolution"] (Cairo, 1963), p. 28.

23 Muḥammad Anīs and Sayyid Harāz, *thawrat thalātha wa-'ishrīn yūliū*

*wa-uṣūluhā at-ta'rīkhiyya* ["The July 23 Revolution and Its Historical Origins"] (Cairo, 1963), p. 102.

24 Rajā' an-Naqqāsh, *"risālat al-qāhira"* ["A Letter from Cairo"], *al-Ādāb,* August 1963.

25 'Awda, *The Search for Theory – III,* p. 61.

26 *Ibid.*, pp. 61–63.

27 *Ibid.*, pp. 63–64.

# 6. PLACING ARAB SOCIALISM

It has often been remarked that Afro-Asian revolutionary movements against Western domination are themselves essentially Western in their ideology, their motivation, and their political character. Owing to the inevitable time and culture lags, however, it has been the lot of these movements to adopt ideas and concepts which now tend, in their original Western environments, to be somewhat out of date or suffer from the fate of so many political ideologies – namely, enter a phase of conflicting interpretations and heresies. The European doctrine of nationalism, for instance, arrived in the East at a time when it was beginning to be widely discredited in the West, while socialism, which almost all of the new nations of Asia and Africa have adopted as their chosen way of life and government, has since the aftermath of World War One been going through a phase of ideological confusion so acute that no one can now pretend to give a definition of it on which all "socialists" would agree. This has largely been responsible for the fact that in the Arab East socialism has never been clearly and satisfactorily defined by any of its theorists and proponents. This is as true of Arab Socialism, which grew out of what President Nasser in 1957 had termed the doctrine of the democratic, socialist, and cooperative society that the Revolution was endeavouring to build, as of any other brand of Afro-Asian socialism.

Speaking broadly, socialism can be defined as a political and economic doctrine according to which the means of production, distribution, and exchange are owned and controlled by the people, everyone is given an equal opportunity to develop his talents and potentialities, and the wealth of the community is equitably distributed. Whether or not one agrees with these aims or considers them feasible, one feels entitled to consider this definition of socialism sufficiently simple and comprehensive for it to be acceptable to all socialists of whatever school or predilection; any added qualifications or adjectives should mean no more than they actually appear to denote.

The founders and advocates of Arab Socialism, however, do not seem to have taken such a straightforward view of things. For them, the question as to whether Arab Socialism is an independent, brand-new doctrine or just ordinary socialism applied to Egypt and the Arab world is capable of provoking heated and sometimes angry controversy. This was so right from the start, when the heat and anger were directed at those who chose to raise the question in the first place: they were accused of lacking in good faith, in that by choosing to raise the question at all they were trying to arrogate to themselves the exclusive right of being called socialists.

The prevalent idea was that, though Arab Socialism indeed had a hard core of classical socialist doctrine, socialism was the monopoly of no one. The implication was that the Egyptian Revolution was as entitled to create its own kind of socialist doctrine as anyone else. As Muḥammad 'Awda argued in 1962, Arab Socialists believe that the tenets of socialism cannot be considered as final and as rigid as the tenets of the Church, and accordingly that those socialists who want to close the door in the face of any innovation or revolution do socialism more harm than good.[1]

Since Karl Marx, 'Awda writes, a great deal has happened: "New nations have emerged, ancient civilizations and cultures have been revived . . . . These new nations and people want to think and to create for themselves, to assert their own identities and personalities, and to create new theories and new systems. The true Marxist, who sees Marx as a socialist and not as a priest . . . has to go to the roots of these new experiences and phenomena, to learn from them and to develop his ideas accordingly."

The fact is, 'Awda continues, that the new, liberated nations did not accept communism as inevitable, at the same time rejecting capitalism as the natural law for man and the universe. "Thus there exists in the world now three forces, each with its doctrine and its political system and its own way of life."

If we do not want to see these three great forces go round in a vicious circle or suffer a collision that would annihilate everything, "we have to see to it that there evolve between them mutual influences, mutual understanding and ideology as well as physical coexistence."[2]

It is here that Arab Socialism can be of help, 'Awda implies. "In this field, history has given the Arabs and the Arab Revolution a role for which they are ideally suited. In the days of its highest [cultural] tide, Baghdad assimilated Greek civilization as well as the civilizations of India and China, and created a purely Arab, purely human [sic] heritage that lives on until this day. Cairo and Cordova did the same thing."

If the Arabs are now searching for a new theory of socialism, "in which they seek to combine their religion and spirituality, their nationalism and their Arabism with the general science of socialism, this is only in keeping with their true selves and with their historical and cultural role. In so doing, they would do harm to no one. On the contrary, they will be augmenting the life of the age and enhance the cause of peace as well as that of socialism."[3]

'Awda's claims may sound somewhat extravagant, but he was not alone in making such claims. In an article entitled "The National Charter and the Evolution of the Science of Socialism," printed in Egypt's leading cultural review *al-Kātib,* 'Abd ar-Raḥmān Shākir takes to task those who explain Nasser's use in his *National Charter* of the term "scientific socialism" as being aimed merely at ending the communists' monopoly over that particular phrase.

To imply, Shākir writes, that there is a vital difference between Arab Socialism and scientific socialism "is to ignore the most significant impact that the Arab experiment has made on the evolution of the science of socialism – an impact thanks to which this experiment is now entitled to be described, without any hesitation, as being a new phase in socialist thought, with a programme which is more instrumental in the implementation of socialism than any that has preceded it."

This, the writer goes on to say, is not only because Arab Socialism is the newest among leading socialist experiments, but also "because of its faithful depiction of the spirit of the age and of the change that has taken place in the world." The *National Charter* itself implied in more than one place that other reform programmes were no longer in keeping with the spirit of the times, "and that the main difference between us and the others lies in [our] awareness of the real and continuous change taking place in the world in which we live."

This, according to Shākir, is the foremost factor to be considered in studying the relation between the Arab experiment and the science of socialism. After all, the socialist doctrine has been formulated as far back as the middle of the nineteenth century, in an age of laisser faire and free competition and before capitalism entered its imperialist phase. Many things had changed since then, and neither capitalism nor communism was now practicable or advisable.

On the contrary, "the continued existence of communist parties – with their loyalties given to foreign powers – is one of the main causes of tension in the world today." The deterioration of the dictatorship of the proletariat into a tyrannical autocracy, too, made people look askance at communism.

All this had made it quite impossible for Arab Socialism to want to follow the example of those whose behaviour had disgusted the whole world [read: the communists]. Instead, it tried to learn from past experiences and act accordingly.

Arab Socialism believed that collective ownership was an effective way of accelerating industrialization in developing countries; but it refused to turn this belief into a fetish or – as Nasser put it in the *National Charter* – to sacrifice whole generations for the sake of those still unborn.[4]

On the other hand, Arab Socialism realized the error of those socialist schools which advocated the elimination of private ownership in agriculture; instead it decided to effect an equitable distribution of land among the peasants.

Seeing how the dictatorship of the proletariat had deteriorated into savage massacres and horrible tyranny, Arab socialism adopted the principle of "democracy for all the people" and advocated the settlement of all class conflicts peacefully, "unless the intrigues of reaction force it to take a different course of action."

Summing up, Shākir writes that Arab Socialism "has chosen the most humanitarian path to change, a path that is nearest to the requirements of human nature and most in keeping with the nation's ancient spiritual and ethical values." Thus, "what Arab Socialism contributes to the human heritage is no mere quantitative addition; it is a qualitative change and a scientific revolution." Moreover, Arab Socialism's programme is "the maturest of all socialist programmes and the farthest removed from emotional crudeness and dogmatic fanaticism."[5]

This was written relatively early in the proceedings – a few months after the publication of President Nasser's *National Charter* in May 1962. But the bulk of the early discussions concerning the nature of Arab

Socialism had taken place before the *National Charter* was made available – as a sort of preparation, in fact, for the final formulation of the *National Charter.* A sample of these discussions, as well as of those of more recent date, reveals the remarkable range of socialist opinions – moderate, militant, Marxist, "scientific," non-communist or even anti-communist – that have been taking refuge under the broad wings of Arab Socialism.

In November 1961, Nasser convened a meeting of leading intellectuals and representatives of the workers, the peasants and the professionals from all walks of life. The gathering, called the Preparatory Committee for the National Congress of Popular Forces, listened attentively to the President while he propounded before them what he wanted to see done and achieved in Egypt. He seemed to know exactly what he wanted; but he admitted that he and his revolutionary colleagues were "still in the coils of an experiment." "In our Revolution," he explained, "practice has preceded precept and theory."[6]

It was in response to this subtle appeal for ideological guidance that the theoreticians of the regime started to make their contributions to a search for the meaning of Arab Socialism. One of these was Iḥsān 'Abd al-Quddūs, who was among the first to try to tackle this thorny problem. He wrote shortly after the beginning of the National Congress of Popular Forces' deliberations, with reference to Nasser's statement concerning the precedence given by the Revolution to practice over theory: "Doctrine always precedes the revolution." The Prophet Muḥammad spent years in preaching the doctrine of Islam before he mustered enough followers and led them in a revolution against the pagans. Communism "started as a philosophy, then became a doctrine, and in the course of long and exhausting years the doctrine managed to obtain a popular basis to stand on." It was only then that the revolution came in Russia. Likewise, the socialism of the Labour Party in England was first formulated by the leaders of the Fabian Society. Not so our socialist Revolution, 'Abd al-Quddūs goes on to explain:

> The doctrine which preceded our Revolution was not a socialist one in the strict sense of the term . . . . Ours was a national revolution in the broad sense of the word "nationalism," and its doctrine was independence and the eradication of corruption.[7]

Here the writer becomes somewhat apologetic. This does not mean, he hastens to add, that the leadership of the Revolution was not a socialist one; it means merely that the Revolution relied on "a broad national basis" and not on "a narrow socialist" one.

This, he explains, was what made the Revolution in the early days after its victory open to the strife of many contradictory nationalist doctrines, ranging from the extreme Left to the extreme Right, without, however, any of these doctines being able to determine the Revolution's real orientation or to offer it the essential theoretical base.

But though 'Abd al-Quddūs recognizes the need for clarification, he does not succeed in making a real contribution towards a clear definition of Arab Socialism. He prefers to leave it to members of the Preparatory Committee for the National Congress of Popular Forces to tackle the job, he writes, and as a member of this Committee himself, he attempts no more than to describe the difficulties facing it. We have therefore to look elsewhere for guidance.[8]

The most coherent and detailed exposition of the points of difference between Arab Socialism and communism has been undertaken by one of its leading adherents, Muḥammad Ḥasanayn Haykal, editor of Cairo's influential and authoritative daily *al-Ahrām,* and President Nasser's chief spokesman. Haykal lists seven such points of difference, after carefully explaining that it is not his aim to attack communism, but merely to put his finger on the characteristics that distinguish the two ideologies.

The first difference between Arab Socialism and communism, according to Haykal, lies in their dissimilar views of the classes. Communism advocates the dictatorship of the proletariat as represented by the communist party, whereas Arab Socialism advocates "the melting away of class differences." In other words: "Communism asks the destitute to revolt against men of property and make them in turn destitute . . . while Arab Socialism asks them to revolt in order to obtain their right in property and their title to an equitable share in the national wealth." Communism wants one class to destroy the other classes completely, while Arab Socialism seeks the abolition of class contradictions "in the framework of national unity."

The second point of difference follows from the first: "Communism considers every man of property an exploiter, and therefore seeks his destruction . . . Arab Socialism differentiates between property belonging to the exploiting classes and property which represents work and endeavour." While communism liquidates the exploiter physically, Arab Socialism tries to disarm and disable him and then welcomes him into the new society, which is to be one in which all classes are transformed into a single class.

The third difference lies in the fact that communism advocates "expropriation" while Arab Socialism advocates "compensation"; its aim is justice and equity, not punishment and revenge.

The fourth point of difference between communism and Arab Socialism concerns the place of the individual in society. In communist society, the State owns everything, while the individual is a mere "working tool" who receives what is enough to satisfy his minimum needs. In Arab Socialism, on the other hand, the individual "is the basis of the social structure," while the State is "a popular tool for attaining justice and providing safeguards for it."

The fifth difference springs from the fourth. Communism, "especially during the period when Stalin directed the experiment," was based on sacrificing generations of human beings in order to attain affluent production. Communism is completely preoccupied with the future and cares nothing for the present while Arab Socialism does care for the present and refuses to sacrifice it for the future.

The sixth point of difference between communism and Arab Socialism, Haykal continues, is "the difference between literal copying and free adaptation . . . between inertia and movement, between blind dogmatism and free thought." The communist, "even if he conforms to Marxist analysis, cannot deviate from the fixed lines . . . otherwise he would be called a deviationist, like Tito." The Arab Socialist, on the other hand, "feels that the intellectual heritage of the whole world is open to him, that . . . he can add to it and participate in its growth. He can add to it his nationalist experience and can develop it with his own historical legacy." As Nasser put it, "we do not open books and copy from them; we open the book of our reality and try to find solutions for our situation." The difference, in short, seems to be one between the doctrinaire and the empiricist.

The seventh and last point in which Arab Socialism is said to differ from communism concerns political organizations. "Communism requires that the organization of political action be exclusively in the hands of the communist party . . . Arab Socialism believes that the organization of political action should embrace the whole nation, and should be based on a frame of national unity." Haykal concludes his comparison with a brief polemic against the communists. "Those," he writes, "who believe that evolution has only one way before it, a way whose beginning is capitalism and whose inevitable end is communism, imagine that History marches in a blind alley. Such a blind alley never existed! "[9]

Haykal's article, and especially his concluding remarks, came not so much as a reply to Arab communists as it did to the then growing Soviet criticism of Nasser's treatment of the communists in Egypt and Syria, at that time part of the United Arab Republic. Khrushchev himself, during a visit to Moscow of a UAR parliamentary delegation in May 1961, took up the subject in an address he delivered before the visitors. According to the official version of this address, Khrushchev told Anwar as-Sādāt, then President of the National Assembly and head of the delegation: "You say that you seek socialism, yet you do not fully understand what socialism, which leads to communism, really is. If we view socialism as a scientific phenomenon, then it is the first stage toward communism . . . If you really want to attain socialism, you ought not to say that you are anti-communist since thereby you will be falling into the trap of the imperialists."[10]

In his reply, which was prepared only after his return to Cairo, Sādāt throws further light on the subject of Arab Socialism. On the crucial point of the inevitability of communism he wrote: "The socialism in which we believe is based on the emancipation of the individual and on his liberty . . . We aim at abolishing exploitation and work for the disappearance of class differences; we want to provide equal opportunities for all, especially in the spheres of health, education and work." Although we believe that the class struggle restricts the forward movement of society, Sādāt added, "we think that it is possible to avoid bloodshed in the class war."[11]

It will be noted that Sādāt's arguments add nothing material to Haykal's list of differences: on the contrary, the latter seems to be only an enlargement on the former's theme. It would, in fact, seem that the vagueness and the apparent confusion which characterize Arab Socialism are an inseparable part of its terminology. Speaking as far back as

November 1958, Nasser himself tried his hand at a definition of the kind of socialism his regime was seeking to attain.

"When we speak of socialism," he told his listeners, "we have to understand the meaning of the term . . . Socialism, in its content, consists of negative and positive aspects. The negative aspects are presented by the liquidation of the legacy left us by the hated past, and the positive are symbolized in building for a future that is sought by all citizens." "Socialism," he finally summed up, "is the destruction of feudalism, monopoly and the domination of capital; [it consists of] building a national economy and working for the growth of this economy and its development in order to meet the needs of society, as well as action to establish social justice."[12]

These pronouncements, stressing as they do the socio-economic aspects of Arab Socialism, were all made before the collapse of the United Arab Republic, the first and most serious experiment in pan-Arab unity made in recent times. Syria's secession in September, 1961, threatening Cairo's position as leader of the Arab nationalist movement, confronted the Egyptians with a dual task, i.e. to find a suitable scapegoat on which to blame the failure of the experiment and, at the same time, to establish an alternative rallying-point for Cairo's Arab leadership.

To attain these objectives, the process of socialist implementation was sharply intensified, thus presenting socialism as an alternative attraction, or at least an important appendage, to pan-Arabism. In an address delivered on October 16, 1961, Nasser identified his enemies by listing mistakes which he said his regime had committed and which he maintained were ultimately responsible for the downfall of the UAR. They again throw a certain amount of light on the shortcomings of the kind of socialism he envisaged. They were given in the form of "enemies" and they were four in number:

The first was Reaction. To continue striking out at imperialism in the form of pacts and military bases, Nasser argued, was no longer adequate, since in the meantime imperialism had taken refuge in the palaces of the millionaires and the reactionaries.

The second enemy was the weakness of popular revolutionary action, a weakness that had led to the infiltration by reactionary elements of the National Union [the predecessor of the Arab Socialist Union as the regime's popular organization].

The third enemy was the lack of sufficient popular consciousness as to the implications of the revolution.

The fourth and final enemy was the existing old machinery of government, which Nasser said was not suited to the task of executing a real social revolution.[13]

Nasser's speech, in addition to giving the signal for an intensification of socialist measures, served to lay greater stress on the political-organizational aspects of Arab Socialism than ever before, and consequently a more searching enquiry into the meaning and political implications of socialism for Egypt was started. Among other things, the subject of freedom in a socialist society claimed a good deal of attention, as will be shown in the next chapter.

In the course of an interview over West German television, President Nasser was asked early in 1965 about the nature of the Arab Socialism which he advocated and claimed to put into practice. Was it a totally different brand of socialism, something unique that he alone had devised? Nasser's answer was quite clear: "When we speak of Arab Socialism," he said, "what we actually mean is the *Arab implementation* of socialism." Other Egyptian leaders take a similar stand on this intricate question. Former Deputy President Kamāl ad-Dīn Rif'at, for instance, has spoken about "the *Arab road* to socialism"[14] [italics mine – N.R.], while 'Alī Sabrī, then Prime Minister, wrote a book entitled *Socialist Implementation in Egypt.*[14]

Even this measure of charity is not to be found in the books on socialism prepared by Egyptian professors and lecturers for their third-year students as part of the compulsory "nationalist subjects" courses introduced in Egyptian universities in 1960. For one thing, in almost none of these books do we find a clear definition of socialism or the things for which it is thought to stand. Dr. 'Alī al-Barūdī, Associate Professor at the Law College in Alexandria, tells us in his book on the subject: "The idea of socialism, even supposing that it can be found in one distinct theoretical form – a possibility ruled out by many students of the subject . . . We shall therefore avoid giving a definition of socialism." This said, Dr. Barūdī proceeds to call a certain Egyptian religious leader a socialist solely because he had dared to criticize Farūq, then King of Egypt.[15]

Partly as a result of their reluctance to define socialism, some of the authors fall into dismal contradictions. In a book called *Arab Society and Arab Socialism,* for instance, co-authors Dr. Aḥmad Fu'ād and 'Abd al-Mun'im Shawqī speak of "differences in implementing the socialist system as they emerge in the various societies that adopted socialism, such as the Soviet Union, the British Labour Government, the French Socialist Government, Hitler's German Socialism, etc."[16]

The same thing occurs in *On Socialist Society,* by Dr. 'Abd al-Mu'izz Abulnaṣr, also of Alexandria University, who points out that Egypt "adopted neither the Soviet nor the Nazi experience in attempting to achieve progress and build the new society."[17] Other authors (such as Dr. 'Abd al-'Azīz 'Izzat, head of the Sociology Department at Cairo University, in his *Arab Ideology*) lump together such specimens of socialist societies as Mussolini's Italy, Franco's Spain, and the Turkey of Kemal Atatürk.

Not a little of this apparent confusion must be laid at the door of official pronouncements on the subject made in Egypt since the introduction of Arab Socialism. For although there may now be a kind of consensus that Arab Socialism is no more than "the Arab road to socialism" (itself a not entirely clear concept, it is true, but having the advantage of making it clear that Arab Socialism is not a *new brand* of the doctrine), the regime's own idea of Arab Socialism has seldom been quite clear and comprehensible. Nasser himself has somehow always implied that his socialism is something unique, since it rejects the domination of any single class of society over the others and seeks to cater to all the classes – an obvious contradiction in terms of true socialist terminology.

This obviously accounts for many a strange-sounding statement in Egyptian university textbooks on socialism and kindred subjects. The dominant theme is that Arab Socialism is a purely Arab "invention" having no relationship to the rich heritage of socialist thought anywhere in the world. Dr. 'Izzat, in the book quoted above, asserts for instance that Arab Socialism is "this new nationalist, social philosophy devised by President Jamāl Abdel Nasser." Again: "We can give the new Egyptian system a novel name: Populist Socialism. This is a unique, brand-new name, as is proved by the fact that the most famous professor and great researcher Borgans [? ] does not mention such a thing."

The head of the Department of Sociology in Cairo continues: "Nasser's system in the spheres of government, economy, and social policy is neither Eastern nor Western; it has no relation whatever to any brand of socialism, whether capitalist or communist: it is quite unique. True, there is some similarity between this system and *solidarisme,* or what in Europe is sometimes called *socialisme solidariste* – a doctrine of neutralism between communism and capitalism."[18]

Another academic who sees no relation between Arab Socialism and the socialist doctrine as such is Dr. Rif'at al-Maḥjūb, who argues that Arab Socialism was created to deal with the specific problems, and in line with the special values, of the Arab world, and that its principles were selected and put together in the light of these problems and those values. Dr. Maḥjūb rejects the theory that Arab Socialism implies no new brand of socialism but only the Arab *application* of Socialism. He writes that in order for this theory to be acceptable we have to accept two suppositions neither of which is valid or true, i.e. that all socialist thought leads to one doctrine, and that, given the existence of more than one brand of socialism, the socialism practised in Egypt today is but an application of some specific, already existing brand of socialism. Since neither of these suppositions is tenable for Dr. Maḥjūb, he concludes that Arab Socialism is something unique and unlike any other brand of socialism.[19]

One feature of these writings on socialism, common almost to all of them, is an incipient anti-Marxism. Thus Dr. 'Abd al-Mun'im al-Beih in his book *Arab Socialism,* asserts that Marxism "is wrong in its premise and misguided in its objective . . . because Karl Marx decided to take as his starting point a certain social phenomenon, when the truth was that the problem existed inside man himself and the conflict raged in his own individual self."[20] Dr. Ṭu'ayma al-Jurf says in his book *The July 23 Revolution:* "We reject Marxism root and branch as a purely materialistic philosophy."[21] Dr. Barūdī attacks Marxism as "amoral," as "a hate-ridden, demoralizing doctrine of domination," and as a system for economic achievement that has no reference to the happiness of man.[22] Dr. 'Izzat goes even further, rejecting Marxism, as practised in the Soviet Union, because of such sins as preaching equality between man and woman and allowing marriage between prison mates.[23]

The fact that so various and sometimes quite disparate shades of socialist doctrine were able to masquerade as the true embodiment of Arab Socialism has had its advantage for the regime. But it also had its disadvantages, and opponents of Marxism outside and inside Egypt herself were quick to seize the opportunity. The fiercest attacks came from outside Egypt. A book published in Beirut in 1965, and bearing the unusual title *The Socialist Deception* by Dr. Ṣalāḥ ad-Dīn al-Munajjid argued bluntly that Arab Socialism was nothing else than downright Marxism. The author had nothing but scorn for those Arab Socialists who assiduously try to establish that the Prophet Muḥammad was "the first socialist," that the first Caliphs were pioneers of socialism, and that the early Muslim visionary Abū Dhar al-Ghaffārī was a regular communist and "a precursor of Lenin and Stalin." After examining over fifty works of Arab Socialism, Munajjid concluded that this ideology was identical with Russian Marxism, especially in that, like the latter, it preaches revolution. The irony of it was that many of the works examined by Munajjid were indeed written by Egyptian Marxists masquerading as Arab Socialists.[24]

Inside Egypt, the tone of the critics of Arab Socialism was naturally subdued. Such writers, lacking as they are in sympathy for any kind of socialism, have in most cases taken refuge in obscure philosophical disputations in order to prove that Arab Socialism has in fact very little in common with Marxism, dialectical materialism, and historical determinism. After thus drawing the line between Arab Socialism and the Marxist creed, they proceed to attack Marxist socialism to their heart's content, paying the merest lip service to Arab Socialism while trying to undermine its ideological foundations.

Two such attempts are worth dwelling upon. Dr. 'Iṣmat Sayf ad-Dawla, a lecturer in one of Egypt's universities, published a weighty 400-page book in 1965 called *The Foundations of Arab Socialism,* in which he tried, as academically as possible, to show that Arab Socialism had not only nothing to do with Marxism, but that it was Western neither in theory nor in practice but a genuinely and authentically Arab creed both in its theoretical and its practical ramifications.

Following this sharp distinction between Arab Socialism and all that in the West is taken as socialist doctrine, Dr. Sayf ad-Dawla proceeds to demolish the philosphical, social, and economic precepts of Marxist socialism, starting with dialectical and historical materialism and ending with the Marxist attitude to nationalism. Only then does the author proceed to define what he considers to be the principles of Arab Socialism. In brief, he finds that, unlike Marxism, Arab Socialism has its roots in the values of the Islamic faith. Among other features which distinguish Arab Socialism from Marxism is that the latter advocates the abolition of private ownership altogether whereas the former contents itself with abolishing the exploitation of man by his fellow-man.

Dr. Sayf ad-Dawla uses another, more obvious device: for some reason he seizes upon the three slogans of Arab Socialism – emancipation, unity and socialism – and insists that these three objectives have to be attained in that order, thus making socialism seem just about unattainable by stipulating that its realization must be preceded by the emancipation of all the Arabs from the yoke of foreign rule and their unification. Objecting to those who argue that socialism should be viewed as the best foundation for Arab unity, Dr. Sayf ad-Dawla insists that unity is the only possible basis for socialism.[25]

Another Egyptian academic who has taken up the anti-Marxist crusade is Dr. Zakī Najīb Maḥmūd, Professor at Cairo University and editor of the "Journal of Contemporary Thought." In an essay in that journal,[26] Maḥmūd discovers an "inner contradiction" in the Marxist doctrine.

Marxism, he points out, preaches two diametrically contradictory principles. On the one hand, it teaches historical determinism, whereby history moves in a predetermined course leading inevitably to socialism and the disappearance of classes. On the other hand, Marxism acknowledges man's influence on events and his will to change his condition. But, Dr. Maḥmūd argues, you cannot believe both in determinism and in free will; hence the contradiction. Needless to say, the implication of all this is that Arab Socialism has no relation – indeed can have no such relation – to a doctrine that is so plainly self-contradictory.

Arab Socialism, which purported to be a doctrine for all Arabs and not confined to Egyptians, was at this stage a subject of controversy in other parts of the Arab world. However, whereas the Egyptians debated the question of what type of socialism was Arab Socialism, certain Arab political intellectuals in Syria and Lebanon were asking themselves what was for them a more critical question: Is Marxist socialism compatible with Arab nationalism? This question was first opened to discussion in the ranks of the Arab Ba'th (Resurgence) Socialist Party. However, the controversy in fact concerned Arab Socialism, whose Marxist connotations were at the time being increasingly stressed.

Broadly speaking, two opposing stands were taken on the question, one finding no incompatibility between Marxist socialism and Arab nationalism, and the other considering the meeting of the two ideologies inconceivable. Respectively, these two stands were represented by the Lebanese Ba'th leader 'Jubrān Majdalānī and the prominent Syrian Ba'thist Ṣalāḥ ad-Dīn al-Bīṭār.

In a lecture on "Socialism in the Arab World" read before the political science class at the American University of Beirut in November 1965, Majdalānī made two rather clear-cut points: "There is no such thing as Arab Socialism, socialism being one and deriving from one and the same single source. There is no fundamental difference between Ba'th socialism and communist socialism." Ba'thists and communists believe in the same socialist doctrine, the only difference between them being in methods of application, phases, and timing.[27]

Bīṭār, former Vice-President of the United Arab Republic and subsequently Prime Minister of independent Syria after the Ba'th *putsch* of March 1962, held a diametrically opposing view. In a series of two articles published toward the end of 1965 simultaneously in Damascus in *al-Ba'th* and in Beirut's *al-Aḥrār,* organs of the Ba'th Party in Syria and Lebanon respectively, Bīṭār declared in quite unambiguous terms that there was a clear and rather irreconcilable opposition between Arab nationalism and Marxian socialism – and that he himself puts Arab nationalism first.

Bīṭār attempts a brief critique of Marxism as a whole. Marxism, he writes, faces constant criticism nowadays not merely from its opponents but also from its adherents themselves. As a tool for interpreting social and economic conditions, Marxism was valid at a certain time and in a certain place (Europe of the 19th century); it cannot serve as such a tool at all times and in all places and societies.

According to Bīṭār, the trouble started when half-educated Arab *littérateurs,* eager to understand the world around them, became enamoured of the Marxist-Leninist doctrine and accepted it as an ultimate and irrefutable truth. Grafting it onto Arabism, they believed in their innocence that Arab nationalism could be made to be a mere appendix of Marxism, which in fact was no more than an alien, intruding philosophy. It was to be regretted, Bīṭār adds, that some Ba'thists fell into the same ideological snare, believing they could be Arab nationalists and Marxists at the same time, "whereas the truth is that the Marxist is an internationalist."

Bīṭār further explains that, as each country must pave its own road to socialism, the only socialism that can suit the Arabs is a nationalist one: "Any socialism that is cut off from Arab nationalism, whether it be Marxian or not, cannot be considered revolutionary, because real socialism is that which springs from nationalism."[28]

From this rather muddled statement it becomes clear that Bīṭār, while dismissing as unrealistic the proposition that Arab nationalism and Marxian socialism can be merged into something called "Arab socialism," still tried to have it both ways. For he never completely discarded the idea of *revolutionary* socialism – and if this is not Marxism-Leninism itself then it is difficult to see quite what it is.

Majdalānī and Bīṭār were not the first non-Egyptians to take an interest in such questions. In 1962 there was published in Cairo in book form a collection from a socialist periodical printed in Beirut by a group of young intellectuals and called *al-Ḥurriyya* (Liberty). The main points made by the group were, first, that there was need for a socialist doctrine that could live and grow and provide a socialist future "whether the present ruling leadership stays or goes"; and, secondly, that the failure of the multi-party system in Egypt must not be taken as a general indictment of the party system. Popular organization, the *al-Ḥurriyya* group argued, cannot be imposed from above, but has to emerge from below – otherwise it would reflect the mentality of the bureaucrat and represent the official administration. Past experiences have shown that popular organizations imposed from above cannot have the spontaneity of action and the organizational capacity essential for such bodies.[29]

For many a reader these views would seem to be the simplest elements of political common sense. Not so for the editors of *Rose al-Yūsuf,* however, one of whom, Jalāl Kishk, in the course of replying to *al-Ḥurriyya's* arguments, insists that they "actually constitute the rift within the Arab socialist movement." Differences over means, the writer explains, are nowadays not less grave than those involving ends; for what is now needed, after fixing the goal, is merely to draw the outlines of the path leading to that goal and guaranteeing that any deviations from this path will be discovered and put aright.

The most revealing part of *Rose al-Yūsuf*'s argument, however, is that relating to the question of leadership. To the *al-Ḥurriyya* group's call for a coherent socialist doctrine that can have a status independent of the present "ruling leadership," Kishk juxtaposes "two philosophies." On the one hand, he says, there is the philosophy "which believes in the trusteeship of socialist thought and the ability of socialists to determine the fate of man and society and to anticipate their future problems and plan solutions for these problems." On the other, there is the philosophy of Arab Socialism, "which considers itself an expression of the needs of the masses and is able to offer the best solution for the specific problem at hand." This socialism, though no mere follower of the masses, does not believe in the determinism of the Marxists. This leads to the significant difference of opinion over the question of leadership: "We do not worship personalities, but we do not believe in the mechanical [working of] history . . . We do not believe that the victories attained by the Arab Nation and the emergence of Arab Socialism were inevitable whether or not the [present] revolutionary leadership was to emerge." [30]

This, obviously, is the crux of the matter. If one starts to belittle the significance of the ruling leadership [i.e., Nasser], one inevitably goes on to meddle in such subjects as the nature of the socialist state! The *al-Ḥurriyya* group's claim that in socialism "the state's point of view represents only one of several trends of thought within the broader nationalist-socialist compass" is dismissed out of hand, "because the state in our Republic is the quintessence of all socialist ideas, not of one of them." *Al-Ḥurriyya's* argument to the contrary not only implies that the right course can conceivably be found outside the state, and that at some stage the state can represent the position of a minority, but suggests also that the government can represent one party, with other parties with different points of view remaining in the opposition. These are, plainly, extremely shocking views. According to Kishk, "socialism is not such a difficult subject," and the fear that for the ordinary Arab citizen it may come to mean no more than a series of arbitrary measures is nothing but a reflection of "the crisis of the intellectuals . . . "

In his *General Theory of Employment, Interest and Money* the late Lord Keynes writes: "Practical men, who believe themselves to be quite exempt from any intellectual influences, are usually the slaves of some defunct economist. Madmen in authority, who hear voices in the air, are distilling their frenzy from some academic scribbler of a few years back. . . . Soon or late, it is ideas, not vested interests, which are dangerous for good or evil."[31]

Who are the defunct economists and the academic scribblers from whom the founders of Arab Socialism distill their various doctrines? In terms of political ideologies and "isms" the claim was made that the system to be implemented in the democratic, socialist and cooperative society which in the late sixties the Egyptian Revolution claimed it was determined to build, was based on the premises of a brand-new, self-contained, and independent ideology having to do neither with capitalism nor with communism. In an article entitled "Where Stands Our Socialism in Relation to Capitalism and Communism," Fatḥī Ghānim tries to place this new system half-way between these two ideologies, drawing on Nasser's occasional pronouncements on the subject.[32]

Ghānim introduces his article with some general remarks. "The basic reality on which our political system is founded is that we are a nation in a state of growth, [a nation] which has awakened from several centuries of deep slumber and found itself lagging behind in the march of civilization and culture. This nation wants to hasten and overtake those who have arrived before it, so as not to remain long behind the caravan, and to cease being weak and dominated by the strong."

There are, however, two opposing ways which can lead to advancement and growth, Ghānim adds. These are the capitalism of the West and the communism of the East. Examining the two systems from the point of view of their respective impacts on the individual citizen, Ghānim rejects capitalism as a system which pampers the individual and inflates his ego, while discarding communism for paralyzing the individual and his activities and asking him to sacrifice his individuality for the common good. "We do not adopt the system of private exploitation nor do we follow that of collective exploitation," the writer asserts. Turning to more practical questions, Ghānim continues significantly:

> We are throwing ourselves today into a sharp contradiction when we ask people simultaneously to consume and to produce, to consume as little as possible and to produce as much as possible. The communists tell us that to resolve this contradiction it is appropriate to establish an authoritarian regime and get people accustomed to privations and sacrifices in the interest of future generations. . . . We

> reject this opinion, which does not conform to the nature of our nation. . . . That is why it is wise to seek incessantly to conciliate the imperative need to hasten development in the interest of society, with the equally imperative need to preserve the personality of individuals, despite the contradiction that this effort carries. The way to do this is to view this contradiction not as an occasion for embarrassment but rather as the reality of our life. It follows that we do not have to suppress this contradiction but rather try to overcome it in recognizing and understanding its reality.[33]

A somewhat more serious attempt to explain why the regime rejected both capitalism and communism as an ideology was made a few months later by Haykal, who in June and July 1961 wrote a series of weekly articles in anticipation, and justification, of the impending socialist measures and decrees. Describing the regime's task as one of achieving both "sufficiency" and "justice," Haykal offered an analysis of Egypt's position in the context of W.W. Rostow's famous theory regarding stages of economic growth *(The Stages of Economic Growth: A Non-Communist Manifesto).* The way in which Haykal chose to use Rostow's theories is instructive. Haykal cites the five stages listed by Rostow as being: a traditional society; the pre-conditions for take-off; the take-off; the drive to maturity; and the age of high mass-consumption.

Thus, he concludes, "take-off" is the key to increasing national wealth as it is the stage at which the nation's economy becomes sufficiently diversified and dynamic to sustain its own continued growth.

Haykal rejects as models for imitation by Egypt both the capitalist path to take-off and the Stalinist communist one; the former on the ground that it relied on plundering the wealth of colonial peoples, the latter for ruthlessly squeezing the savings of the Russian people. In Egypt, Haykal writes, "the need was urgent for a comprehensive plan in whose service the entire national energy would be placed – a plan that would assure the increase of production and at the same time not forget the need to satisfy the consumption demands and the need for basic services of the masses who have suffered long deprivation."[34]

Haykal's comments on the applicability of Rostow's theory of economic growth, and his seeming rejection of its implications for Egypt, may have well been meant to constitute an authoritative pronouncement on the subject following the publication of an Arabic rendering of Rostow's book and the attraction which his ideas were proving to have for a number of the regime's spokesmen. To give one example: as early as May 1, 1961, 'Abd al-Quddūs published a lengthy article in which he tried to apply Rostow's theories in their entirety to the Egyptian economy. The results were interesting, if somewhat muddled.

In the first place, 'Abd al-Quddūs seeks to translate Rostow's theory into a language intelligible to him and to the general reader. In this process he attributes to Rostow the division of societies into four categories – the "backward," the "on-the-move," the "mature," and the one which "reached the highest stage of maturity." This latter category represents a society in which everyone acquires "a high capacity for consumption, so that he buys a car and an electric refrigerator, and spends every summer in Switzerland."

Where, 'Abd al-Quddūs finally asks, does the United Arab Republic fall within this division? "Until 1953," he replies expertly, "our society was . . . backward, since we were not a productive society. We were wholly dependent on cotton planting, i.e., production depended on one branch only, namely agriculture; agriculture depended on one product, namely cotton. . . . We used to produce cotton not on our own behalf but on behalf of others. That is why we remained backward, because a productive society is that which produces on its own behalf and not on behalf of others."

In 1955, however, things changed. "Three years after the Revolution, we were transferred to the stage of take-off: our society was on the move. A society which is on the move is that which enters the stage of production – and production means industrialization." Lest the reader may become despondent, however, 'Abd al-Quddūs hastens to add: "We were late in reaching this stage, lagging behind many of the Great Powers. Yet, in my opinion, we did not lag behind too much."

"Things are not as bad as they seem," 'Abd al-Quddūs implies. "Britain, according to Rostow, started her take-off stage in 1780. . . . France in 1840; the United States in 1860; Japan in 1900; and Russia in 1918." (In his book, however, Rostow allocates the take-off of both France and the U.S. to "the several decades preceding 1860"; of Japan to "the fourth quarter of the 19th century"; and of Russia to "the quarter century or so preceding 1914.")

Moreover, there are great societies whose take-off started at the same time as did that of Egypt and Syria. "China started in 1952, India in 1954 – according to Rostow's division" (" . . . during the 1950's India and China have, in quite different ways, launched their respective take-offs" – Rostow).

Be that as it may, 'Abd al-Quddūs asks another interesting question – and answers it. "As we have already started the take-off stage, when will we reach the stage of maturity? " Here, "we find that we have to keep pace with states which overtook us by decades. . . . We find that, in order to keep pace, we . . . cannot afford to pass through the same long phases which Britain, for instance, had to undergo. We have to rely on revolutionary methods of industrialization and on economic planning."

'Abd al-Quddūs casts a glance at the stages of economic growth as experienced by various societies and draws relevant conclusions as to what is to be done. The transition from the stage of take-off to that of maturity took Britain 70 years (1780–1850), while it took Russia a mere 21 years (1918–1939). Why was this so? 'Abd al-Quddūs asks. "The reason was the revolutionary methods followed by Russia. And revolutionary methods here do not mean political systems or doctrines; what is meant are the revolutionary methods used in administration and in the direction of society's forces."

But this is not all. "If we wish to keep pace with other societies, we are compelled to complete [this stage] in less time than did Russia. We too will have to adopt revolutionary methods in the drive to concentrate and direct our productive potential." The achievements of the past five years (1955–1960) show clearly that "we will reach [the stage of maturity] in far less time than did many states. The force which drives us is a stunning one – the force of the Revolution."[35]

Haykal's approach was far less uncritical towards Rostow than that of 'Abd al-Quddūs. On the subject of Arab Socialism proper, Haykal continues to propound the same sort of "class neutralism" said to constitute the regime's economic and social policy. The regime kept arguing that it was "after the blood of neither the capitalists nor the workers; it can accomodate both." However, Nasser himself, in his traditional anniversary speech on July 22, 1961, repeatedly referred to the "struggle of the working class" against the "exploiting capitalist class." Nasser defined the working class as being "the workers, the peasants, the office workers, and everyone who draws a wage in order to live." He continued:

> The working class begins with the President of the Republic who lives on his salary and goes on to the worker who lives on his salary. ... Today we must get rid of the contradictions we inherited from the aristocracy and pseudo-aristocracy. In the past everyone used to hate having it said that he belonged to the working class, even though he didn't get enough at the end of the month to eat. The others had to call him "your excellency the Bey" and treat him with deference, even though at the end of the month if he didn't get his £E10 he wasn't going to pay his rent or pay the grocer or get enough to eat. ... They went so far as to split us up within factories, saying: There is a union for the labourers and a union for the office workers. What's the difference between the two? The labourer works and gets his wage, and the office worker works and gets his. At the end of the month neither of them is going to eat if he doesn't get paid. In other words, the two of them are equal in everything.

Contrasting with these is

> the dictatorship of capital [which] exploited every means to preserve the ruling classs ... exploiting capitalism which ruled in alliance with feudalism. ... The weapons of landed feudalism and of exploiting capital are the means of production by which the people are exploited.

However, Nasser adds, exploitation doesn't mean that anyone who owns something is an exploiter.

> By the capitalist exploiting class I mean those who used their money to exploit the people and suck their blood. ... There are owners who are not exploiters, whose wealth is the product of their work, who have not used this wealth for exploitation. We are not against ownership in an absolute way, but against exploitation. Otherwise we would have confiscated property without giving bonds bearing interest. We would have confiscated everything and prohibited ownership. But we say that ownership is a social trust. If it is directed towards exploitation then it goes beyond its trust.[36]

Where, then, does Arab Socialism stand ideologically? There is of course a good case to be made for the argument that the question is somewhat irrelevant – that time was when such abstract ideological discussions were meaningful and fruitful. In the article quoted above, Ghānim asserts that the regime's chosen political ideology does not mean "mere vacillation between capitalism and communism" but an ideology "in its own right." A close scrutiny, however, of the statements and theoretical formulations produced by the regime – some of which are quoted in this chapter – tends to lead one to the conclusion that Ghānim's so-called ideological alternative to capitalism and communism is little more than a strange mixture of various "isms," such as Karl Kautsky's social democracy, Mussolini's corporate state, and Tito's socialism – all suitably proportioned with state capitalism.

The affinity to Mussolini's ideas is perhaps the most controversial. Yet Arab Socialism, with its strong nationalist undertones, does call to mind the teachings of Mussolini, who once wrote that an all-inclusive popular organization was needed so that "political discipline may prevail and the bond of common faith may bind everyone above contrasting interests."[37] Nasser's Arab Socialist Union (ASU) claimed to represent the people "as a whole" and not merely this or that economic class. It is defined as an "alliance" of the various "social forces" in Egyptian society. The whole concept of the National Congress of Popular Forces – from which the ASU sprang – represented the regime's idea of a single political organization embracing all classes and sections of the people. Similarly, Arab Socialism identified itself with the highest national authority and tried to make "the people" part of the State.

NOTES

1 Muḥammad 'Awda, *Ākhir Sā'a,* 5 September 1962.

2 *Ibid.*

3 *Ibid.*

4 'Abd ar-Raḥmān Shākir, *"al-mīthāq wa-taṭawwur 'ilm al-ishtirākiyya"* ["The National Charter and the Evolution of the Science of Socialism"], *al-Kātib,* August 1962.

5 *Ibid.*

6 Nasser quoted in Nissim Rejwan, "The Political Ideas of Arab Socialism," *Jewish Observer and Middle East Review* (London), 15 November 1963, p. 28.

7 Iḥsān 'Abd al-Quddūs, *Rose al-Yūsuf,* quoted in Rejwan, *op. cit.*

8 *Ibid.*

9 Muḥammad Ḥasanayn Haykal, *al-Ahrām,* 4 August 1961.

10 *Al-Ahrām,* 9 June 1961.

11 *Ibid.*

12 Nasser, *thawratunā al-ijtimā'iyya* ["Our Social Revolution"] (Cairo, 1959), p. 142.

13 Nasser in an "Address to the Arab Nation," *R. Cairo,* 16 October 1961. Full text in *al-Jumhūriyya* (Cairo), 17 October 1961.

14 Kamāl ad-Dīn Rif'at, *"muqābala ideolojiyya ma'a kamāl rif'at"* ["An Ideological Interview with Kamāl Rif'at"], conducted by Muḥammad 'Awda, Kamāl Zuhyarī and Aḥmad 'Abbās Ṣāliḥ, *al-Kātib,* January 1964, pp. 57–58. Ṣabrī's thesis is expounded in his book, *at-taṭbīq al-ishtirākī fī miṣr* ["Socialist Implementation in Egypt"] (Cairo, n.d.).

15 'Alī al-Barūdī, *al-ishtirākiyya al-'arabiyya* ["Arab Socialism"] (Cairo, 1953), p. 9.

16 Ahmad Fu'ād and 'Abd al-Mun'īm Shawqī, *al-mujtama' al-'arabī w'al-qawmiyya al-'arabiyya* ["Arab Society and Arab Nationalism"] (Cairo, 1963), p. 178.

17 'Abd al-Mu'izz Abulnaṣr, *fī al-mujtama' al-ishtirākī* ["On Socialist Society"] (Cairo, 1963), p. 217.

18 'Abd al-'Azīz 'Izzat, *al-ideolojiyya al-'arabiyya* ["Arab Ideology"] (Cairo, 1964), p. 240.

19 Rif'at al-Maḥjūb, *al-ishtirākiyya al-'arabiyya* ["Arab Socialism"] (Cairo, 1963), pp. 68–69.

20 'Abd al-Mun'īm al-Beih, *al-ishtirākiyya al-'arabiyya* ["Arab Socialism"] (Cairo, 1963), p. 72.

21 Ṭu'ayma al-Jurf, *thawrat yūliū wa-mabādi' an-niẓām as-siyāsī fī al-jumhūriyya al-'arabiyya al-muttaḥida* ["The July Revolution and the Principles of Government in the United Arab Republic"] (Cairo, 1962), p. 64.

22 Barūdī, *op. cit.*

23 'Izzat, *op. cit.,* p. 256.

24 Ṣalāḥ ad-Dīn al-Munajjid, *al-taḍlīl al-ishtirākī* ["The Socialist Deception"] (Beirut, 1965), pp. 30–31. A fuller exposition of Munajjīd's

thesis is to be found in the sections: "Arab Socialism," pp. 25–33 and "The Similarities between Marx's Principles and Those of the Charter," pp. 35–42.

25 'Iṣmat Sayf ad-Dawla, *usus al-ishtirākiyya al-'arabiyya* ["The Foundations of Arab Socialism"] (Cairo, 1965), *passim.*

26 Zakī Najīb Maḥmūd, *"al-marksiyya manhajan"* ["Marxism as a Programme"], *Majallat al-Fikr al-Mu'āṣir* ["Journal of Contemporary Thought"]. Quoted by Maḥmūd Amīn al-'Ālim in *ma'ārik fikriyya* ["Intellectual Disputations"] (Cairo, 1965), pp. 202–203.

27 Jubrān Majdalānī, "Socialism in the Arab World," a paper read at the Political Science class at A.U.B. in November 1965. Quoted in Nissim Rejwan, *Jewish Observer and Middle Eastern Review.*

28 Ṣalāḥ ad-Dīn al-Bīṭār, *al-Ba'th* (Damascus), *al-Aḥrār* (Beirut), October 1965.

29 Reported in *Rose al-Yūsuf,* 14 May 1962.

30 Jalāl Kishk, *Rose al-Yūsuf,* 14 May 1962.

31 Lord Keynes, *The General Theory of Employment, Interest and Money* (London, 1936), p. 383.

32 Fatḥī Ghānim, *"ayna ishtirākiyatunā min ar-rāsmāliyya w'ash-shuyū'iyya"* ["Where Our Socialism Stands in Relation to Capitalism and Communism"], *Rose al-Yūsuf,* 13 February 1961.

33 *Ibid.*

34 Muḥammad Ḥasanayn Haykal, *al-Ahrām,* June and July 1961. Quoted in M. Kerr, "The Emergence of a Socialist Ideology in Egypt," *Middle East Journal,* Vol. 16 (1962), No. 2, pp. 133–134.

35 Iḥsān 'Abd al-Quddūs, *Rose al-Yūsuf,* 1 May 1961.

36 These excerpts from Nasser's address of 22 July 1961 are given in Kerr, *op. cit.,* pp. 136–137.

37 Quoted in Hannah Arendt, *The Burden of Our Time* (London, 1961), pp. 258–259.

# 7. THE PROBLEM OF FREEDOM

The study of politics has been defined as that discipline which seeks to explain, or justify, the exercise of coercive power by some men over others. Accordingly, the function of political theory would be to try to expound the mode of the exercise of such power, the limits to which it should be subject, and the aims of the exercise of power.[1]

In denouncing the old party system in Egypt as a minority, dictatorial rule, Nasser proclaimed his ultimate goal to be a true democracy, in which "senators and deputies will serve all Egyptians rather than a few."[2] To that end the Constitution of 1956 proclaims the Egyptian people as establishing themselves as a democratic republic and as affirming that "sovereign power is invested in the nation." Again, Nasser asserted: "Our ultimate aim is to provide Egypt with a truly democratic and representative government, not the type of parliamentary dictatorship which the Palace and the corrupt "pasha" class imposed on the people."[3]

Yet the exercise of power remained in the hands of the country's rulers, new though they were. This was bound to take some explaining and justification, and this was done in various ways and by various spokesmen of the regime ever since the issue became a public one, especially since the plebiscitory election of an Egyptian National Assembly in 1957. Nasser himself took the lead in this campaign, defining the new Egyptian regime as "a socialist, democratic and cooperative society." The goal of democracy, he said, was to be reached through "the creation of a socialist, cooperative society."[4]

But what is democracy?

> Democracy is not mere phrases, or parties. We had parties and we had a Western democracy which they imitated blindly. We had about seven or eight parties, each of which comprised two parties and each of these was two parties in its own turn. We all know the story.

> There also was a parliament and a Speech from the Throne. Every year they used to make speeches and talk about feudalism, occupation, the British, the High Commissioner, the British Ambassador and all that kind of well-known talk.
>
> In order for us to realize the democratic society we have to liberate the individual. We cannot say we have a democratic society when we have feudalism, and if the free individual cannot earn his livelihood he will never be able to express his views on any subject and there will thus be no democracy. Democratic society does not mean letting a group of feudalists own the country, indulge in corruption, become capitalists and dominate the country. [Democratic society] is not one in which a minority dominates the majority. . . .
>
> Democracy does not mean that we establish parties, because it is possible to establish reactionary parties or ones whose leaders take their orders from the Ambassador . . . . Real democracy is that the individual should be liberated and that the society should be liberated and built on sound foundations . . . . The road to this democracy is by building the socialist, cooperative society, after the accomplishment of which there will not remain anyone who would sell out the country or dominate it, because the country will be in the hands of its sons and of each of its individuals. No one will be able to deceive us as they used to deceive us in the past. [5]

Returning to the same subject four years later, Nasser had a more articulate, better-organized version of what amounted to the same thesis. There were, he suggested, two kinds of freedom – political freedom, i.e. democracy, and social freedom, i.e. socialism. Political freedom, he asserted, was not "the copying of formal constitutional facades." Following the popular revolutionary movement of 1919, he explained, Egypt "fell under the great deceit of a sham democracy . . . . After the first recognition of Egypt's independence by imperialism, the revolutionary leadership surrendered to a pseudo-democracy with a constitutional facade that did not embody any economic content."[6]

But a democracy that did not embody any economic content was at best "a sham democracy," and Egypt's experience after the 1919 revolution proves beyond doubt "that political democracy or freedom in its political form has no meaning whatever without economic democracy, or freedom in its social form."

Here Nasser provides the most elaborate statement offered by the Revolution of a doctrine of freedom that comes quite close to a full-fledged Marxist view:

> It is an indisputable fact that the political system in any state is but a direct reflection of the prevailing economic state of affairs and an accurate expression of the interests controlling this economic state. If feudalism is the economic power prevailing in a certain state, then undoubtedly political freedom in that state can mean nothing more than freedom for feudalism. It controls economic interests and dictates the political shape of the state, forcing it to serve its own interests. The same applies when economic power is in the hands of exploiting capital.

In Egypt before the July 23 Revolution, Nasser asserts, economic power was in the hands of an alliance between feudalism and exploiting capital – and it was therefore inevitable that the whole political set-up, including the parties, should represent that power and that alliance. "Democracy on this basis was merely the dictatorship of reaction."[7]

After a brief survey of the evolution of democracy and democratic institutions in Egypt following the 1919 revolution, showing how feudalism in alliance with reaction made a travesty of parties, parliaments, and constitutions, Nasser lists six principles embracing "sound democracy" – "democracy of the people, the whole of the working people." These principles include three which have a direct bearing on the subject of freedom.

The first principle stipulates that "political democracy cannot be separated from social democracy." No citizen, it says, can be regarded as free to vote unless he is given the following three guarantees: he should be free from exploitation in all its forms; he should enjoy an equal opportunity to have a fair share of the national wealth; his mind should be free from all anxiety likely to undermine the security of his life in the future.

The second principle asserts that political democracy "cannot exist under the domination of any one class; democracy means, even in its literal sense, the domination and sovereignty of the people as a whole."

Finally, the fifth principle asserts that "criticism and self-criticism are among the most important guarantees of freedom." Yet it adds this important qualification: "The most dangerous obstacle in the way of free criticism and self-criticism in political organizations is their infiltration by reactionary elements."[8]

These "final" formulations of the Revolution's concept of freedom did not, however, come without certain birth pangs: it was preceded by quite a stormy public discussion of the subject in which several of the regime's spokesmen and supporters among the intellectuals took part. Besides, there were lengthy deliberations in the Preparatory Committee of the National Congress of Popular Forces, which ostensibly prepared the *National Charter* and was to be the first body before which Nasser was to read that statement of Egyptian policy and ideology. Right at the outset of these deliberations, Nasser announced that freedom was to be granted "only to the people." The people alone, he asserted, will enjoy freedom of expression, freedom of criticism, and freedom of assembly. "No freedom and no democracy to the enemies of the people," he decreed unambiguously.

This vague though ominous formulation by Nasser of the regime's attitude to the subject of freedom was received in silence by the Preparatory Committee – whose members included cabinet ministers, university professors, journalists, authors, and peasants – were it not for the lone voice of Khālid Muḥammad Khālid, a Muslim *'ālim* (religious savant) well known for his modernist and liberal views. Khālid, who had always held what may be described as the classical liberal concept of freedom, believed fervently that religion in general, and Islam in particular, taught the granting of freedom to all men. "I know of no difference," he once wrote, "between people's right to oppose [their rulers] and their right to breathe, since both activities are indispensable for ensuring existence and the continuation of life." Not only does religion grant people political freedom, give the people the right to choose its own ruler, and invest it with the authority to dismiss him for deviating or becoming tyrannical; religion advocates freedom of criticism and urges the believers to practise it. Khālid had been a consistent supporter of the Revolution and as a member of the Preparatory Committee, he stood up and challenged Nasser's restrictive idea of freedom and asked for the granting of liberty of expression and criticism to all – "including the communists."[9]

Khālid's lone dissenting voice did not fail to provoke answers from the regime's supporters among the intellectuals. One of the most vocal of these was Iḥsān 'Abd al-Quddūs, then owner-editor of Cairo's leading political weekly *Rose al-Yūsuf.* 'Abd al-Quddūs admits that Khālid had raised "an important issue." But, 'Abd al-Quddūs adds, "when he spoke of freedom he spoke of it in a general way, in a rhetorical style; he relied more on emotional enthusiasm than on systematic and logical study." For freedom, it transpires, "has several meanings"; it has one meaning in capitalist society, another in socialist society. "We," 'Abd al-Quddūs declares significantly, "are looking for a new meaning of freedom – a meaning that would suit our socialism and our society."

In a socialist society, he adds, "freedom is a means, not an end; it is social freedom rather than political freedom. . . . Capitalist doctrines neglect social freedom and grant political freedom, because capitalism knows that when it eliminates the former it can dominate the latter." 'Abd al-Quddūs, however, fails to explain to his readers precisely where this "new meaning of freedom" differs from its meaning in communist society.[10]

Subsequently, in a series of articles 'Abd al-Quddūs propounded the political concepts of the regime's ideology, then in its formative phase. In an article entitled "The Pitfalls of Elections" 'Abd al-Quddūs tries to show, taking care not to give too much offence, that the elector cannot in fact be much more than an idiot. Democracy, he argues, has its defects; and the most prominent of these defects are elections as a means of giving the people a share in government.

'Abd al-Quddūs proceeds to tell us why he thinks so. Whatever the electoral system, he submits, and no matter what precautions are taken to guarantee genuine popular representation, elections always boil down to the same thing: the voter has to cast his vote. The trouble, of course, is that this voter, when he finally sets out to choose between the candidates, usually follows his own personal interests and emotions, he is short-sighted in that he concentrates on the present and ignores the future, and is generally unmindful of the common interest. Candidates know all this and exploit it to the full, appealing to the voter's narrow interests and scattering easy promises. 'Abd al-Quddūs adds that the retort that the public interest is after all the sum total of these personal interests, and that easy popular gains constitute a first step to more difficult, long-range ones, ignores the facts of the situation. For you can sometimes satisfy these interests and promise such gains by merely giving the voter a pound or inviting him to an election banquet or promising him things that are at variance with the public interest.

What then is to be done? ‘Abd al-Quddūs claims that some election laws (he does not say where) tried to overcome this democratic defect by stipulating that a fixed number of the deputies be officially appointed instead of popularly elected, while "some socialist states" have resolved the difficulty by allowing the ruling socialist party itself to name alternative candidates from amongst whom the electorate has to choose its representatives. This latter practice, ‘Abd al-Quddūs points out, guarantees that all the candidates are advocates of the socialist society. The difficulty here, he continues regretfully, is that this can be done only where the party precedes the revolution: in Egypt, however, the Revolution was not brought about by a particular party, but by the people as a whole.

In conclusion, ‘Abd al-Quddūs reluctantly decides that in such an impossible situation the only thing to do is to rely on . . . popular consciousness, which he rather inconsistently describes as "a big guarantee" for all electoral systems. "The whole future," he concludes, "depends on the consciousness of the voters."[11]

‘Abd al-Quddūs also has his own ideas about such subjects as liberty and the party system in a democracy. Writing in a previous issue of his weekly he deplored the fact that most of those who spoke about democracy did so on the assumption that it was equivalent to liberty and the multi-party system. "Democracy is not liberty," he wrote. "It is the form, or the organization through which the people enjoys its freedom."

As to political parties, ‘Abd al-Quddūs submits that "a party, in the correct sense of the term, represents an interest; differences of interest represent class differences." Thus, only a class society can be a multi-party society, while a classless society is one in which there are no parties. "It is because a capitalist society is a class society that capitalist democracy is based on the multi-party system." In the socialist society, on the other hand, classes disappear and the interest of the people becomes one; here, "democracy can be maintained with only one organization, one body, one party."[12]

Up to the internal turmoil following the defeat of June 1967, this official view of the meaning and implications of freedom confronted no serious vocal challenge from leaders of opinion and members of the Egyptian intelligentsia. The contrary was rather the case. Journalists and other political footdraggers were by no means the only ones to come out with further explanations and elucidations of the dominant doctrine. Dr. Muḥammad Mandūr, a leading literary critic and professor of literature who had taken up political and cultural journalism and was a member of the National Assembly, wrote more than once in defence of the prevalent attitude to freedom. In one of his articles he relates how the Ministry of Culture and National Guidance once asked him to deliver two lectures early in 1963, one entitled "The Free Man in the Free Society" and the other "Freedom of Expression is the First Requisite of Democracy." Dr. Mandūr marvels at the close connection between the two subjects, which, he says, comprise "a clear intellectual and ideological unity." He explains:

> For freedom of expression can be practised in our new society only by the free citizen in the free society. In both cases, however, the reference is not to that idealistic, imaginary freedom advocated by the bourgeois French Revolution when it laid down that people are born free and have to remain free – and which then proceeded to announce rights and freedoms for man which remained ink on paper except for those who – because of their social wealth – are to enjoy them for their own interests and often against those of others. For instance, [the French Revolution] advocated the freedom and the right of every citizen to obtain an education; yet the common people were unable to enjoy this freedom or benefit from that right because they could not bear the high cost of education especially in its higher stages. Then it advocated freedom of opinion; but it is well known that such freedom is useless where the citizen is unable to reach the medium which can communicate such an opinion.[13]

A remarkable feature of the official view of freedom and democracy as embodied in the *National Charter* is that, while not really Marxist in its essence, it proved quite acceptable to intellectuals with pronounced and known Marxist leanings. This no doubt was one result of the ideologically highly elastic nature of much of the *National Charter's* formulations – a circumstance which allowed writers with the most varied approaches to the subject to lean on parts of the *National Charter* for support of their respective attitudes.

This was to be true even in the case of known Marxists. During the period preceding the promulgation of the *National Charter* and following it, known Egyptian communists found themselves in prisons and concentration camps, where they were detained following the break with General 'Abd al-Karīm Qassem's Iraq in 1959. Among these was Maḥmūd Amīn al-'Ālim, who together with the majority of detained communists was released early in 1964, partly, no doubt, as a token to the then Soviet Prime Minister Nikita Khrushchev, who paid an official visit to Egypt. Following the release of these communists, voices began to be heard in Egypt in mild dissent from certain formulations in the *National Charter* concerning the meaning and content of freedom – or rather from the interpretation of these formulations that was generally accepted as authoritative by the local intelligentsia. The Marxist monthly *aṭ-Ṭalī'a* and the leftist *al-Kātib* were particularly active in this respect.

The argument raised against this interpretation tended toward a Marxist stance rather than a liberal one. A leading exponent of this approach was 'Ālim himself, who shortly after his release from jail was entrusted with the editorship of the literary-cultural monthly *al-Hilāl.*

'Ālim presents the case for what is virtually a purely Marxist view of freedom when he asks: "Does freedom mean free competition in the capitalist system or is it economic planning in the socialist system? " His answer is quite plain. After giving his views on what freedom means in capitalist and socialist societies, he turns to Egypt and asks which of the two regimes was "freer," the pre-1952 or the post-1952? He admits that before 1952, the year of the Free Officers' revolt, there were political parties, constitutional battles, a parliament, elections, cabinets that fell and were re-formed, as well as party or privately-owned newspapers, an organized opposition, and so on.

In the Egypt of the Revolution, on the other hand, there are no political parties, no parliamentary opposition in the traditional sense, no private ownership of newspapers and magazines, and no political struggles. Yet there is no doubt that in pre-revolutionary Egypt "freedom was essentially the freedom of reaction, feudalism, the big capitalists and imperialism." Parliaments did not represent the peoples' true will or their control of the social machinery. In contrast to this state of affairs, 'Ālim adds, "higher bases for freedom" were built after the 1952 Revolution, though they were not immediately apparent. The transfer of power from the hands of reaction and imperialism to those of the national forces was itself a change in the general content of freedom, while a further step forward was taken with the transition from the national Revolution to the social one, i.e. from change effected by the army under the Free Officers to more radical change in which workers, peasants, and revolutionary intellectuals participate in the millions.

Thus, despite the absence of the various trappings of liberal democracy and democratic institutions as known in the capitalist world, the concept of freedom in Nasser's Egypt is taking, according to 'Ālim, "broader and more fertile depths and dimensions." He finds no contradiction in this. As "social necessity" changes from society to society, he says, so does the form of freedom. The reason why, in capitalist society, freedom takes the form of a multi-party system, elected parliaments, and privately-owned media of communication is that in such a society the various classes struggle among themselves for power. This is why this particular form of freedom is not fit for a classless society, or for one in which class distinction is in the process of elimination. In fact, the call for a multi-party system, an organized opposition, and the other trappings of liberal democracy amounts to no less than advocating a return to the class system. At best, it springs from "a purely sentimental, liberal concept of freedom." [14]

An almost diametrically opposed view has been taken by other liberal intellectuals who also invoke the *National Charter.* The most outspoken of these, as shown above, has been Khālid, who, true to his conviction that freedom ought to be granted to all, continued to propound a view of freedom which, though purporting to reject both the capitalist and communist approaches to the subject, is a straightforward version of the liberal case as so often presented by Western thinkers of that school. Basing himself on Nasser's *National Charter*, Khālid comes out strongly in favour of all basic freedoms for the individual, going so far as to advocate political opposition and the licencing of political parties. He submits that freedom of speech, a free press, and the right to criticize were essential parts of the democracy which President Nasser's

*National Charter* advocated. He saw the new Egyptian society as one that is free both of capitalist restrictions and communist rigidity.

The reason why Khālid speaks of "the crisis of freedom in our world" is that he finds that both of the dominant political systems prevalent in our world, the capitalist and the socialist, "regard freedom as a device for serving their own ends," whereas freedom is democracy, and democracy is a system that embraces the whole of life, whose goal is to put everything in the service of man, relying in this effort on the concepts of justice, truth, and freedom.

After thus indicting both Western democracy and Soviet communism for their neglect of freedom and its prerequisites, Khālid turns to the position in Egypt's new society. Relying on the *National Charter,* he calls for the institution of all the freedoms on which democracy is based – the freedoms of opinion, of expression, of criticism, as well as the individual's freedom to shape his life and make his place in society.

As to the ways of realizing these freedoms, Khālid advocates representative government with all its ramifications, calling on the proposed National Assembly to elect, side by side with its Speaker, the leader of the Opposition. This Opposition, however, should not represent a class or a party and ought not to be allowed to turn into a political organization. Khālid also recommends that the press be regarded as an independent estate on which no authority can be imposed other than the law and in whose affairs no other authority should interfere.[15]

Few other intellectuals dared to voice similar demands for the liberalization of political life before 1967. Only as a result of the defeat, and the events of its aftermath, did the conditions for voicing such protest become more suitable. During Nasser's last three years of rule, slogans such as "the sovereignty of the law," "civil rights," "political freedom" became the rallying cry of various groups of students, professionals, and intellectuals.

## NOTES

1 E. A. Kedourie, "The Study of Politics," *Philosophy,* Vol 27 (July 1952), No. 102, p. 3.

2 Nasser, "The Egyptian Revolution," *Foreign Affairs,* January 1955, p. 208.

3 *Ibid.*

4 Nasser, in an address to the Egyptian National Assembly late in 1958 – see Nasser, *"thawratuna al-ijtimā'iyya"* ["Our Social Revolution"] (Cairo, 1959), pp. 183–184.

5 *Ibid.*, pp. 184–186.

6 *Charter,* see Appendix, p. 219.

7 *Ibid.*, see Appendix, p. 220.

8 *Ibid.*, see Appendix, p. 225.

9 Khālid Muḥammad Khālid, *ad-dīn fī khidmat ash-sha'b* ["Religion in Service of the People"] (Cairo, n.d.), pp. 26, 32.

10 Iḥsan 'Abd al-Quddūs, *Rose al-Yūsuf,* 4 December 1961.

11 *Ibid.*, *"mazāliq al-intikhābāt"* ["The Pitfalls of Elections"], 11 December 1961.

12 *Ibid.*

13 Muḥammad Mandūr, *"al-insān al-ḥurr fi'l-mujtama' al-ḥurr"* ["The Free Man in A Free Society"], *al-Kātib,* February 1963, p. 5.

14 Maḥmūd Amīn al-'Ālim, *"ma'na al-ḥurriyya fī mujtama'inā al-jadīd"* ["The Meaning of Freedom in Our New Society"], *al-Hilāl* (Cairo), July 1964. Reprinted in Maḥmūd Amīn al-'Ālim, *ma'ārik fikriyya* ["Intellectual Disputations"] (Cairo, 1965), pp. 164–165.

15 Khālid Muḥammad Khālid, *azmat al-ḥurriyya fī 'ālaminā* ["The Crisis of Freedom in Our World"] (Cairo, 1964), p. 138.

# 8. ATTITUDE TO WESTERN CULTURE

In November 1956, shortly after the Suez War, the American writer Dwight Macdonald asked Dr. Ṭāha Ḥusayn in Cairo what he thought of the Hungarian revolt. Ṭāha Ḥusayn, the grey eminence of Egyptian letters and one of the chief disseminators of Western culture in the Arabic-speaking world, had this to say in reply: "I am not informed of what has been happening in Hungary, because I have only seen the reports in the British and French press *and they are not trustworthy.*"[1]

Ṭāha Ḥusayn's reply was typical of the attitude of the Egyptian and Arabic-speaking intelligentsia vis-à-vis a civilization with which they had the strongest of cultural and material ties, and which was in large measure responsible for the emergence and training of that very intelligentsia. Nor did this process of disillusion and hostility start with the Suez conflict or even with the establishment of the State of Israel. The attitude of the Arabic-speaking world to the West had always been one of ambivalence – of admiration and an urge for emulation on the one hand and of resentment and rejection on the other. But following World War Two the general mood began to be dominated by a variety of sharp sentiments ranging from suspicion and hostility to soaring self-confidence; sometimes, indeed, there was discernible in their attitude a feeling of scorn, derogation, and downright superiority. Several factors can account for this growing hostility, such as the Palestine debacle and the feeling of frustration which followed the consistent failure of pan-Arab objectives to make any headway. But there were more deep-seated factors at work. Professor von Grunebaum has pointed out that, from the standpoint of the West, "the greater the success of Westernization, the greater the political resistance to the West, but all the greater, too, the resistance to every feature of full Westernization, the political utility of which is not immediately discernible."[2]

A good deal has been written about encounters between cultures and the ways in which an assaulted culture tends to respond to the challenge of alien cultural encroachments. Yet though some historians, notably Arnold Toynbee, have tried to establish certain patterns for these encounters, no hard-and-fast rules have ever been discerned as to the workings of these processes. In the case of the Arabs, the situation remains rather fluid although over a century and a half have passed since their first encounter with Europe was made in modern times.

As a matter of fact, Arab-Islamic reactions to the impact of Western civilization have at no time been uniform. Since it started to make its presence felt in the Arab world, the West has been encountering three types of response in the area. One has been uncompromisingly hostile and unreceptive; another was extremely hospitable, whose proponents were willing to become uncritically Westernized; and the third lay somewhere between these two extremes, showing willingness to learn from the West while remaining fully aware of the shortcomings of its culture and the advantages of their own culture and tradition.

By the mid-fifties of this century, however, the first type of Arab reaction to the West had almost disappeared, apart from some scattered pockets of resistance represented by religious zealots who appeared half-convinced themselves. The enthusiasts, on the other hand, had equally dwindled in number, and it was scarcely possible to find one thinking Arab advocating full and unconditional Westernization. As for the preserve-the-good-aspects-of-both-cultures school of moderates, there were signs already that some of them were beginning to have doubts as to the practicability of their chosen course. At present, however, the trend seems to be moving in a distinctly anti-Western direction.

At first these reactions used to be rather unsophisticated, the war cries being such terms as "cultural tutelage," "cultural imperialism," and even "cultural enslavement." What is more significant, these cries came from conservative, older-generation Muslim intellectuals whose attitudes to things non-Muslim were predictably hostile. Two examples of this kind of reaction can be given here, one from Egypt, the other from Iraq. The first comes from Anwar al-Jundī, a prolific Egyptian writer and historian and author of a four-volume work called *Landmarks of Contemporary Arabic Literature up to 1940.* The fourth and last of these volumes, *Contemporary Arab Thought in the Battles of Westernization and Cultural Mobilization,* offers a survey – in 648 pages – of "various attempts to impose cultural tutelage on Arab thought, beginning with those made by Turkish imperialism and ending with those of Western imperialism and Zionism."[3]

Jundī's book covers a wide range of subjects in which these attempts at cultural subordination were made: education, politics, society, women, journalism, religion, Arab nationalism, and the Arabic language. The tone of the book and its generally defensive stance can be seen from the fact that, although it is common knowledge that in each and every one of the fields dealt with the West has left a permanent impact on Arab society, Jundī finds it possible to conclude with the following assertion:

> All that can be said about this campaign is that Arab thought has not given in, notwithstanding all the troops, armaments and conspiracies that joined forces to overthrow it – that Arab thought has been able to resist with prowess and with violence, and to show originality, vitality and a capacity for evolution and for learning without losing its original traits.[4]

However, Jundī's conclusion that all is well on the cultural front, and that the Arabs have emerged victorious from the intellectual battle forced upon them by western rule, was not shared by all.

'Abd ar-Raḥmān al-Bazzāz, then Director of the Arab League's Institute of Higher Arabic Studies in Cairo and later Prime Minister of Iraq, argues that Western imperialism has left behind it a sizeable cultural legacy of which the Arabs must try to rid themselves.

He grants that, with Algeria finally independent, the Arabs were well on their way to political independence, and that, everything being equal, they would sooner or later attain economic independence as well. What they would then need would be "cultural independence," since "no nation ought to consider itself completely independent unless its political and economic independence is accompanied by the lofty ideal of intellectual or spiritual independence."

Intellectual independence did not mean that the Arabs should avoid the West and discard everything western, Bazzāz writes; it was a call for self-realization and for a feeling of uniqueness, and a desire to contribute to the human heritage on a basis of equality and true partnership, free of submission and tutelage.

Right now, the Arab world abounded with the bad effects of intellectual imperialism, in fields such as language, literature, social habits, and standards of living. Everywhere you turned you found them: "In our everyday language, in the names we give things . . . in our political and social outlook, and in every walk of life." Colloquial Arabic contained hundreds of Italian, Spanish, French, English, Turkish, Persian, Indian, and other terms.

One of the worst effects of intellectual imperialism in the Arab world today, Bazzāz argues, "is to acquiesce in calling our homeland 'the Near East' or 'the Middle East'," which implied that Western Europe was the measure of all things, and that the Arab world was given only a relative status, since it was "East" only vis-à-vis the Westerner. To the Arab, however, the appellation signified "absolutely nothing."

But this was not all. The West went even further by adopting the term "Middle East" instead of "Near East," thus making it include Turkey, Iran, Ethiopia, and Israel. The West could not reasonably be blamed for inventing these terms, which were "in keeping with its strategic, political and imperialistic blueprints"; the blame must be roundly laid at the door of the Arabs for agreeing to be given a relative and inaccurate geographical name.

"The term 'Middle East' did not, for instance, include the Arab countries of North Africa, such as Tunisia, Algeria and Morocco. How, then, could we accept a name that kept out a significant part of our Arab homeland? . . . . The correct thing would be to call ourselves Arabs . . . Arabs of the Mashriq [East] and those of the Maghrib [West]."

Bazzāz, who was once Dean of Baghdad's Law College, was of the firm opinion that the West's choice of the term "Middle East" hid some very subtle and sinister aims.

The West, he argues, "wants to delude us into thinking that we and Turkey, Iran and Pakistan, for example, are one and the same thing, and that since we are all countries of the Middle East, what is good for these lands in the way of pacts and policies is also good for us."

Even more deplorable, however, was the fact that "the Middle East" included, in the West's eyes, Israel as well. The West's argument, according to Bazzāz, ran as follows: "Israel is in the Middle East; it is an established fact, being actually there and no longer merely one of the goals of Zionism; it is there to stay. It remains for you Middle Easterners to live together and to find ways and means for friendship and co-operation leading to peace."

It was to the Arabs that this piece of Western logic was addressed – and it was therefore incumbent upon them to insist on calling their homeland the Arab world, "thus wiping out Israel intellectually, and affirming that the Israelis are people who are foreign to us and usurpers of our land."

Bazzāz finally mentions, as a "curiosity," Mr. Nehru's habit of calling the Arabs West Asians. The description, Bazzāz submits, was geographically correct, but it too failed to give an adequate idea of the existence of one Arab nation. "We Arabs are one of those large nations that inhabit two great continents, and whose being extends from the East to the West. Therefore, any attempt to define us vis-à-vis one continent, or in relation to some imperialist Western countries, will fail, since it gives no adequate expression to our actual scope and status."[5]

The causes of this growing anti-Western trend in the cultural sphere are too complex to go into here in any detail. One of the more apparent, and important, of these causes has been the contemporary Arab intellectual's intensified quest for a distinct identity and personality of his own. As one young Egyptian writer, Rajā' an-Naqqāsh, implied, this quest seems to have been undertaken in sheer self-defence: "When you are confronted with a foreign invasion while you are without a personality and a cultural heritage of your own, the invader will overrun you; but when you face an invasion when your ranks are joined and when you are armed with a strong personality and an identity of your own it will be difficult to defeat you."

In the same article Naqqāsh, who is a typical "Westernized" Arab himself, deplores the attitude of "some Lebanese," who he claims despise and reject the Arab cultural heritage, and advocate thorough Westernization. Naqqāsh's main argument is that, in recognizing the distinct personality of the Arab nation and stressing the positive aspects of the Arab heritage, "we thereby acquire a solid basis on which we can build and which would enable us to face the destructive invasion made by the West in various forms."[6]

Naqqāsh's are fairly militant views, but a more reasoned and far maturer approach to the problem also obtains in recent Egyptian writing. Aḥmad 'Ābbās Ṣāliḥ, a well-known Egyptian writer, has indeed described the state of the Arab intelligentsia today as one of "intellectual adolescence." Though the description was indignantly rejected by some, he writes, there were others who pointed out that, by attacking the contemporary writer and rejecting his thesis out of hand, the Arab intellectual was in fact providing the best proof that he really was adolescent intellectually, since the first sign of intellectual maturity was to treat adverse opinions objectively and calmly. Indeed, Ṣāliḥ adds, one of these writers has pointed out that a certain measure of adolescence in the behaviour of the Arab intellectual of today was rather inevitable. For if adolescence is the unconscious revolt against parental authority, then it is natural that the Arab intellectual should feel, at this phase in his nation's liberation from Western dominance, "like the adolescent who discovers his body anew."[7]

The parental authority against which the Arab intellectual has been rebelling, writes Ṣāliḥ, is Western culture, "that teacher from whom he had learned his ideas and conceptions of the modern world – the sum total of the attitudes and the rules according to which he behaves in his everyday life." In the beginning, this rebellion was so violent and so blind that it led to the advocacy of complete intellectual withdrawal from the outside world, on the ground that everything brought by Western culture was evil and wrong. Thus a trend was started, which rejected all other cultures and sought the recreation of a pan-Arab one. Opposed to this trend, however, were the intellectuals of the previous generation, for whom Western culture was the very air they breathed. Taken by surprise by the new generation's violent revolt, members of the older generation of intellectuals launched a lame attack on the former, seeking protection under the only culture they knew and were brought up upon – that of the West.

Now all this must stop, says Ṣāliḥ. A new, calmer appraisal must be attempted so that the new energies are set in the right direction. The starting point here, he writes, should be "a reappraisal of what we have and what the others have, a reappraisal which would start from the beginning, with no hatred, no adversity, but also without awe either." It should be kept in mind, too, that Western culture itself was not created by Westerners alone, but was a product in whose making all cultures have had a share, "and our Arab culture probably more than others." Western culture is thus not something completely foreign, the product of a different species. It is merely that "the historical process and the requirements of evolution have resulted in the accumulation of mankind's intellectual heritage and scientific genius there [in the West]."

It so happened, however, that the end product of Western evolution, says Ṣāliḥ, was the cause of the world's, and ultimately even the West's, misery and suffering. For the message of Western culture was not one that aimed at the happiness of mankind; "it was a tendency toward superiority, dominance and overlordship . . . [and] has produced only this conflict-ridden world in which blood was shed everywhere." Now Western culture has proclaimed its bankruptcy: "Tens of writers have written its death certificate, among them Oswald Spengler, Arnold Toynbee and Walter Schubart [author of "Russia and Western Man"]." At a time when Western thinkers and men of letters thus proclaim the death of their own culture, the Arab intellectual can be excused for being so sceptical about the values of that culture. This attitude cannot be described as "adolescent"; there is, after all, an obvious difference between rejection and scepticism.[8]

From here Ṣāliḥ turns to analyzing the causes of the West's decline as they are seen by the Arab intellectual. "What matters to us here, however, is not the fact of its death, but the reasons which have led to that death. The most important of these reasons is that Western culture was not objective, especially when it was exploited by the bourgeoisie in order to preserve itself in face of the logic of history." Ṣāliḥ sets his point of departure from the assumption that Western culture was that of the bourgeois, imperialist adventurer, and proceeds: "In the past we used to live within the bourgeois framework, since we were in fact a bourgeois society borrowing its concepts from the Western bourgeoisie, and it was natural that we absorb bourgeois culture. . . . Now, however, a great deal of the conflict experienced by the Arab intellectual springs from his dependence on this Western culture in a changing society – a society which negates the fundamentals of that culture."

The difficulty of the Arab intellectual's position resides in the fact that it is no longer enough to say that Western culture is dead, and proceed to quote Western authors to that effect. It is no longer sufficient to produce translations of Western books in defence of, or against, this theory or that. What the Arabs need is "an independent, creative and objective outlook of their own," Ṣāliḥ asserts. The position now prevalent is the contrary of what it should be: one picks up any book in Arabic dealing with some aspect of Western culture – and it is invariably either a straight translation of a Western book or a collection of ideas collated from the work of various Western thinkers and which the author often attributes to himself. "Our history itself is a repetition of the findings of Western researchers," Ṣāliḥ complains, and calls for intellectual leadership – "a leadership that would plan, organize and carry out an overall survey of our cultural condition."[9]

Before turning our attention to more recent manifestations of this ambivalence it may be useful to give at least one example of it in its less extreme forms, and from an earlier period. Aḥmad Amīn (1886-1954) was a prominent Egyptian Muslim author, educator, and man of letters. As far as the influences of the West were concerned, Amīn was in no way hostile to them; in fact, as the editor-in-chief and the leading light behind *lajnat at-ta'līf w'at-tarjama w'an-nashr* (The Authorship, Translation, and Publishing Committee) as well as the editor of the cultural weekly *at-Thaqāfa,* he was responsible for bringing to the reader of Arabic many of the philosophical, literary, and scientific products of Western culture. This did not seem to conflict with his traditionalism as a Muslim, nor did it impede his own work as a historian of the old school.

Before 1947, the year in which he paid a visit to London, Amīn did not pay much attention to such topics as Westernization, East-West contrasts, or the comparative merits and demerits of these two civilizations. Following his visit, however, he wrote his book in which he set out to discuss these subjects. Here Amīn, who in the past had taken a rather positive position on the influence upon Islam of Greek, Jewish, and Christian cultures, and thus sought to justify and encourage contemporary borrowings from Western civilization, suddenly announced that his whole attitude to the West had undergone a basic change, and that his visit in a Western country had led him "to doubt the soundness of the prevailing belief that, in point of civilization *(ḥaḍāra),* the West was ahead of the East." Among the things which Amīn found wanting in the West were its worship of power, its pride, the excessive freedom which it grants women, and the lack of balance between the material and the spiritual. Besides, the West was already in decline.[10]

Amīn's revised ideas about the West and its culture were pursued five years later with an even greater bitterness and intensity of feeling in

*Yawm al-Islam* (Islam's Day), a volume which concluded his seven-volume study of Islam's social and cultural history. Here the hostility is so overt that Amīn accuses Christians in general of hating Muslims, a hatred which he says is evidenced in their support of the Jews against the Arabs in tearing off Palestine out of their hands. He also takes issue with Ṭāha Ḥusayn's assertion that the East does not differ so much from the West, and again makes a sharp distinction between the spirituality of the former and the materialism of the latter.[11]

Amīn's strictures against the West illustrate fairly the prevalent Arab-Muslim attitude to Western cultural encroachment. This attitude, however, was to grow in the intensity of its hostility, and it is safe to assume that had Amīn lived to see the Suez War and its aftermath he would have been even more resentful of the West than his more Western-oriented contemporary Ṭāha Ḥusayn.[12]

That the Westernized Muslim-Arab's negative reaction to the West should have intensified seems, even in limited retrospect, to have been natural. For as the Arabs gained political independence, and as many of their young intellectuals came to know Europe more closely, they – perhaps paradoxically – started to learn more about themselves, and to appreciate more those characteristics of their culture which, rather than revealing their affinities to the West, distinguished and set them apart from it. Inevitably, too, the more thoughtful amongst them found that they were not entirely pleased with the results of their now century-old encounter with Europe. Rightly or wrongly, some of them started to see that Europe's "cultural invasion" of their way of life and habits of thought had in the end given them very little while virtually robbing them of their distinctive traditions, their true personality, and their authentic cultural identity.

As has already been indicated, the most interesting – though not unexpected – feature of this consciousness has been that its most vocal exponents have been those who themselves were most affected by Westernization, and who have had a fairly intimate knowledge of Europe and its ways.

The sharpest and most articulate expression of this state of mind came in the mid-sixties from a non-Egyptian source. It was, however, so symptomatic of the new Arab-Muslim reaction to Westernization that it could have come from any Arabic-speaking country. Characteristically enough, in fact, it came in the form of an address before the Fifth Arab Writers' Congress, which convened in Baghdad early in February 1965. The address, closely argued and full of deeply-felt eloquence, was given by Nāzik al-Malā'ika, a young Iraqi poetess who is also one of the few leading poets writing in Arabic today.[13]

Malā'ika's lecture, entitled "Literature and Mental Invasion," started with a comparison between military and mental invasion: while military invasion aims at physical conquest and can succeed in destroying only cities and material civilizations, mental invasion aims at men's minds and souls and its damage, once done, is more difficult to rectify or undo.

Following this distinction, she recalls that throughout their history the Arabs have experienced only military conquest, while remaining immune to mental invasion. The reason for this was simple: being a source of light and knowledge for the whole world, the Arabs succeeded in invading their neighbours culturally and intellectually even when they were themselves subdued militarily by these neighbours.

Thus while the Persians were actually ruling the Arabs, the Arabs managed to dominate them culturally, so that when the Persians finally left they had adopted the Arabs' own religion, and their language still bears signs of the influence of Arabic.

It was only in recent times, when the Arabs lost their leadership in science and industry, that they had to succumb to an effective mental invasion. Europe's onslaught came on all fronts, while the Arabs assumed a passive attitude: "We allowed them to change the style of our dwellings and the type of our town planning; we let them teach us their social customs, their behaviour, their way of dealing with people, and their conversation; and we started wearing their clothes and eating their type of food."

It is not as though none of these acquisitions was useful, but the Arabs' general attitude to the invading culture was wrong: "We started discarding what was essential in our culture, including those traits which made us superior to the West, and took cheap and harmful wares in their place."

In the intellectual sphere, Malā'ika goes on to say, the collapse has been no less complete, and it had now reached its limit. "Open an Arabic periodical and you will find one article on Arthur Miller, followed by another on Marcel Aymé, a third on Bruno Walter and yet another on

Voltaire. What is more, the writers and critics who produce these articles write them not from an Arab point of view but from a purely Western one, so that if you translate the whole periodical into a European language the Western reader will find nothing novel or interesting in it."

A fate worse than this can hardly befall a nation, she laments – "not because we deny the merits of these Western men of letters, but simply because we are a nation with its own literature, its own religion, and its distinctive culture. . . . To admire all their writings unquestioningly means nothing less than that we have lost our identity and abdicated our intellects."[14]

Malā'ika enumerates four spheres in which the West's intellectual invasion manifests itself: morality, religion, language, and spirit *(ma'na-wiyya).* Starting with the invasion's destructive impact on Arab morals, she traces the decline of the moral approach in Arabic literature. In Arabic, she points out, literature *(adab)* was closely linked with propriety and good behaviour (also *adab*). But this word has now lost its moral connotations, as the Arabs' approach to literature has become identical to that of the West, where since the days of Aristotle there has been no relationship between aesthetics and morals, and where a work of literature can be judged aesthetic even though it may be immoral.

This divorce between aesthetics and morals has had disastrous effects on modern Arabic literature, which abounds in works lacking in all propriety and morality, is destructively degenerate, unrepresentative of the Arab mentality and temper, and does not give expression to the Arabs' current phase of national upsurge and cultural revival.

Turning to the sphere of religion, Malā'ika suggests that Europe's cultural invasion has resulted in a considerable amount of harm, in that it made the Arabs acquire the West's attitude to religion and its materialistic outlook on life. The Western attitude to religion radically differs from that of the Arabs. In Islam, religion is closely linked to life – nay, it is life itself; while in the West there prevails "this strange divorce between life and religion."

The adoption by the Arabs of this attitude has led to their estrangement from religion, and it threatens their severance from their cultural roots and ultimately the overall loss of their true spirit.

In language, the damage has been no less substantial. Here the cultural invasion takes mainly the form of bad translations from European languages, weakening and bowdlerizing the Arabic language by introducing foreign expressions and un-Arabic forms of grammar and syntax. Malā'ika cites many examples of this phenomenon, but her most damning accusations concern the Arabic translation of the Bible.

This rendering of the Old and New Testaments was done several decades ago in Beirut with the help of Christian missions, and has since been distributed free in hundreds of millions of copies. Being just about the worst translation made of any work from any language into any other, Malā'ika seems on sure ground in claiming that the Arabic Bible has been a factor in weakening the general literary taste and spreading ungrammatical and unidiomatic Arabic.

But it is in the Arab *ma'nawiyya* (spirit, morale) that the mental invasion of the West had wrought the most harm. Here the invaders worked with the aid of spiritual baits to ensnare the minds of impressionable youth. Chief among these baits had been the constant invocation of lofty ideals such as humanism, liberty, and freedom of thought.

Through the ideal of humanity, the European invaders introduced the harmful concept of a "world literature," implying that there is such a thing as a world literature that knows no national boundaries and which expresses the spirit of all nations, irrespective of their individual circumstances and their distinct personalities. Among the creators of this "world literature" Malā'ika cites Jean-Paul Sartre, a much-translated writer who, though possessing undeniably high literary merit, is irrelevant to the Arabs, and whose ideas are actually "opposed to our spirit and our civilization: we have no business adopting them unless we want to destroy ourselves."

The other bait used to ensnare the minds of young Arabs was the ideal of freedom, depicted as an absolute value bearing no relation to anything else and acknowledging no bounds or limitations. The acquisition of these absolute values from the West resulted, among other things, in the spread of pessimism in modern Arabic literature, which reeks of a feeling of nausea and a conviction that life is absurd, that nothingness is better than being, and that man is responsible to no one.

This type of feeling and thinking could not be more alien to the Arabs. For one thing, Malā'ika asserts, the Arab individual is today far better off than he was before, and has no apparent cause for being so pessimistic and despairing. For another the Arab, unlike the Westerner, has high regard for things spiritual and, with the aid of his belief in God and because of his fatalistic view of life, he is serene and free of anxiety.

Finally, the Arabs do not suffer from that feeling of guilt which plagues Western man, as a result of living off the sweat and labour of subject peoples. There are some who seek to justify the gloom, the despair, and the emptiness prevalent in Arabic writing today by pointing out that this is "the generation of tragedy" that witnessed the loss of Palestine. Malā'ika rejects this explanation. "The tragedy that took place in 1948," she asserts, "has fired the whole of the Arab homeland with the fire of struggle and Arabism, resulting in great revolutions sweeping Cairo, Algeria, Beirut, Baghdad and the Yemen."

According to Malā'ika, then, the real problem lies in the fact that "our writers have ceased to express their own feelings and content themselves with repeating the pronouncements of the Western writer." This is why we find, she concludes, that "while Arab nationalism sings joyously, the scribblings of these writers exude lamentations and cries of emptiness and loss."[15]

The opinions expressed by Malā'ika are by no means universally accepted amongst thinking Arabs. For although it would be true to say that no Arab intellectual would today advocate full and unquestioning Westernization, or would even say that the encroachments of Western culture on his own culture were an unmitigated blessing, there are many who would look for a solution somewhere between the two extremes of rejection and acceptance. In this respect it is instructive to notice the reactions which Malā'ika's outspoken indictment of Western cultural influences has provoked among Arab intellectuals. These reactions have on the whole been neither too heated nor quite convincing – a fact which can be taken as an indication that her views are, generally speaking, not quite unpopular in these circles.

Yet as far as can be made out, there has not been a single attempt to defend Malā'ika's views *en bloc.* The only reactions to her views available appeared in the leading cultural monthly *al-Ādāb,* which published the text of Malā'ika's lecture, and they all took issue with her views. These criticisms, submitted by three leading intellectuals of three different nationalities, dwelt on two main aspects of her attitude, namely the idealization and romanticization of the Arabs' cultural and literary heritage and the wholesale condemnation of Western literature and her dismissal of it as totally irrelevant to the Arabs' specific experience.

First among Malā'ika's critics was the Lebanese writer and editor Dr. Suhayl Idrīs. He submits that the picture depicted by Malā'ika of classical Arabic literature as being invariably great, moral, and creative has no basis in fact. According to Dr. Idrīs, too, Malā'ika's vision of Islamic society as an ideal one is also distorted, for the purity and goodness of the Islamic faith as such did not prevent its religious leaders at certain periods of Arab history from persecuting scientists and philosophers and suppressing free thought. Strangely enough, though rather typically, Dr. Idrīs avoids taking issue with Malā'ika over her central thesis, namely that Western culture is completely alien to the Arabs' tradition and temperament and world-view, and that the adoption by the Arabs of Western cultural traits tended to destroy the Arab's specific personality and estrange him from his own self and identity. In dealing with her strictures in this area, for instance, Idrīs merely makes a defence of Western literature *per se* and submits that Arabic literature, being still in a formative stage, inevitably has to borrow and even imitate other, maturer literatures. He justifies this view by arguing, not quite convincingly, that since Europe itself in medieval times drew upon the riches of Arab civilization, it would not be "shameful" for the Arabs now to borrow and take from Europe.[16]

This refusal to face Malā'ika's central thesis is significant in that it further emphasizes the deep ambivalence with which contemporary Arab intellectuals relate to the West. It is noticeable in the rejoinder to Malā'ika written by Dr. 'Alī az-Zubaydī,an Iraqi Arab nationalist intellectual and a professor of literature. Repeating the argument that the Arabs should refrain from idealizing and romanticizing their past and their heritage, which he says contain both good and bad, he makes the point that, though the Western imperialists were responsible for a number of the Arabs' present failings and misfortunes, "our responsibility is greater and our stocktaking should be fiercer with ourselves than with them, for had we not ourselves failed our countries and our minds, the foreigner would have found access neither to our minds nor to our countries."

Zubaydī also cites President Nasser and other leaders of Arab nationalism to the effect that Arabism is progressive rather than regressive, positive rather than negative, and humanistic *(insāniyya)* rather than racial. Zubaydī's article actually lapses into sheer polemics and contains a few highly rhetorical statements, such as that the Arabs should reject "reactionary ideas," that their culture and personality are strong enough to withstand Europe's influences, that in condemning Western literature one ought to distinguish between its good and its bad aspects, and that attention should be paid to the fact that the Arabs' fear of innovation is exploited by their enemies as proof of their stagnation and as a justification for foreign domination. Zubaydī, in fact, makes no serious attempt whatsoever to come to grips with Malā'ika's charges and reservations.[17]

Little light on this subject, again, is shed by Malā'ika's third critic, the Syrian writer and novelist Muṭā' Ṣafadī, though he does touch upon some of the specific points raised in her lecture. Accusing her of generalizations and inaccuracies, Ṣafadī disagrees with the statement that Islam is basically different from Christianity, in that the former is organically linked to life – nay, is life itself – while the latter, with its doctrine of original sin and its otherworldly tendencies, is divorced from life. In this he too fails to convince since he tends to overlook the crucial fact that unlike Christianity, which allows for the separation of Church and State, Islam is both a religion and a worldly system, and in this significant respect at least it does differ essentially from Christianity.

Ṣafadī's uncertainty about the whole issue becomes apparent when again he manages to avoid the real issue in replying to Malā'ika's charge that the Arabic language has been adversely influenced by translations from foreign languages and, even more important, by the borrowing of certain aspects of Latin grammar and syntax and their introduction into a language that is structurally different from European tongues. All he has to say in justifying these innovations is that they make for greater variety of expression and are useful in different literary forms such as the novel and poetry. Finally, Ṣafadī keeps significantly silent about Malā'ika's argument that the whole temperament, personality, and spirit *(ma'nawiyya)* of the Arab are different from those of the European, and that any attempt to graft the latter onto the former tends to lead to harmful results.[18]

## NOTES

1 Dwight Macdonald, "Ten Days in Cairo," *Encounter* (London), January 1957, pp. 12–13. [Italics mine, N.R.]

2 Gustav von Grunebaum, *Modern Islam: The Search for Cultural Identity* (Los Angeles, 1962), p. 177.

3 Anwar al-Jundī, *ma'ālim al-adab al-'arabī al-mu'āṣir ilā sanat 1940* ["Landmarks of Contemporary Arabic Literature up to 1940"], Vol. IV: *al-fikr al-'arabī al-mu'āṣir fī ma'rakatay at-taghrīb w'at-ta'bi'a ath-thaqāfiyya* ["Contemporary Arab Thought in the Battles of Westernization and Cultural Mobilization"] (Cairo, 1962).

4 *Ibid.*, p. 43.

5 'Abd ar-Raḥmān al-Bazzāz, *"lughatunā al-'arabiyya"* ["Our Arabic Language"], *al-'Arabī* (Kuwait), July 1962, pp. 17–20.

6 Rajā' an-Naqqāsh, *"al-mas'ala hiya rū'yat at-turāth?"* ["The Issue is: How We View the Heritage?"], *al-Kātib*, January 1965, p. 23.

7 Aḥmad 'Abbās Ṣāliḥ, *"mawqifunā min ath-thaqāfa al-gharbiyya"* ["Our Attitude to Western Culture"] *al-Kātib*, February 1964, p. 7.

8 *Ibid.*, pp. 7–8, 9, 11.

9 *Ibid.*, pp. 13, 15–16.

10 Aḥmad Amīn, *ash-sharq w'al-gharb* ["East and West"] (Cairo, 1955), Chapters 11 and 12, pp. 136–146, and 147–161.

11 Aḥmad Amīn, *yawm al-islām* ["Islam's Day"]. Quoted by Nadav Safran, *Egypt in Search of Political Community* (Cambridge, Mass., 1961), pp. 162–163.

12 See Note 1.

13 The full text of Nāzik al-Malā'ika's address *"al-adab w'al-ghazū al-fikrī"* ["Literature and Mental Invasion"] is printed in *al-Adāb*, March 1965, pp. 30–34.

14 *Ibid.*

15 *Ibid.*

16 Suhayl Idrīs, *"a'māl mu'tamar al-udabā' al-'arab"* ["Proceedings of Arab Writers' Congress"], *al-Ādāb*, March 1965, pp. 120–121.

17 'Alī az-Zubaydī, ibid., p. 122.

18 Muṭā' Ṣafadī, *"qarā'tu al-'adad al-māḍī min al-ādāb: al-abḥāth"* ["I Read the Previous Issue of al-Adāb: Articles"], *al-Adāb*, April 1965, pp. 76–77.

# 9. LITERATURE AND SOCIETY

In the summer of 1961 a new phrase began to gain currency in Cairo's political and cultural circles – *azmat al-muthaqqafīn* (the crisis of the intellectuals). The phrase was certainly not a new one in the Arab world, though its connotations were. Previously, when one heard people talk about the crisis of the intellectuals, one automatically took the phrase to refer to the problem of those thousands of young men and women who every year complete their secondary schooling and find themselves unable to get suitable employment. (The confusion between "intellectual" and "literate" or "educated" stems from the fact that in Arabic these terms are usually used interchangeably to denote *muthaqqaf,* which properly speaking means "cultured" or "intellectual." In Egypt, however just before the issuance of the far-reaching socialist measures, the term was in a way rehabilitated, and "the crisis of the intellectuals" referred mostly to intellectuals properly so called.) The phrase *azmat al-muthaqqafīn* was coined by Muḥammad Ḥasanayn Haykal in an article in *al-Ahrām* whose theme was the current state of relations between the Egyptian intelligentsia and the Revolution. According to Haykal, the crisis is not one of the intellectuals' political loyalty to the regime "but has something to do with their revolutionary loyalty to the Revolution."

The intellectuals, it appears from the article of this leading spokesman of the regime, have three grievances against the present regime – and three demands: that the Army should have gone back to its barracks after having effected the Revolution of July 23, 1952; that there should be a return to parliamentary life and a revival of political parties, since these are the basis of democracy and its unchanging form; that an end must be put to the preference given to the "trustworthy" *(ahl ath-thiqa)* over the "experts" *(ahl al-khibra).* (This grievance, Haykal maintains, originates in the fact that army officers were appointed in various companies and institutions to jobs that are purely technical and can be properly filled only by experts.)[1]

Haykal's article touched off quite a controversy, and in subsequent issues of *al-Ahrām* he took care to reiterate that the question was not one of political loyalty to the Revolution but of participation in it, and of "complete interaction" with it. "The Revolution," Haykal repeats, "has found in the intellectual groups precisely what it needed in terms of political loyalty; the intellectuals cooperated with the Revolution in all the plans which it sought to put in force, and with all their ability." Yet, Haykal hastens to add, the Revolution is not merely projects executed: it is a basic change in the structure of society.

But then, what is it exactly that Haykal, and the regime for which he has been so able a spokesman, want of these intellectuals? "The collaboration of the intellectuals with the revolutionary drive after July 23, 1952, " he explains, "is not the ultimate aim." The natural and inevitable role for the intellectuals to play was not "merely to collaborate with the Revolution"; it should have been "to interact with it, to adopt its cause, to take it in, to give it . . . its national ideology, to distill from their consciences and their knowledge its revolutionary doctrine, i.e. its road to the radical basic change in the structure of Egyptian society."

According to Haykal, the reconstruction of society, and participation in this reconstruction with one's knowledge, experience, and whole consciousness, is what constitutes revolutionary action in this phase of the popular struggle. What Haykal seems to be after, in short, is the intellectual's whole soul, not his mere collaboration which sometimes looks more like passive agreement than wholehearted support.[2]

It all seemed very hard on the intellectuals. And so completely against the grain, too! In the mid-thirties Julien Benda, the French philosopher and essayist who himself was a passionate supporter of "extreme democracy," wrote *La trahison des clercs* denouncing intellectuals who allowed their attitudes to be tainted by political bias and warned against any compromise over the intellectualist approach to life.[3] What Haykal was advocating, of course, was the very opposite of an intellectualist approach: he was, in fact, asking the Egyptian intellectual to surrender his thinking faculty in favour of total submersion into the current revolutionary process.

Haykal's article was only the first of a series, but it provoked quite a controversy. For one thing, having set out the intellectuals' main grievances against the regime and deplored the lack of reciprocation between them and the revolutionary drive, Haykal subsequently found out that he could not produce a satisfactory definition of the term "intellectual." Flooded by enquiries from his readers as to what, precisely, he meant by the term, Haykal was wary. The crisis, he implied, was in fact confined to one type of intellectual – namely the political intellectuals, the professionals whom the discarded parties had succeeded in attracting to their ranks and who gave their loyalty to the old ruling class, trying to be part and parcel of it. . . .

This definition did not prove satisfactory, and Yūsuf as-Sibā'ī, writing in *Rose al-Yūsuf,* rightly points out that, if that were the case, "our criticism should be directed against these [intellectuals] in their capacity as associates in the political, not cultural, life." The real subject of the controversy, Sibā'ī concludes, are those intellectuals who have preferred to devote themselves to their technical work either in government offices or in the private sector. "Yet I do not believe that the Revolution would be materially affected whether or not these reciprocate with its revolutionary drive," Sibā'ī decides.[4]

But this was obviously not what Haykal had in mind. To dismiss the whole matter in this way amounts to cynicism. Another contributor to *al-Ahrām,* a university lecturer in literature, Dr. Louis 'Awaḍ, offered a different definition of the term. "The intellectuals," he writes, "are not only the group of university professors and writers. The term denotes everyone who reacts, whether he be a reader, a student or just a plain citizen who cares about serious matters – everyone who has a clear view . . . about prevalent conditions . . . or about ways to correct these conditions."[5]

Such a definition embraces a wide group of thinking citizens whose existence seems to be hardly felt these days. The question is: where are these intellectuals now, and why have they ceased to take any part in public life? As Muḥyī ad-Dīn Muḥammad, the young Egyptian writer, puts it in *al-Ādāb:* "Was the divorce between the intellectual and the popular tide known in the days of political parties . . . or is it something peculiar to the present state of affairs? "

The writer suggests that the phenomenon was peculiar to the present regime: The intellectuals, he asserts, had the door half open for political action, for leading the people against the government of the day, and there was reciprocation between writers and the public, whom they sought to lead in the popular struggle. The reason for this, according to Muḥammad, was that these writers knew for certain that the old regime was about to crumble, and were willing to sacrifice "a year or two in prison" since it was merely a question of time. . . .

Now things have changed. "Perhaps the most important factor leading to the present isolation of the intellectuals," Muḥammad goes on to say, "is this new conception of democracy, a conception which the Revolution has not revealed with the same clarity and starkness with which it revealed its other ideas. Perhaps the only justification for this failure is its preoccupation with foreign affairs." But this lack of attention to "the old democratic conception of liberty" is very temporary, since it will stop as soon as the pressures of foreign policy cease to hold the regime's whole attention. . . .

At last coming round to the point, Muḥammad lets it slip that the Revolution's inattention to the old view of democracy "has created a sort of weakness which can be called fear." This fear, he explains, "was a very natural reaction to the suppression of every word spoken against the Revolution in its first stage." Muḥammad writes in a way which suggests that he does not believe a word of it, that the intellectuals now ought to stand up and announce the end of this state of affairs. If this has not yet happened, he adds, "it is because fear still reigns supreme in the hearts of the writers and intellectuals, a fear which has killed everything that is liable to give them confidence in what they write and what they think."[6]

Haykal's expansively liberal offer to Egyptian intellectuals to speak their true minds was reminiscent of Ilya Ehrenburg's famous good tidings about a literary "thaw." In fact, Haykal used the term in one of his articles on "the crisis" and maintained that his was an attempt to bring about such a thaw. However, such a gap seemed to have yawned between Haykal's wish and the actual state of intellectual freedom in Egypt that his words were not taken quite seriously. A strange commentary on his whole approach came in the form of an anonymous letter sent to him in reply to his call for plain speaking. The writer of the letter – apparently one of the intellectuals to whom Haykal's articles were addressed – bluntly told *al-Ahrām*'s editor that "the free discussion" to which he had invited his readers was nothing but "a trap to unmask [the regime's] opponents! "[7]

Despite Haykal's passionate call for free discussion, however, there was no gainsaying the fact that in Egypt as well as in the majority of other Arabic-speaking countries freedom of expression did not exist for those who had anything fundamental to say in criticism of the existing order of things. Indications of a realization that this state of affairs was not conducive to literary creativity – that without a certain measure of freedom of thought, literature and other cultural activities could hardly continue – came not only from Egyptian intellectuals but from others in the Arab world as well. Some of these even expressed the belief that whatever the value of the immediate political gains achieved by the military regimes, these regimes had the side-effect of stifling literature and culture, thus turning an era of political nationalist revival into a period of marked intellectual decline.

Because of the prominent cultural role which she had always played in the Arab world, the acutest example of this decline was Egypt herself. Though credited with almost every Arab nationalist victory since the mid-fifties, it was beginning to be generally realized that Cairo, once the unrivalled centre of Arabic thought and culture, was gradually surrendering that status to Beirut, which could claim no spectacular successes in the field of international or inter-Arab politics. Already in the late fifties the Arab cultural centre of gravity was fast shifting to Beirut.

The realization did not come all at once, and was by no means universal. At first, faced with this steep literary decline, enthusiastic "new critics" like Muḥammad Mandūr, Shawqī Ḍayf, and Muḥyī ad-Dīn Muḥammad decried the dearth of "a literature of Revolution" that seeks its subject-matter and its inspiration in the life of revolutionary Egypt. Then these critics started to seek reasons for the decline in the fact that these things take time and that, in the words of Muḥyī ad-Dīn Muḥammad, no great literature or immortal poetry can be expected "as long as the air is polluted with the smoke of hatred, repression, poverty and restrictiveness."

In the end it took a Lebanese – himself a staunch supporter of Cairo's policies – to find the cause in the absence of freedom of expression. Writing in the same issue of *al-Ādāb,* Dr. Suhayl Idrīs maintains that it was futile to advocate a revolutionary literature, "because we do not believe in 'committing' but in 'commitment,' a commitment springing from the writer's own spontaneity."

"Yet this," Idrīs goes on to explain, "does not absolve us from pointing out that the gravest problem confronting modern Arabic literature, in its present revolutionary phase, is that of freedom of thought. The writer, since he is called upon, by the nature of the age in which he is living, to participate in demolishing old concepts and replacing them by revolutionary ones, cannot possibly fulfil his mission if he is not granted a sufficient measure of intellectual freedom, that freedom which we would not be unjustified in saying is absent in most of the Arab countries." It is only when this freedom is granted, Idrīs concludes, that modern Arabic literature will be able to fulfill its mission.[9]

All this sounds convincing enough. But when one delves a little deeper into the writing of these revolutionary intellectuals one immediately discovers how limited and restricted is the freedom which they advocate. The behaviour and reasoning of Muḥyī ad-Dīn Muḥammad himself provide an instructive illustration of this point. In his article quoted above, entitled "A Revolt Against Modern Arabic Thought," he demands:

> Let us open the doors for ideas to strive, collide, fight, and annihilate each other! It is only thus that we can find out which of them can survive in the face of logic, criticism and traditionalism. . . . Freedom of belief and freedom of expression are inseparable parts of life in the modern age, and without them literature can never grow and progress. . . . Authority is an expression of the will of the people; it is not illegitimate pressure over that will. Let us always remember this and fight injustice, repression and dictatorship, in order to establish a civilization which the East has been dreaming of for hundreds of generations, i.e., a democratic civilization.[10]

This spirited plea for freedom was written towards the end of 1959. Subsequently, Muḥammad wrote dozens of monthly letters from Cairo as *al-Ādāb's* correspondent there, and in almost every one of his reports he invariably found cause for deploring the behaviour and pronouncements of certain Egyptian intellectuals and writers standing in the way of the so-called "revolutionary upsurge." More than once he urged the authorities to mete out suitable punishments to these "reactionaries." In one of these reports, indeed, he attacked a whole assortment of people whom he calls "spreaders of poison and haters of this great socialist revolution which is trying to achieve goodness, justice and freedom," and promises his readers that they will be destroyed. . . .[11]

The problems which confronted Egyptian writers and men of letters were not all of the ideological variety. They had more to do with cultural planning *(takhṭīṭ thaqāfī)* than with ideology. According to Rajā' an-Naqqāsh, a leading young Egyptian cultural critic and author of a book entitled *The Crisis of Egyptian Culture,*[12] the main problem confronting the Egyptian creative writer in the early sixties was publishing. This, according to him, was the thing about which all Egyptian writers complained – young and old, aspiring and well-established, completely unknown and quite famous. Yet, he adds, "while publishing constitutes a serious crisis in our literary life . . . books are published every day in endless profusion." Where then did the crisis lie? What was the secret of this apparent contradiction? To Naqqāsh, the root of all the trouble rested in the fact that many publishing houses in Egypt were not subjected to what he called detailed "cultural planning." Such lack of cultural planning may be excused where commercial publishing is concerned, he submitted, but it was plainly indefensible when one talked about publishing "institutions" of an official or semi-official character, concerns that were established first and foremost to promote culture and literature.[13]

One such publishing enterprise was the National Publishing House *(ad-dar al-qawimmiyya l'in-nashr),* which became a "state institution"(i.e., incorporated into the public sector system) and which was supposed to play an important role in the cultural and literary life of the country. This huge publishing firm, one of whose declared goals was "to contribute to the accomplishment of the cultural revolution," put out an average of four books a day, including original works and translations from foreign languages; but Naqqāsh considered its choice of titles unfortunate, slipshod, and arbitrary. After listing some glaring examples of the publishing house's failure to choose suitable titles, Naqqāsh repeats his call for "detailed cultural planning" and counsels that special "responsible committees" be named to supervise the endless stream of books being published those days. But would this "literature-by-committee" accomplish the desired cultural revolution and still remain worthy of the name? On the occasion of the 10th anniversary of the Revolution, the General Egyptian Institute of Theatre and Music announced a competition for a one-act play, establishing the play's theme as "glorifying positive, fruitful work for the public's welfare under socialism."[14] Cultural planning of a more "detailed" character was hardly thinkable, one might say. But even Dr. Mandūr, a fervent advocate of socialist realism and a man with open Marxist sympathies, who sat on the committee that was to award the prizes, in the end admitted that to set literature the task of eulogizing any specific human value creates highly difficult problems for the writer. Applause and glorification are liable to turn literature into mere oratory and propaganda, thus making it lose its special characteristics and become indistinguishable from other forms of political and sociological writings. The works sent in by the majority of those who participated in the competition, he writes, consisted of "endless political debates between the old reactionary mentality and the new socialist one." In the few cases where the plays submitted contained proper plots, moreover, these invariably revolved round the cruelty shown by the capitalists and feudalists of the old regime towards workers and peasants, or the arrogance and superior airs of the old, idle propertied classes. The dialogue was naturally of the lowest quality, since it consisted merely of "speeches."[15]

After reminding young writers that glorification of work and other values in literature cannot be attained through reciting speeches but ought to be embodied in the plot and in the actions of the characters, Dr. Mandūr cites the plot of one of the plays submitted which he thinks satisfied this particular demand. It tells the story of a poor gardener and his daughter. As a young girl the daughter worked as a maid in the same palace in which her father worked, but when he discovers that the Pasha's wife, a heartless Turkish lady, is ill-treating his daughter he decides to send her to school, doing extra work as a pedlar in order to pay for her education. Eventually, the daughter graduates in medicine and sets up a successful clinic. In the meantime the Pasha dies, leaving a son who, after failing in his studies, joins the ranks of the idle heirs. Our rich heir then asks for the gardener's daughter's hand in marriage, but both father and daughter reject him, making it clear that they will tolerate no idlers in their hard-working, productive family. It is only after the Pasha's son decides to start to do some useful work that the marriage is finally effected.[16] Cultural planning of the rigid variety, then, never gained ground in Egyptian literary circles, even among its more radical members.

Those who sought to learn from the experiences of the Soviet system in this particular field laid stress on the post-thaw frame of mind in Soviet Russia rather than on the practices of the Stalinist regime. The questions asked by these writers can be formulated as follows: What can modern Arabic literature in Egypt learn from the Soviet literary experience? Should Egypt's Arab Socialism practise the kind of rigid intellectual terror which plagued the Soviet literary scene? Or ought it to let all flowers bloom? What attitude should the present socialist regime adopt between "the literature of drum-beating" and genuine creative literature, even when this latter seemed to oppose socialism and differed from it in viewpoint?

This was a sample of the kind of questions then being asked in Egyptian literary and intellectual circles following the apparent dearth in outstanding creative work in Egypt since the 1952 Revolution. The answers were far from uniform.

Both advocates and opponents of literary freedom professed adherence to socialism, but the differences in approach were rather pronounced, with the old generation feeling the suffocating impact of socialist regimentation and the new writers – verbally at least – clamouring for total commitment in literature.

In an issue of his monthly, *al-Kātib,* Aḥmad 'Abbās Ṣāliḥ tries hard – but with no apparent success – to reconcile socialist practice with unfettered literary and artistic creativity. He points to the deplorable state of Soviet literature under Stalin, when "most literary works dealt with collective farms, factories and tractors while ignoring man himself."

He then cites the sharp reaction which followed Stalin's death and which "liberated literature from cliches and drum-beating and empty slogans." He finds fault even with the critical attitudes then prevailing in the Soviet Union, which he says were still somewhat rigid and doctrinaire. Yet he offers no better attitude or solution.

Ṣāliḥ draws an analogy between the Soviet and the Egyptian literary experiences under socialism. When socialist practice began in Egypt, he writes, noisy demands were heard clamouring for "committed literature" and, as in Russia immediately after the revolution, these shouts came from people who were the least cultured, the least talented, and the least sincere in their professions of loyalty to socialism. He warns against the danger of "large-scale intellectual terror posing as the sole revolutionary authority and paralysing literature and thought."

Here, however, the writer realizes that he has perhaps gone too far. Letting all flowers bloom, he reminds his readers, "does not mean accepting a literature whose content is reactionary and opposed to the socialist solution; it does not mean that we should accept empty gropings in the name of Art for Art's Sake; and it does not mean welcoming a literature that ignores the problems of modern Arab man to roam in total darkness after some abstract value."

Art being "direct criticism of life and an attempt to change it," the artist was "a revolutionary by virtue of the functional nature of the creative act." Thus equating art and revolution, Ṣāliḥ states his point fairly bluntly: "We naturally ask the artist to live the problems of his times, to be sincere with them and sincere with himself – but we ask of him no more than that." The artist's commitment was essential to the Revolution and the Revolution accepted no other attitude on his part.

One curious feature of Ṣāliḥ's argumentation was that he did not seem aware of the paradox of his line of thought. The Artist, he says – and seems to accept this view – "considers his mission fulfilled when the Revolution has succeeded in seizing power," as this meant that he was then living in harmony with his environment, in that equilibrium for which he had been longing with all his being.

It was not as simple as that, however. The Revolution, once accomplished, was bound to come across many unforeseen obstacles, to commit mistakes and to blunder. This is where it was bound to make more demands on the artist. It accepted criticism and self-criticism, but only within the framework of revolutionary practice. It could not easily see that literature was a pure criticism of life, and would therefore accept nothing less from literature than turning itself into "brass drums to spread enthusiasm among the caravans."

And yet, despite this awareness, Ṣāliḥ insists that literature could not oppose the socialist idea, "because [this] idea, as an ideal and as a tool for elevating man materially and spiritually, is daily renewed." It was also "a scientific reality," and thus feared no hostile views or false visions. It did not ban literary and artistic works hostile to itself or differing from its views, "unless these are mere propaganda stunts totally foreign to art and honest thinking."[17]

Ṣāliḥ's invocation of the Soviet experience could not have been a coincidence. A year or so before he wrote his article, in April 1964, hundreds of Egyptians, among them many writers and journalists, were released from prisons and other places of detention where they had been kept since 1959 when the communists of Iraq stood in the first ranks of those who opposed union with the then United Arab Republic. At that time President Nasser decided to wage a merciless campaign against Arab communism. There can be no mistake about the intellectual ferment caused by the subsequent appointment of many of them to fairly leading positions in journalism, publishing, and the other media of communication. After the summer of 1964, in fact, Egyptian papers and periodicals became full of debates which, though ostensibly dealing with literature and the arts, were really open ideological contests between followers of Arab Socialism and hardcore Marxists who were just not convinced by it.

The extent of communist infiltration of the Egyptian press may not have been as great as it was depicted by outside observers; but its effects were considerable. Early in 1965, for example, Cairo's leading politico-cultural weekly, *Rose al-Yūsuf,* was handed over to a new editor and a new management board chairman who was a known communist, while Iḥsān 'Abd al-Quddūs, its owner-editor and son of its founder, Fāṭīma al-Yūsuf, was removed. Previously, Dāral-Akhbār, which puts out the daily *al-Akhbār,* the weeklies *Akhbār al-Yawm* and *Ākhir Sā'a,* and the monthly *al-Hilāl,* had received a new boss: Khālid Muḥyī ad-Dīn, another reputed Marxist, who in turn appointed new left-wing editors for these publications. Though these changes were made with considerable discretion, they did not fail to give rise to objections and murmurings. The official explanation was provided at the time by Haykal, who wrote that the measure was meant to bring the communists into the light of day so as to make supervision and control of their activities easier. During a private meeting with members of the Parliamentary Committee of the Arab Socialist Union late in February 1964 Nasser answered some questions on this subject by asserting that the appointments were meant to give the communists a chance "to rehabilitate themselves in our society." As long as they do not seek to form their own organization, he implied, the communists will not be molested, while their writings must remain within the framework of the principles of the *National Charter,* like all other journalistic and literary activities.[18]

A somewhat different explanation was offered by Naqqāsh, himself one of the up-and-coming Egyptian intellectuals and journalists. According to Naqqāsh, the changes were essential in themselves, since Egypt was now passing through a new revolutionary era and thus needed "a new press, a press which answers the people's real needs."

Prior to the Revolution of 1952, Naqqāsh explains, the Egyptian press was hostile to the people and represented reactionary and imperialist forces. Egyptian newspapers and journals were either of the cheap sensationalist kind offering sex and violence and ignoring the people's real needs or so-called "neutral, balanced, fair and reasonable" publications.

Since this kind of neutrality and fairness in effect meant "a neutralism between the people and its enemies, between British imperialism and the popular will, between feudalists and peasants, and between capitalists and the workers," it was in actuality nothing but treachery and a failure to deal with the country's real problems. As an example of this latter type of journalism Naqqāsh cites *al-Ahrām*'s attitude until it was given over to Haykal in 1957.

This evil legacy in Egyptian journalism did not end with the Revolution, for the Revolution was too busy fighting its major battles to give enough thought to purging the press of Rightists and opportunist elements. Now the time had come to create "an all-out revolutionary press capable of creating a genuine revolutionary atmosphere among the people." The Revolution must be introduced to the masses rather than remain known only to an elite of intellectuals. "In this phase of our history it is no longer reasonable to leave the press with its old legacy, or make it dependent on the efforts of a handful of journalists, or to become each an island unto itself, with some papers liberated and others lagging behind the realities."

It was in a bid to cure these chronic ills of the Egyptian press, Naqqāsh implies, that the communists were allowed to infiltrate and take virtual control of Egyptian papers and periodicals. According to him, the press was in such a deplorable state "that there was no way other than letting the Leftists, who are loyal to the people and to the Revolution, take control of it, in order to turn [it] into a valuable revolutionary weapon, and to clean it of the dust of a past that was full of treachery." The Left, he concludes, "offers the only salvation for our press, and is the only way of creating high-level revolutionary journalism."[19]

But whatever the real explanation may be for letting the communists into influential positions in journalism and other fields of cultural activity, it would be interesting to see in what spheres of ideology they have been most articulate.

One of these was the subject of literature and society. It was by no means a coincidence that, with several avowed Marxists at the helm of some of Egypt's most sensitive communications media, literary and artistic debates towards the end of 1964 began to be conducted with a heat and an intensity of feeling that seemed out of all proportion to the nature of the subjects discussed. Indeed, in an article in *Rose al-Yūsuf,* 'Abd al-Quddūs remarks upon such differences of opinion among Egyptian intellectuals, adding that these differences "refuse to come to the surface and would not define themselves frankly." This may have been true of political viewpoints; in literary matters, however, the disputants usually gave their emotions full expression.[20]

There is, indeed, ample reason to believe that most of these disputes were in fact used as camouflage for far more serious differences, and that they signify a fierce and basic ideological conflict from whose conduct one could easily perceive the various disputants' positions vis-à-vis the main political ideas which compete for men's minds today.

One of these disputes revolves around the subject of the writer's "commitment" and the social content of literature. Though the subject was not new for Cairo's literary circles it acquired a marked intensity following the emergence of a number of left-wing writers and intellectuals from prison cells and concentration camps to assume leading posts in the Egyptian press and other fields in the communications media.

The discussion over "commitment" started towards the end of 1964, when Maḥmūd Amīn al-'Ālim, a leading communist ideologist, published an article on current Egyptian works of literature and art. It all appears to have started when 'Ālim, released from long imprisonment, decided to take a stroll in Cairo's streets and alleyways. He liked what he saw. He savoured the smell of smoke issuing from factory chimneys; he liked the smiles he noticed on faces he encountered; and he was pleased with the figures he read concerning industry, output, and construction work.

'Ālim's pleasure was marred, however, by the works of art and literature that came his way. Stepping into the nearest theatre house, for instance, he watched *The Servants,* a play by a leading Egyptian playwright, Yūsuf Idrīs. He left the theatre deep in sombre thoughts. He then picked up a book of poems by Ṣalāḥ 'Abd aṣ-Ṣabūr, a leading poet of the Modernist school, only to be even more dismayed and bewildered. Considering those works over-pessimistic and gloomy, 'Ālim started wondering: Is there in this world and age still room for sorrow, gloom, and bitterness?

'Ālim put all these thoughts into his article. The gist of this was that there did not exist any opposition at all between the revolutionary artist and the revolutionary regime, and that the artist should therefore see goodness and light in everything which takes place, provided only that the general direction was the right one. His art should thus be full of optimism and happiness, and if this meant sacrificing art, well and good then, since the loss will not be so great and the stakes are far bigger and more important than mere art: It is a question of destiny as determined by economic and political considerations.[21]

Reaction to 'Ālim's article was immediate and rather violent. Ṣabūr wrote a rejoinder in which he implied that every believer in socialist realism was a Moscow agent, adding that he would never discuss the subject with 'Ālim, but would take it up with Moscow itself, without mediators! Idrīs, author of *The Servants,* asserted that Russia was not exactly the paradise which was promised to the believers, and that she had problems and difficulties of her own, like any other country. He said also that art has great significance, and wondered what people would do without it.[22]

Several other writers and critics took up the issue, all siding with 'Ālim's critics. One of them wrote a cantankerous piece assuring 'Ālim and his followers that he would "wipe them out," that he would never forgive them, and that "they will live to regret it! " Finally, he complained to Khrushchev himself about 'Ālim's behaviour, assuring the then Soviet Prime Minister that though he respects him personally he has nothing but disrespect and scorn for his followers.[23]

It is easy to perceive that this particular controversy in fact went far beyond such subjects as the writer's commitment and the social content of literature. The surprising fact was that all those who took part in attacking 'Ālim do believe, or profess belief, in "commitment" – and they all write with the doctrine of Arab Socialism as their declared point of departure. By taking such a hostile attitude to 'Ālim, however, his opponents exposed themselves to criticism as confirmed "Rightists" who virtually rejected "commitment" and denied literature any social content, which, needless to say, was not quite the case.

It should be pointed out, however, that neither 'Ālim nor his opponents, though each party no doubt commanded a following, represented the prevalent literary attitude in Egypt to these subjects. There was, so to speak, a third group, whose adherents, while acknowledging the social content of literature and agreeing that the writer should be "committed," refused to relegate the arts to a position of propaganda and mere service to the political regime of the day.

One of the members of this group of writers, Ghālib Halsa, presented the case with considerable force and cohesion, rejecting the attitudes both of 'Ālim and his critics. The former, he claimed, wanted to make art a mere servant of authority, thus ignoring the very nature of artistic creativity, which is essentially the expression of a subjective experience not given to conscious control; his critics, on the other hand, concentrated on the artist's experience to the exclusion of his social obligations.

Both these attitudes, Halsa asserted, were harmful in that they leave the door open before the masses, which cannot be expected to be content with mere propaganda when they want to get artistic pleasure, to turn to the "Rightist" school as their only recourse. Pointing out that the real subject of discussion between the disputants was nothing less than the relation between the people and the authorities, Halsa wrote that the only way for providing suitable conditions for artistic creativity was by granting the people full freedom of expression and organization and letting them practise the actual responsibilities of government rather than offering them sermons and commands.[24]

Such reservations notwithstanding, however, the question as to the writer's proper role in society, and whether he has a social role to play at all, had long since appeared to have been settled for the new generation of Egyptian writers and men of letters. In the mid-sixties, discussion of these subjects usually went "beyond commitment," taking it quite for granted that the writer, the creative artist, and the intellectual all work for the progress and well-being of man. The questions under discussion took the discussants another step forward; it was: does the role of the writer and the intellectual end with writing, reading, and conducting literary and artistic discussions, or should it extend to active participation?

This was how Aḥmad 'Abd al-Mu'ṭī' Ḥijāzī, the poet and literary editor of *Rose al-Yūsuf,* opened a series of contributions in that review on "The Artist and Politics." After citing the example of French writers under the German occupation during World War Two and that of some British writers in the Spanish Civil War, Ḥijāzī answered his question by asserting that for the artist "the only possible choice is one between siding with the Revolution and siding with its enemies."

In fact the artist has no alternative but to join the army of the Revolution, "not only to realize socialism but also to solve his own artistic problems, such as reaching the masses . . . and educating the people in the new values of art and literature."[25]

The well-known novelist and literary journalist, Fatḥī Ghānim, tried to answer the question: why and for whom do we write? He then declares that he was all for those artists and writers "who produce for the masses, for the sake of asserting revolutionary values, establishing new [social] relations, aiding social progress, and for the victory of man against all kinds of exploitation." These writers and artists, Ghānim concludes, evaluate political action as a guide and an end, from which they draw justification and incentive for their literary production.[26]

After Ḥijāzī and Ghānim, who wrote from the viewpoint of the creative artist, came the out-and-out socialist ideologues. Writing subsequently on the same topic, Muḥammad 'Awda commences with a violent attack on "capitalist and feudalist society," which he describes as "a society which constantly persecutes the artist's personality and tears up his sensibility, a society with no principles, no morality and no values, and in which no virtues or beliefs or ideals can flourish . . . an opportunistic, unethical and inhuman society whose paramount law is wolf eats wolf and the devil swallows those who lag behind! "

Plainly, 'Awda adds, no literature or art can flourish in such a society. In the socialist society, on the other hand, man's cultural and spiritual needs are considered as important as his material ones, and the artist there "is not only necessary but inevitable." The artist, therefore, must take part in actual politics, in order to build the socialist society.[27]

Under the title "Why I Worked in Politics," Dr. Mandūr, late Professor of Literature at Cairo University and a leading literary critic and intellectual in his day, used his own life experience to prove that the artist should take an active part in tackling the political and social issues of his time and his society. He related how, on returning to Egypt in 1939, after spending nine years at European universities, he was shocked to see the yawning gap between the actual, sorry state of his country and its great potential, and how he reached the decision to do something about it.

Working as a teacher of literature at the university, Mandūr related how he was torn between the liberal education he received in the Classics and the urge toward social reform and political action which filled him. In the end, he found a solution: he left the university to assume the editorship of the Wafd's daily organ *al-Miṣrī,* from where he thought he would be able to combine literary criticism with political activity.

But although his efforts to reform the Wafd Party from within proved unsuccessful because this popular party was controlled by reactionaries, capitalists, and feudalists, Dr. Mandūr did not regret having made the effort. His political work, he asserted, had produced certain changes in his literary criticism; he established a new school called "the ideological method in criticism," whose point of departure was that "literature and art have a social role to fulfil" and that it was in this fulfilment that use must be made of healthy artistic and aesthetic values.[28]

"Art without politics is not art," declares Ṣāliḥ, editor of the monthly *al-Kātib* and the last participant in *Rose al-Yūsuf*'s running debate. He asserts that the impact of a work of art upon the people was "invariably positive, that is to say, it makes us try to change ourselves or our environment." That is why the artist's starting point is primarily political, radical, revolutionary.

But the artist's role does not end with the victory of the Revolution. On the contrary: the writer's duty becomes greater, and his responsibility heavier. It even happens that writers decide to join the political battle directly, fighting it not with artistic methods but with direct political means, or with both at the same time. This is what was taking place in Egypt, Ṣāliḥ asserts, and this was how it ought to be, he implies.[29]

From the above symposium in *Rose al-Yūsuf* the reader will no doubt get a fairly "Zhdanovist" impression of the state of Egyptian letters under Nasserism. This would not be quite accurate. Some writers, novelists, and poets, such as Dr. Yūsuf Idrīs, Ṣabūr, and Najīb Maḥfūz, took quite a sober view of the subject.

Thus the subject of intellectuals, their problems, duties, and standing was once more the cause of discussion and controversy in Egypt in the years which followed Haykal's series of articles on "the crisis of the intellectuals." Yet, whereas in 1961 criticism of these intellectuals was directed at their alleged indifference, apathy, and failure to participate in the people's struggle, discussion later in the sixties revolved round their actual ideological differences, the disparity between their views on such subjects as the function of literature, the social role of criticism, and the revolutionary duty of the intellectual. Above all, these intellectuals were being taken to task for their apparent – and normally rather natural and healthy – failure to agree upon one uniform meaning of socialism and the means best calculated to attain it. Indeed, as was quite to be expected, despite the appearance of ideological uniformity and conformism, basic and far-reaching differences of opinion continued to emerge among members of the Egyptian intelligentsia. Early in 1965 'Abd al-Quddūs – as we saw in Chapter 5 – went so far as to assert that the Egyptian intellectuals were "the most disunited, scattered and mutually-hostile group in the country."

## NOTES

1 Muḥammad Ḥasanayn Haykal, *al-Ahrām,* 2 June 1961.

2 Muḥammad Ḥasanayn Haykal, *ibid.,* 9 June 1961.

3 Julien Benda, *La Trahison des Clercs* [Trans. Richard Aldington, "The Treason of the Intellectuals"] (N.Y., 1956).

4 Yūsuf as-Sibā'ī, *Rose al-Yūsuf,* 19 June 1961.

5 Louis 'Awaḍ, *al Ahrām,* 30 June 1961.

6 Muḥyī ad-Dīn Muḥammad, *"an-nashāṭ ath-thaqāfī fī al-waṭān al-'arabī: al-jumhūriyya al-'arabiyya al-muttaḥida al-iqlīm al-janūbi"* ["Cultural Activity in the Arab Homeland: The United Arab Republic. The Southern Region"], *al-Ādāb,* July 1961, pp. 77–78.

7 Cited by Muḥammad Ḥasanayn Haykal in *al-Ahrām,* 23 June 1961.

8 Muḥyī ad-Dīn Muḥammad, *"thawra 'alā al-fikr al-'arabī al-ḥadīth"*

["A Revolt Against Modern Arabic Thought"], *al-Ādāb,* January 1960, p. 3.

9 Suhayl Idrīs, editorial, *ibid.*, p. 2.

10 Muḥyī ad-Dīn Muḥammad, *op. cit.*, pp. 3–4.

11 Muḥyī ad-Dīn Muḥammad, *"an-nashāṭ ath-thaqāfī fī al-waṭan al-'arabī"* ["Cultural Activity in the Arab Homeland"], *al-Ādāb,* October 1961, p. 79.

12 Rajā' an-Naqqāsh, *fī azmat ath-thaqāfa al-miṣriyya* ["The Crisis of Egyptian Culture"] (Beirut, n.d.).

13 Rajā' an-Naqqāsh, *"ath-thawra ath-thaqāfiyya w'at-takhṭīṭ"* ["The Cultural Revolution and Planning"], *al-Ādāb,* July 1962, pp. 70–71.

14 *Ibid.*

15 Muḥammad Mandūr, *"su'ūbat al-adab al-jadīd"* ["The Difficulty of the New Literature"], *al-Kātib,* August 1962, pp. 6–10.

16 *Ibid.*

17 Aḥmad 'Abbās Ṣāliḥ, *"at-takhṭīṭ ath-thaqāfī"* ["Cultural Planning"], *al-Kātib,* April 1965, pp. 3–8.

18 Nasser reported in Rajā' an-Naqqāsh, *"an-nashāṭ ath-thaqāfī fī al-waṭān al-'arabī. al-jumhūriyya al-'arabiyya al-muttaḥida"* ["Cultural Activity in the Arab Homeland. The United Arab Republic"], *al-Ādāb,* January 1965, pp. 77–78.

19 Rajā' an-Naqqāsh, *op. cit.*, p. 78.

20 Iḥsān 'Abd al-Quddūs, *Rose al-Yūsuf,* 21 December 1964.

21 Maḥmūd Amīn al-'Ālim, quoted in Ghālib Halsa, *"ma'raka ḥawl al-adab w'al-mawqif"* ["A Battle about Literature and Attitude"], *al-Ādāb,* November 1964, pp. 12–13.

22 'Abd aṣ-Ṣabūr's comments as well as Idrīs' are quoted in Halsa's articles, *ibid.*, pp. 13–14.

23 Reported in Halsa, *op. cit.*, p. 14.

24 *Ibid.*

25 Aḥmad 'Abd al-Mu'ṭī Ḥijāzī, *Rose al-Yūsuf,* 16 November 1964.

26 Fatḥī Ghānim, *Rose al-Yūsuf,* 23 November 1964.

27 Muḥammad 'Awda, *Rose al-Yūsuf,* 30 November 1964.

28 Muḥammad Mandūr, *"limadhā ishtaghaltu b'is-siyāsa"* ["Why I Worked in Politics"], *Rose al-Yūsuf,* 14 December 1964.

29 Aḥmad 'Abbās Ṣāliḥ, *Rose al-Yūsuf,* 28 December 1964.

# 10. AN AUTOCHTHONOUS CULTURE ?

The period covered by this survey was one of a marked dearth in creative writing, at least in so far as quality was concerned. This state of affairs, which some have sought to depict as normal in times of revolution and accelerated social change, was not confined to Egypt alone but affected the whole of the Arabic literary scene. Of the various branches of literature, however, drama was not the hardest hit, mainly because of official and semi-official encouragement. There have been numerous translations of foreign plays, classical, modern, and *avant-garde,* and quite a few original productions. But the search, especially in the Egypt of the fifties and sixties, for originality and authenticity, and the emphasis on the popular and the specifically Egyptian, served to accentuate the essential foreignness of much that was being served on the Egyptian stage. This included not only the straight translations but also the original plays, modelled as they all were on European theatre.

But before we tackle this point – this demand for an authentic, native Egyptian theatre – it would be apt to say a word about the place of drama in Arabic literature. It is well known that the art of drama as we know it today has been quite unknown in Arab culture. The relative dearth in this particular art medium in Arabic in recent years thus has rather deep roots in Arab literary history. For no matter how one would view the quality and the richness of the East's cultural heritage, it is evident that the only peoples of the ancient world who knew theatre as we now understand it were the Greeks and the Romans. What theatre was found to have existed in ancient Egypt, China, and India lacked most of the known characteristics of the art. And if the East as a whole lagged behind in this field of literary creation, the Arabs were totally to neglect it until the second half of the nineteenth century, when a number of inadequate and thoroughly adapted versions of certain French plays were introduced on improvised stages in Beirut and Cairo.

The reasons for the Arabs' neglect of theatre are many and cannot be gone into here. Chief among them are, perhaps, the Arabic language and the Arabs' outlook on life.

The advent of Islam in the seventh century did not make things easier or the atmosphere more congenial for the development of drama. This must have been largely to blame for the curious fact that during the Muslims' period of intensive and rather fruitful translation of works from Greek and Latin, into Arabic, not a single play or work of literature was rendered into that language. The fact that these translations were invariably sponsored and subsidized by the rulers of the day, and that these generally did not order the rendering of literary works, cannot wholly account for this interesting phenomenon. In a paper read by 'Azīz Abāẓa before the Arab Academy in Damascus in 1961, he points out that Aristotle's *Poetics* did get translated into Arabic, but that its translators "did not understand the work, so that their version was confused, uneven, and obscure – with the result that it remained a closed book for them." Abāẓa indeed rejects the theory that it was Islam – "the religion of reason and creativeness" – that was to blame for the absence of theatre in Arabic. Rather, he implies, it was the Arabs' own temperament, their psychological make-up and predilections.[1]

It was only after the coming of the West to the area, with its Christian missions, its schools, and its colleges as well as its conquering armies, that theatre was introduced into Arabic in any form. The two countries first to benefit from this innovation were Lebanon and Egypt, where amateur and rather primitive theatrical groups emerged, and in 1869 the Khedive Ismā'īl built the Opera House in Cairo and invited a French troupe to perform in it. In the same neighbourhood, Al-Azbakiyya, another theatre house was built, Comédie. It has been claimed that the cultural renaissance initiated and actively encouraged by Ismā'īl was directly responsible for the birth of Egyptian drama. On the other hand, by encouraging playwrights to translate and adapt European plays, Ismā'īl fostered a climate in which anything else was bound to suffer.[2] One factor which helped in the fostering of such a climate was the fact that the talent which first inspired modern Egyptian theatre came from outside, mainly from Syria, where European influence had quickly, and very early, penetrated the intellectual life of the educated minority. Among the experimental dramatists of this period, in Syria and later in Egypt, the tendency was to begin as a translator and adaptor of foreign plays, and then to launch one's career as an original playwright.

But while these foreign influences militated against the creation of an authentic Egyptian theatre, a remarkable new talent which appeared on the Egyptian cultural scene did much to correct the prevalent Western bias. This was a young Egyptian by the name of Ya'qūb Sanū', a journalist who found in the medium of the theatre a fitting outlet for his radical temperament. Sanū', whom one Egyptian writer has described as "combining in his person the energies of a noble people overcome by tyranny for a long period of time," tried to correct the overwhelmingly European character of the Egyptian stage; and he did this through composing original plays that were rooted in the Egyptian milieu. These plays he wrote in a mixture of classical and colloquial Arabic – a practice adopted by other translators and adaptors of plays for the young stage. The use of the colloquial in these translations has been defended on two counts: It brought the European classics to Arab audiences and it fulfilled a necessary phase in the evolution of a native theatre. Still, "by concentrating on foreign plays . . . so much attention was focused on the European theatre that it unconsciously formed the translators into replicas of their European models."[3]

It is not our purpose in this chapter to survey the development of the Egyptian theatre since its early beginnings in the works of Sanū'. It is worth noticing, however, that at least in the Egyptians' own estimate, this development was so significant and far-reaching that by the middle of the twentieth century they have come to see their theatre as an original one of an international quality. Aḥmad Shawqī with his historical verse plays, which ranged between ancient Egyptian, Roman, Greek, and Islamic history; Tawfīq al-Ḥakīm with his "theatre of ideas" *(masraḥ adh-dhihn)*; Aḥmad Taymūr with his original plays on Egyptian life and culture; and 'Alī Bakathīr with his plays on Islamic themes and history – all these brought to the Egyptian theatre a modernity and a popular scope that made it an important and very prominent feature of the country's literary and artistic life.

The Revolution of 1952, though initially preoccupied almost exclusively with political and social problems, in the early sixties started to take an active interest in the theatre, whose chief problem remained the same since the early days of Sanū' – namely its failure to reach the masses. Until well after the 1952 Revolution, Cairo had only one theatre, the National Theatre, subsidized by the State, and three private companies specializing in light comedy. In the early sixties, the Government undertook a series of measures designed to encourage local playwrights and actors, as well as translation of great plays from foreign languages. Dr. ʻAbd al-Qādir Ḥātim, Minister of Information, had the idea of setting up special "television theatre companies." By the mid-sixties there were nearly twenty such companies, which perform not only for television but tour various parts of the country giving live popular presentations. Their repertoires include plays by such Egyptian dramatists as Ḥakīm, Taymūr, and Bakathīr, as well as young authors. Novels by Najīb Maḥfūz (*al-liṣṣ w'al-kilāb,* "The Robber and the Dogs"), by ʻAbd ar-Raḥmān ash-Sharqāwī (*al-arḍ,* "Earth"), by Iḥsān ʻAbd al-Quddūs and Yūsuf as-Sibāʻī have been adapted for the stage.

Side by side with this official encouragement, the Revolution has also had the effect of bringing to the fore more fundamental questions, concerning the theatre as well as other fields of cultural activities. Reappraisals, re-evaluation, reformulations, and the beginnings of fresh approaches to these questions became very prominent features of the literary-cultural landscape, and some writers began to call for "overall reappraisals," comprehensive "survey operations," and radical reformulations of attitudes. Very few such operations were forthcoming, however – and those that were actually made have not been of the happiest or the most successful. Among these was an attempt to deal with the problem of a native Egyptian theatre. The question posed was: can a genuinely autochthonous Egyptian theatre be created, or even envisaged? The topic was debated at some length, but the result has been a fairly unanimous agreement that there was, is, and can be no possibility whatever of such a theatre ever emerging.

A vivid debate started when Yūsuf Idrīs, one of Egypt's foremost short story writers and critics of the younger generation, and a playwright in his own right, published in 1964 a series of articles in a leading literary review calling for the creation of a theatre that would be genuinely Egyptian, in form as well as in content, and asserting that this was not only necessary but also quite feasible. What theatre there is in Egypt today, Idrīs maintains, is Egyptian neither in form nor in content, and even when the plays were written by Egyptians and dealt with specifically Egyptian themes it remained an essentially European theatre "reflecting neither our true character nor our nature." In order to bring out Egypt's specific personality and identity on the stage, Idrīs argues, it was not enough merely to stumble over an Egyptian theme; there must be found a form for staging these plays which would spring from and be reflected in these terms.

What was needed in order to attain this, Idrīs asserts, was for the modern Egyptians to have another look into themselves and their personalities in order to discover what was genuine and what was acquired. For as it now stands, the Egyptian theatre is copied from the theatre of Europe in literally everything – form, production, acting, décor, etc. He is convinced, however, that every people, no matter how advanced or backward, "has its own unique psychological and spiritual constitution, its own tastes and its own feelings which derive from its specific cultural heritage, climate, history and traditions." Also, that man never existed alone "but was and will always remain a member of a community having its own identity and feeling and taste." This being the case, every people has to have its own distinctive artistic forms and expressions.[5]

Idrīs's articles constitute a detailed and interesting critique of the Egyptian theatre, a passionate indictment of its record since its inception in the second half of the nineteenth century. In his view, the movement which had bestowed on Egypt the art of drama, and which he considers to be still dominant in Egyptian theatre, has been "an illegitimate child of that theatre, so that our theatre grew up as the faked offspring of eighteenth and nineteenth century French theatre. It all started with literal translations [from this theatre], then developed into adaptation and borrowing, not only of texts of theatrical traditions but of schools of thought and even terminology; this last is still current in our theatre, so that we still use foreign words such as 'décor,' 'juene première,' 'vaudeville' and 'drama.' " This Idrīs finds deplorable since "no matter how we adapt, change or develop European theatre its European character will continue to be as distant from our nature as Europe is distant from us. Like water and oil, neither can we mix with Europe nor can Europe mix with us. Every people has its own special nature in response to which it produces its arts."

There is, Idrīs reminds us, "a basic difference between science and art." Science can comprise universal laws which the whole human race can handle, utilize, and put into effect in the same spirit and mentality;

"still, we find that even science, which ought to be general and universal, has its varieties. In India and China, for instance, there are three kinds of medical sciences – the traditional European, the experimental popular Indian, and the Arabo-Greek, which makes use of the prescriptions recommended by ancient Arab and Greek authors. I am indeed told . . . that the results of treatment given according to all these three methods are almost identical in their effectiveness, with the popular experimental and Arabo-Greek ones often proving superior to that of Europe." If this is true of science, Idrīs asks, "what then would be the case with art, which not only is native by nature but which, unless it is native, loses its character and its nature as art? " The art which we call universal "is none other than European art, which we call universal only loosely and because of its very wide currency; but it is a European art first and foremost, so much so that if we were to isolate it from Europe it would lose its artistic effect completely. This is because every art is the product of a people or a group of peoples living in a certain environment and having the same temperament and psychological make-up, so that the product, art, must always be identical to the producer, the people, or the artist who springs from this people."

For this reason, Idrīs writes, the theatre too, in its "universal" form, "is none other than European theatre; all that there is to it is that this theatre has spread in keeping with the spread of European civilization and European languages until it has come to embrace most of the countries of the world." This so-called "universal" theatre, then, "has come to threaten popular native theatres everywhere, except in those lands with their own deeply-rooted theatrical traditions, such as China and Japan." It was this same European theatre, masquerading as universal theatre, that "destroyed our own native theatre which had inevitably to emerge one day. It is not at all possible, either, that this theatre can fill the place of our own native theatre or prevent its emergence, unless it be possible for French or English to render our Arabic language redundant or destroy it or take its place. For, like language, art is an inseparable part of a people's nature and the characteristics of its existence."

Idrīs further explains that what he is referring to here is not only *bona fide* European theatre but the so-called Egyptian theatre which has been a product of the influences of European drama. To this latter theatre belong all the plays that have been written for the Egyptian stage so far, not excluding those belonging to the modern Egyptian school. "The spread of this type of theatre and its popularity do not in the least disprove the thesis that it is not of us and does not spring from our nature; on the contrary, they emphasize our people's need for theatre as well as the importance attached to it; in the absence of a theatre of its own it patronizes the other theatre, and 'something is better than nothing'."[6]

What, then, is to be done? This question brings Idrīs face to face with the wider, far more crucial subject of cultural borrowing in general. There are, he writes, two trends of thought concerning the ways in which such borrowing is to be conducted. There are, first, those who argue that "we borrow from Europe everything that we can borrow, and after we have assimilated it we start creating for our special needs." This, Idrīs says, is exactly like the case of a man who tells the budding young writer: "First you have to read all the literatures of the world and absorb them, and then, but only then, can you sit down and write." However, "the truth is that the only way to write is to read and write at the same time, learn and teach, create your own art while contemplating the art of others, past and contemporary." One writes because, through writing, one can find oneself and one's identity, can discover one's themes and form one's style. One does not read in order to borrow or to emulate, but in order to acquire the general knowledge necessary for giving one the capacity for a better appraisal of one's existence.

The second trend is equally "extremist," Idrīs writes. "It argues that our assimilation of European culture is bound to influence our psychological make-up and stamp it with a foreign character, so that when we write we will find ourselves impelled to tread the same path as taken by the Europeans." This too is dismissed by Idrīs as wrong-headed, because "it means that we lock ourselves inside and try to start from the very beginning, until we have produced the pure Egyptian art which will have no trace whatever of foreign influence."

Idrīs dismisses both schools of thought as wrong, because self-negation is as bad as exaggerated awareness of the self. The first trend results in the depreciation and ultimately the abdication of our personality, while the second would have us avoid everything produced by others on the ground that it is not our own and has no relation to us. Idrīs therefore proposes, as the only solution to the problem, that "we keep our doors wide open to foreign cultures, which we should study and comprehend, and at the same time not put off [doing] what we ourselves can do until we have completed the act of assimilation. We have to open up in order to observe the cultures of others, and then close ourselves in and forget about these cultures and those arts whenever we want to write for ourselves." Interaction with Europe is both necessary and inevitable, "and not only between us and Europe but between us and Asia, Africa, America and the rest of the world." The gravest problem, however, is that this process should be interaction in the full sense of the term, i.e. it ought to be founded on a basis of give-and-take and of mutual influences, "because one-sided borrowing and one-track influence ultimately lead only to the elimination of our personality." The Egyptians, then, must have their own independent personality in the realms of literature, the arts, the sciences, and all other fields of creativity. This personality must develop through two basic methods – by deepening its roots in our heritage and our history and by opening the windows of all cultures to it.

This is Idrīs's central thesis. As far as the theatre is concerned there is, to be sure, such a theatre in contemporary Egypt, and it has been there for a long time. "What is rather doubtful, however, is whether this theatre is representative of our stage personality. My own opinion is that it is not, and that such a personality has not yet been created and that its creation, planting and tending requires great and continuous efforts which must be borne by all those who are interested in the art of the theatre."[7]

In order to accomplish this essential work of rebuilding Egypt's own independent "stage personality," Idrīs adds, "all we need is to forget all those European concepts which we learnt from Aristotle, Shakespeare, Molière and the great theatre critics – and then with keen eyes and an open mind start searching in our life, for it is there that the first seeds lie, the first saplings and the raw material from which we can shape the new embryo and lay the foundations." Such seeds and such saplings are there, to be sure, and they have been there since the time of the great Pharaohs. Idrīs discusses a few of the forms which in his opinion constitute the original popular and folkloristic Egyptian stage, such as *Karagoz* (mimicry) and *Khayal aẓ-ẓil* (shadow theatre), seeking to show the characteristically Egyptian nature of these theatrical forms. But it is in his treatment of tragedy that he brings out the radical difference between what he calls the "drama features" of the Egyptians on the one hand and those of the Greeks – and ultimately the Europeans – on the other.

Greek tragedy, he notes, is a theatrical form through which the Greeks sought to depict man's heroism in his struggle against Fate. The tragic hero in Egyptian, Arab, and Eastern lore differs radically from the Greek.

> He is not the victim of a criminal or capricious fate; he is a real hero, not because of the heroic deeds he performs, but because it is he who is the master of his destiny and he who conducts his own life: He makes his own choice and his destiny is decided in accordance with that choice. Thus man's tragedy here is that of the choice he makes – of man who holds and controls his destiny. He is not the victim of some power that lies outside himself; he is the victim of himself, of his ability to make choices and of his own free will. For instance, he can be the man of ambition who starts working his destiny by a burning desire to lay his hands on the possessions of others, and whose desire leads him to ever more tragic circumstances until in the end he commits the great crime – murder, rape or the sacrifice of those most dear to him – on the altar of his own desires. It is then that his fate is sealed and he receives the just penalty, so that he ends up either murdered, or landing in the same trap he had set for others, or going to Hell on the Day of Judgement.

Plainly, Idrīs writes, these two types of tragic hero represent two totally different outlooks on life.

> According to the Greeks, man is a victim, his struggle is that of the helpless victim whose life and fate have been determined for him [by the gods]. With us, on the other hand, it is man himself who makes his life and his destiny and is thus held responsible for the way in which he makes his choice, and is ultimately punished or repaid for this conduct. With us, man is boundlessly free, but at the same time equally responsible for his choice: responsibility is as boundless as freedom. With the Greeks, man is not endowed with any freedom, and he is ultimately not responsible: Oedipus is not in the least responsible for murdering his father and marrying his mother, since

> this was a crime forced on him; in the whole drama he is merely a puppet moved by the fingers of Fate – and how can a puppet be held responsible?

Summing up this section of his survey, Idrīs writes: "The concept of tragedy is entirely different [in the two cultures]. There, tragedy is purely metaphysical; here, purely social. There it treats of the relationship between man and his creator and the master of his destiny; here it treats of the relations between man and man – it deals with man's crime against man, not that of Fate against him."[8]

From all this, Idrīs takes us back to the main theme of his articles, namely the existence of an authentic, native Egyptian theatre. On the strength of all that has been explained above, he writes, "we can say that there does exist an Egyptian theatre; it is there in our life and in our being, but we fail to see it because we want to see it as a replica of the Greek and European theatre which we knew and which we translated, borrowed, adapted and emulated from the last decades of the nineteenth century and until our own days." "All that this Egyptian theatre lacks in order to acquire a form and to take its rightful place in our lives," Idrīs adds, "is that we take a fresh look at ourselves and our life, so as to distinguish between the authentic and the acquired there; it is to learn how to respect our identity and the arts which that identity gives rise to." To do this in the sphere of theatre "it is not enough merely to stumble onto an Egyptian theatrical theme; we have to create for this theme the theatrical form which springs from it, is capable of bringing it out and of developing it to its greatest and widest possibilities."[9]

Reactions to Idrīs's novel thesis came from almost all the leading men in Egyptian theatre; they were immediate and unequivocal – and all vehemently critical. "This call seems to me to be like a call to re-create the Universe! " declared Dr. Muḥammad Mandūr. True, he said, Egyptians once had some kind of popular theatrical forms that can be likened, remotely, to what is known as theatre; "but it is historically proved that the art of the theatre in its modern sense did not develop out of these popular forms but was taken by us from Europe." Even Idrīs's own new play *The Servants,* which he wrote in support of his thesis, is similar in theatrical form and intellectual content to some European plays, both modern and ancient. The very theme which Idrīs tackled in this play, the theme of relations between servant and master, "he tackled on a cosmic, metaphysical basis, when he tried to show that tutelage is an inevitable, external relationship embracing not only man in society but extending to the world of matter, where electrons are destined to circle around the nucleus of the atom." It is clear, Mandūr adds, that Idrīs in this play was influenced not only by the peasant theatre of Fayyūm but also by European culture, philosophy, and literature. "And no harm in that, either. It is his duty, and ours, to benefit from all cultures, to assimilate these cultures and to turn them into a part of our general cultural and literary heritage, guided by our originality and specific character." Finally Dr. Mandūr, who was considered avant-garde in his views and tastes, went on to deplore chauvinism in matters pertaining to culture, literature, and the arts. "We did not resist the material aspects of civilization and the amenities of life which we borrowed from the West," he writes. "Why then should we be so rigid against Western culture, literature, and art when they are not the West's exclusive property but the common property of all humanity?"[10]

Dr. 'Alī ar-Ra'ī, another prominent critic and literary editor, explained that there were only two forms of theatre in existence today – the Western theatre and the Far Eastern (Shadow) theatre. These two dramatic forms are in fact "two sides of the same coin, and in my opinion it is impossible to attain a form of theatre that can be much different from these." It is to be noted, writes Ra'ī, that the traditional theatre of the Far East has remained stagnant for hundreds of years, and that modernist playwrights there today write their plays in the same form prevalent in Egypt and other Arab countries. This, Ra'ī adds, is due to the fact that "the nature of life in the modern age differs completely from the material and intellectual conditions in which this [traditional Far Eastern] theatre grew up." For this reason Dr. Ra'ī believes that Idrīs's call for the formulation of an authentic Egyptian theatrical theory on the basis of what theatrical forms there are in the Egyptian tradition is untenable, since there is not enough in that tradition from which to formulate such a theory. Idrīs's own play, *The Servants,* offers "nothing new that can be described as Egyptian by way of artistic forms."[11]

Again, while granting that the advocacy of an authentic art and a distinctive literature is a plausible thing in itself, Dr. 'Abd al-Qādir al-Qiṭṭ, one of Egypt's most respected critics, believes that Idrīs went too far in his advocacy, "so far, indeed, that his views cannot be implemented unless we ignore all that has happened in Arab theatre in nearly a century and start to look from scratch for new theatrical forms representing the true spirit of the Egyptian people."

According to Qiṭṭ, in advocating an authentic Egyptian theatre both in form and in content Idrīs "ignores the vicissitudes of civilization and its shiftings between peoples, and that those peoples which were left behind culturally must borrow from other civilized peoples, so that when they have reached a level at which they can again be original and creative they will stop borrowing and adapting in order to start building on what they have attained – not to start all over from scratch."

Qiṭṭ further disputes Idrīs's cultural relativism. The degree of superiority of an art or a language, he argues, "cannot be measured merely by the extent to which it satisfies the needs of its environment without reference to the degree of backwardness of that environment." There is, he adds, one universal human society, in some of whose sections are embodied the heights of achievement attained by man's intellect and his capacity for artistic expression. "In this sense, there is no doubt that we are entitled to prefer the symphony to the red *mawwāl,* because the former represents a special musical apogee . . . in expressing the complex varieties of feeling and in its control of a multitude of musical instruments." True, the red *mawwāl* may prove more satisfying to the Egyptian who has not become used to listening to a symphony; but this does not mean that it is impossible to draw an absolute comparison between these two art forms, unless we can argue, for instance, that the unclean waters of the canal are better than purified waters because some people like to drink water from the canal! [12]

Another prominent playwright and literary historian who took up Idrīs's challenge was Dr. Rashād Rushdī, Professor of English Literature at Cairo University. Rushdī rejects the thesis that form is important. The significant thing is not the theatrical form nor the style in which the play is written, "but the degree to which the theatre can give expression to people's personalities, their fears, their hopes, and their sufferings." A playwright can utilize any theatrical form, whether this is to be found in Egyptian or other theatres, Rushdī argues. He then dwells on Idrīs's own plays and says that his work is a mixture of Brecht and the old Italian theatrical form known as art comedy. Summing up, Rushdī writes:

> It is impossible to build an Egyptian theatre on an abstract idea that cannot take on a national character. In order for us to create an authentic Egyptian theatre we must, I believe, depict on the stage Egyptian characters, with their dreams, their apprehensions, and their reality. This has not been attained yet, and this is the heart of the matter. For the difference between, say, the Italian and English theatres . . . though they both share the same essentials of the theatrical form, is the respective ways in which they depict characters who are truly representative of the land in which the play is written. Without this there can be neither a place nor a life for theatre.[13]

There were many other reactions to Idrīs's call, none of which were quite sympathetic to his basic premise, and none of which even partially conceded that his own attempt at resuscitating the true, authentic, and specifically Egyptian theatre – his play *The Servants* – succeeded in what its author set out to do. This is not in the least surprising. Idrīs's call for the creation of an autochthonous Egyptian culture – for that is in fact the real burden of his argument – raised a problem not unknown in countries just emerging from foreign rule and trying to assert their specific personality and cultural identity. Yet the problem was seldom formulated in the same stark, radical way in which it has been presented by Idrīs. Nor, save for the militant traditionalists, had any Egyptian writer of importance seriously advocated a total return to inherited culture.

In the Cultural Congress of Havana, held between January 4 and January 12, 1968, this same question was raised by some delegates from developing countries. Among these was Mammeri Mouloud of Algeria, who said that the intellectual of the Third World "finds himself faced with the double necessity of assuming an inherited culture and using an acquired culture." Yet, he added, neither of these can simply be put on like a ready-made suit. Traditional culture, which was the product of a cultural system which is already in part disrupted, cannot serve as the basis of the new culture, Mouloud said, even though parts of it may be capable of being preserved. Attempts to make it so either fail, as in sub-Saharan Africa, or produce the *espectáculos folkloricos* of the modern tourist trade, or – as another delegate to the Congress put it – the even more dangerous "accelerated indigenization of the violence and tribulations of other times."[14]

## NOTES

1 'Azīz Abāẓa, reported in *al-Adīb* (Beirut), September 1961, p. 62.
2 Irene L. Gendzier, *The Practical Visions of Ya'qūb Sanū'* (Cambridge, Mass., 1966), pp. 31, 33.
3 'Abd al-Mun'īm Ṣubḥī, *"ya'qūb sanū': rā'id al-masraḥ al-miṣrī"* ["Ya'qūb Sanū': Pioneer of Egyptian Theatre"], *al-Kātib,* August 1963, pp. 99–100.
4 Yūsuf Idrīs, *"naḥwa masraḥ miṣrī"* ["Towards an Egyptian Theatre"], *al-Kātib,* January 1964, pp. 67–79; February 1964, pp. 109–120; March 1964, pp. 86–97.
5 *Ibid.,* January 1964, pp. 78–79.
6 *Ibid.,* February 1964, p. 115.
7 *Ibid.,* February 1964, p. 115–118.
8 *Ibid.,* March 1964, pp. 89–90.
9 *Ibid.,* March 1964, pp. 90–92, 94–95.
10 Muḥammad Mandūr, *Ākhir Sā'a,* 19 April 1964.
11 *Ibid.*
12 *Ibid.*
13 *Ibid.*
14 Quoted in E. J. Hobsbawm, "The Cultural Congress of Havana," *The Times Literary Supplement,* 25 January 1968, p. 79.

# 11. CONCLUSION: NASSERISM AS AN IDEOLOGY

"A living ideology," observes Erik H. Erikson, "is a systematized set of ideas and ideals which unifies the stirrings for psychological identity in the coming generation."[1] Viewed within this mainly psychological context, the set of ideas, aspirations, and ideals that we habitually call Nasserism has no doubt largely fulfilled its function. In Egypt – and to a large extent in the Arab world as a whole – the mixture of radical nationalism and socialism propagated by Cairo throughout the sixties has become, to paraphrase Erikson's definition, a stratum in every Arab's imagery.

Whether this set of ideas and aspirations, however, has ever been satisfactorily systematized is a rather different matter. In fact, any serious survey of the subject would tend to show that as an ideology Nasserism remains far from coherent, self-complementary, methodical, or consistent. In this brief appraisal I propose to deal with two questions, however tentatively: how far are the adherents and advocates of the ideology themselves aware of this inadequacy and how do they explain it? and what are the main challenges which Nasserism faces in the seventies, especially now that its founder and leading light has departed?

The two questions are plainly closely interrelated, and can perhaps best be tackled from the vantage point of a recent historical perspective. Sāmī Khashaba, one of the more independent-minded younger intellectuals of the Nasserist era, has described the sixties as "shattering" – shattering not only because of the bitter experiences of the 1967 defeat and its aftermath but also, and perhaps mainly, because of the nature of the challenges which the decade held in store for the Nasserist experiment. These challenges did not, Khashaba implies, take the regime by surprise; they simply confronted it with tasks for which it was not prepared, long-term tasks designed to confront and obliterate the traces of "thirty generations of slavery, coercion, cultural forgery, and the perpetuation of ignorance through superstition, mimicry, and economic, mental, and spiritual impoverishment." In the face of these challenges, the task of the revolutionary Egyptian intellectual of the sixties was two-fold: in the first place, he had to rediscover Egypt's specific national identity while at the same time underscoring man's intrinsic worth as man and avoiding the pitfalls of nationalist bigotry on the one hand and national self-deprecation on the other. He also had to explore the people's oral and written lore and heritage with a view to reevaluating them, subjecting them to critical scrutiny, and distilling their lessons. This act of reappraisal and selection had to accomplish two complementary tasks – the elimination of the mystical and superstitious traces of these heritages on the one hand and the articulation of the progressive, humanistic features of the Egyptians' national identity on the other. Secondly, he had to spread the message of intellectual and individual freedom and to probe deep into the cultural and actual problems confronting the society, including all those subjects which had been considered taboo. However, at the same time as these problems were openly and fearlessly attacked, the revolutionary intellectual had to advocate and adhere to social solidarity and intellectual steadfastness, avoiding the pitfalls of negating the national heritage and national tradition altogether.

These, according to Khashaba, were in brief the tasks undertaken by the Nasserist Revolution and its intellectuals during the sixties on the ideological and cultural planes. However, the decade brought its own grave socio-political challenges. Indeed, the sixties opened with the crisis in Egypt's relations with the Arab Left as a whole, when Arab communists came out openly against Cairo's pan-Arab sentiments and designs. Then came the dissolution of the Egypt-Syria merger, a severe blow to the newly-formed Arab nationalist consciousness of the Egyptians.

This was on the Arab nationalist, political front. On the home, or social, front, difficulties were raised by those internal enemies who had a vested interest in perpetuating the prevalent illiteracy and ignorance, and who sought to preserve the supremacy of traditionalism and mental backwardness over reason and free thought. These factors, coupled with what Khashaba describes as the age-old frustrations inherited from centuries of slavery, cultural stagnation, and lack of any solid tradition of intellectual and individual freedom have resulted in two interrelated phenomena – bewilderment and confusion among the revolutionary intellectuals as to their precise obligations on the theoretical-ideological plane, and the emergence of reactionary elements which, while pretending to adhere to the aims of the Revolution, acted covertly against these aims by standing in the way of all revolutionary endeavour and resisting the rising wave of intellectual and cultural emancipation.[2]

As one among several reasons for the lack of ideological clarity, Khashaba's explanation is certainly valid. However, there were more deep-seated reasons having to do with the fact that, apart from general dissatisfaction with the prevalent state of affairs and eagerness to seize power themselves, the Free Officers who staged the revolt of July 23, 1952 had no political philosophy of their own and lacked even an organizational framework. Thus, instead of submitting a programme of action they took to improvisation based on a partial, second-hand, and rather fragmentary understanding of certain fashionable ideas and ideals. The situation was only partially rectified with the publication, in 1962, of Abdel Nasser's *National Charter,* which, though presenting the regime's ideas and intentions in a fairly systematic way, suffered both from ideological confusion and a total lack of coordination between ideals and realities.

However that may be, it is hardly possible to deal with the ideological prospects of the seventies in post-Nasser Egypt without reference to the regime's traumatic experience in the war of June 1967 with Israel. The defeat of the Egyptian army in that war started a process of reappraisal and self-criticism which, less thorough and less far-reaching though it was than might have been expected, was only in its preliminary stages when Nasser passed away in September 1970. As one noted Egyptian critic pointed out, the first reactions to the defeat were – in their chronological order of appearance – three: "sorrow and disbelief," "anger," and "defiance."[3]

More recently, however, there has been another type of reaction, one which concentrated on ideological reassessment and tried to fathom the deeper causes of what has been termed variously "the ideological crisis" or "the crisis in contemporary Egyptian thought." In a brief but highly instructive article entitled "Contradictions in Contemporary Egyptian Thought,"[4] Amīr Iskandar opens by wondering whether this crisis is an extension of the ideological crisis which now besets Western thought as a whole – that crisis whose chief manifestations have been a revolt against reason and modern science, escape and alienation from reality, disorientation, and resort to mythology and irrationality. His answer is unequivocal: there is no connection whatsoever. The fact, he explains, is that whereas Western culture and Western thought face "a crisis of extinction" *(azmat fanā')*, "we face what can be termed 'a crisis of construction' *(azmat binā')*." Nevertheless, our world having become what it is ("a global village") the crisis in Western thought and civilization has left certain minor traces in modern Egyptian moods and thinking.

The West's ideological crisis, however, has not been confined to the boundaries of capitalist Europe but has affected socialist Europe as well, even though the form and content of the crisis may be different in the two camps. In its socialist form, this crisis has had three leading symptoms – the fall of Stalinism and its various myths, the ideological division in the socialist world, and the proliferation of different schools of Marxism. This has indeed contributed to the current ideological crisis in Egypt in a substantial manner.

The reason is two-fold. In the first place, Marxism and the civilization which Marxism promises present the natural alternative to the disintegrating bourgeois thought and its withering civilization – and every setback suffered by this Marxist alternative is bound to lead to disappointment, anxiety, doubt, and bewilderment in the societies which have opted for it. Secondly, any proliferation in Marxist schools of thought must naturally open the way to fresh ideological endeavours, variously motivated by considerations of principle or political opportunism. The result has been, in Egypt as elsewhere, a tendency to stress variety at the expense of unity, division rather than solidarity, and the worst thing was that this division has not been confined to problems of practice and implementation but has affected issues pertaining to theory and ideology as well.

While all this is quite true, however, Iskandar insists that neither the ideological crisis in the capitalist world nor the crisis in Marxist thought has been the main cause of the current crisis in Egyptian ideology, since, as he puts it, "we are part of a world that is different from either of these two worlds, a world sometimes called 'the third world,' sometimes 'the developing world' – and in both cases what is actually meant is the underdeveloped world." Moreover, rather than speaking of "a crisis," Iskandar chooses the term "contradictions," which he considers "more accurate and more relevant to our conditions." Those who speak of a "crisis," he explains, actually mean "contradictions" – "since they believe that contradiction is a symptom of crisis, when the truth is that it is the real, permanent essence of every natural, sociological, and human phenomenon".[5]

The writer then enumerates four contradictions from which contemporary Egyptian thought suffers. The first concerns the roots of this thought, the second its "horizons," the third its general orientation, and the fourth concerns "the nature of its fabric."

The first contradiction is generally formulated in the context of a linkage between authenticity and contemporaneity, between past and future. There are three schools of thought on this subject – that of the traditionalists, which is the largest in terms of size though not the most influential; that of the innovators and Modernists, which is the smallest in size though currently the most influential in policy-making and institution-building; and that of the vacillators, which stands somewhere in the middle both in size and in influence. All of these schools suffer from a mechanical, one-track, and static view of the issue of Egypt's heritage and cultural personality, thus ignoring the continuous mobility and interaction which play so prominent a role in socio-cultural evolution and development.

The second contradiction pertains to the two basic concepts of nationalism and internationalism. This contradiction – which in some ways parallels the first, with the nationalists clinging to tradition and heritage and the internationalists propounding a Western orientation, whether socialist or capitalist – is artificial and even fake. "In today's world there is no such thing as purely nationalist thought, nor is there anything remotely practicable that can be termed purely internationalist thought. . . . The narrow nationalist trend, like the wide-open internationalist trend, represents a deviation from our Egyptian thinking. It would befit us more to say that our national thinking will have to be erected on internationalist premises, and that internationalist thinking is bound to acquire a national aspect within our [geographical] boundaries."

The third contradiction, which concerns orientation, comes in the form of a struggle between Left and Right. While forces of the Right cannot openly assault those of the Left, their campaign takes various undercover forms. Chief among the subjects on which these forces have been active is the question, raised several years ago, as to whether Egypt's socialism was "Arab Socialism" or "an Arab road to socialism," with advocates of the former interpretation trying virtually to rob Egypt's socialism of all its content and cut it off from the main current of international socialism. Under the slogan of Arab Socialism, Iskandar points out, many wrong ideas and concepts were disseminated, true scientific socialism was rejected, and intellectual innovations were condemned as "imported ideas."

The fourth and last contradiction listed by Iskandar concerns the structure and fabric of contemporary Egyptian thought and has to do with the rivalry between technology and ideology. Three trends are discernible in this struggle – one which advocates "the technological revolution" as a panacea; one that insists on "ideological clarity" as the main tool for building the new man, and sees in the technological trend a hidden anti-socialist and pro-American design; and the third is that which considers both of the two other trends erroneous in their programme, short-sighted, and fundamentally arid. The correct formulation of this question, Iskandar maintains, can be attained through linking technology with ideology, the scientific revolution with the ideological revolution.[6]

Though he proposes no solutions, and despite the extreme brevity of his thesis, Iskandar has done what no Egyptian intellectual has in recent years: he has thrown the door wide-open for a critical consideration of the premises of the prevalent ideology and put his finger on Nasserism's leading and most damaging shortcoming, namely its lack of clarity and its perpetual vacillations. The "contradictions" which Iskandar says plague "contemporary Egyptian thought" are in fact those same contradictions which beset the prevalent Nasserist ideology but which no one in Egypt has dared to describe as such. The seemingly endless ideological debates which raged in Egypt in the years preceding the Six-Day War were manifestations of these inner contradictions in the ideology itself: the fact that such views as those of Iskandar's were being aired indicates that the time was ripe, even before Nasser's departure, for a reevaluation of the doctrine of Nasserism. Nasser's death only hastens the process.

Seen in retrospect, however, it now appears rather remarkable that so little substantial criticism was voiced against the regime and against the underlying assumptions of its official ideology. Not unexpectedly, too, such criticism came mostly from outside Egypt, and since one of the inherent features of Egypt's revolutionary ideology is that it tries to embrace the whole of the Arabic-speaking world it will be in order to consider here both Egyptian and non-Egyptian Arab reappraisals of that ideology. The severest and most systematic critique of the ideology of the Egyptian Revolution has come from a young Arab university lecturer in philosophy reportedly closely connected with one of the more radical of the Palestinian guerrilla organizations – The Popular Democratic Front for the Liberation of Palestine. A Syrian by nationality and one-time lecturer at the University of 'Ammān, Ṣādiq Jalāl al-'Aẓm is a new kind of Arab radical – fearless, outspoken and completely free from the stifling age-old mental habits and socio-cultural inhibitions from which his fellow-Arabs are prone to suffer. In 1968, 'Aẓm published a highly controversial book called *Self-Criticism After the Defeat,* in which he severely criticized many aspects of Arab life and politics, mercilessly dissecting his people's individual and public behaviour. One section of the book is devoted to what the author calls "the negative features at work in what we habitually call the Arab Socialist revolutionary line" – by which he obviously means Nasserism.

A host of questions, he writes, involving the very essence of revolutionary socialism are left unanswered by the Arab revolutionaries. A sample of these questions: Does the Arab revolution seek mere agrarian reform or a radical transformation in the spheres of agriculture and the ownership of land? Does it aspire merely to transferring ownership of the means of production from private to public hands, or does it intend to introduce a true revolution in industry, class relations, and the distribution of the national income? Does the revolution plan radical change in the present legal apparatus and a revision of age-old religious laws? Finally, does it seek mere reform or true revolutions in such fields as education, social relations, scientific research, etc.? [7]

The criticism of Nasserist ideology and practice implicit in these questions is amply developed in 'Aẓm's book. Many Arab socialists now talk about "an Arab Vietnam" and make endless analogies between the Arab revolution and the great socialist revolutions, such as the Russian and the Chinese. All these comparisons and analogies, 'Aẓm asserts, are unfair to these revolutions, since in his opinion there can be no comparison between them and the superficial, improvised and show-off-type revolutions of the Arab world.[8]

One basic difference which the author cites is that, unlike other socialist revolutions, the Arab revolution has so far failed to proclaim its socialism as both scientific and secular. As we have seen, a number of questions touching upon the very essence of socialist revolutions are left unanswered by the Arab revolutionaries. The truth, ʻAẓm asserts, is that the Arab revolution, as we have known it during its various stages, had offered no answer to any of these questions, especially on the level of actual practice.

From this ʻAẓm turns to his own critique of Nasserism. One of the consequences of this lack of ideological clarity, he writes, is the "middle-of-the-roadism" which characterizes the Arab revolution in general and Nasser's Arab Socialism in particular. The avoidance of any serious confrontation with the problem of classes in Egyptian society, the half-hearted nationalization measures, the still inadequate representation granted to workers and peasants in the country's political institutions – all these are regarded by the author as manifestations of the "middlism" *(wasaṭiyya)* which has always been a feature of Nasser's regime. What the Arabs need now, ʻAẓm concludes, is the emergence of "new revolutionary forces whose leadership is totally committed to [solving] the problems of the great majority of the Arab people, i.e. the toiling masses and the working class." Only such leaderships can bring out the social content of the Arab revolution; only they can transform the present "guerrilla" warfare into a real popular war of liberation in which the mobilized masses can play an effective role.[9]

It is noteworthy, in this connection, that a good deal of the criticism directed at the Arab Socialist ideology of Cairo is often based on an unfavourable comparison which the critics draw between this ideology and what they call "the Palestinian Revolution." In a sense, the steady growth in influence and popularity of the Palestinian fidayeen (guerrilla) movements after the Israeli-Arab war of 1967 was itself not only a standing rebuke to Nasser and other Arab rulers for their failure to solve the Palestinian problem; it also seemed to constitute a partial refutation of the Egyptian President's hard-core pan-Arab doctrine. In the first half of 1970, indeed, some Egyptian writers and spokesmen for the regime found themselves engaging in a growing "dialogue" with the Palestinians, accusing the guerrilla organizations of "regionalism" *(iqlīmiyya)* in the sense that they call for "Palestine for the Palestinians" rather than join forces with the pan-Arab nationalists who believe that a united Arab world is the answer not only to Zionist aggression but also to the Arabs' socio-economic plight.[10]

But this is only one of the ways in which Nasser's whole style was being questioned. The Free Officers' revolt of July 23, 1952 – which remained sacrosanct except with certain Marxist Arab circles and with writers of the ultra-Right – was itself coming under fire as the sixties were coming to a close, and was now being downgraded in favour of "the Palestinian Revolution." The issue of Beirut's leading organ of the radical Arab Left *Mawāqif* dated November–December 1969 is devoted to a rather novel enterprise – a re-examination of Nasserism. Under the general title, "The July 23 Revolution on Trial," the special issue carries six major contributions on the subject, and of these only one comes out in defence of the Nasserist experiment and calls for identification with the July 23 Revolution. Among the five "prosecutors" of this Revolution, the most outspoken – and articulate – was 'Aẓm, whose indictment of Nasserism rested upon three major premises:

1. The Egyptian Revolution is responsible for two Arab defeats (1956 and 1967) and has thus proved impotent.

2. In view of this, Arab revolutionaries as a whole – and Nasserists first and foremost – must revise their attitude toward the July 23 Revolution.

3. There is an ultimate opposition between the Nasserist Revolution and the Palestinian Revolution, and the latter must in the end supersede the former. In this sense Nasserism has become an obstacle in the "new Arab path." [11]

As has been indicated, in his *Self-Criticism After the Defeat* 'Aẓm furnishes a more "ideological," though less outspoken, case against the Egyptian Revolution when he bluntly charges Nasserism with equivocation and "middle-of-the-roadism." The Arab Socialist Revolution, he writes, "was neither revolutionary enough nor socialist enough, especially when judged by the stern standards imposed by the June defeat." He also takes strong exception to President Nasser's plea that, when speaking of Arab nationalism or patriotism, "we must, at this particular juncture, forget about many other concepts: the patriot of the Right is just like the patriot of the Left. When Israel occupied the West Bank, she made no distinction between a Right-wing patriot and a Left-wing one, so long as both of them were patriots." Such sentiments, 'Aẓm asserts, are indicative of a lack of sufficient socialist and revolutionary content in the current Arab nationalist doctrine. Indeed, he views these manifestations as a sign that there does not exist any real socialist Arab Left capable of leading the Arab nation through its present predicament. [12]

These are serious charges with far-reaching implications. Not only Nasser's leadership and ideology were being questioned here but the very basis of the pan-Arab nationalism which he came to represent. For what 'Aẓm is saying is that it is ideology and class affiliation, rather than "national" belonging, that really matter. To ask – as the Egyptian President does ask – that one should cease making distinctions between rich and poor, Right-winger and Left-winger, and make "Arabism" the only criterion for admittance into the fold – such sentiments appear to 'Aẓm to spell total ideological bankruptcy.

It is probably not entirely satisfactory, in a study of Nasserist ideology and its position in the seventies, to cite non-Egyptian Arab sources of criticism, despite the fact that on its own showing this ideology claims to encompass the entire "Arab revolution." The truth, however, is that there is much covert criticism of Arab Socialism inside Egypt herself. As has been shown in Chapters 5–7, this criticism is implicit in the writings of the Marxists who, instead of mounting a frontal attack on the doctrine as a middle-of-the-road, spineless concoction – as does 'Aẓm – normally choose to incorporate it into their own Marxist ideology, often citing the *National Charter*'s reference to it as "scientific socialism" as proof that it is none other than Marxist socialism.

More serious even than this ideological challenge to Nasserism, however, is the position with regard to the other leading component of that ideology, i.e. pan-Arabism. In fact, some years before the 1967 war with Israel, following the collapse of the Egypt-Syria merger in 1961, Nasser's pan-Arab plans already lay in ruins. But the defeat of 1967, and the subsequent emergence of the Palestinians as a factor in Arab politics, have brought the problem to the forefront in Arab ideological discussion. A growing number of Egyptian intellectuals allowed themselves to express disenchantment with the Arab world, which in spite of Egypt's sacrifices for its causes remained ungrateful and uncooperative. One way to express indirectly the tendency to somewhat withdraw from the Nasserist pan-Arabism of the late fifties was to challenge the doctrine of Arab Popular Liberation War and its advocates the Palestinian fidayeen. The debate, which was conducted between the fidayeen, their theoreticians and apologists, on the one hand, and defenders of the established Arab revolutionary order, on the other, took many, sometimes quite unexpected, forms. In the Cairo daily *al-Jumḥūriyya,* for example, there appeared an article by the paper's editor, Dr. Muḥammad Anīs, a Professor of History at the University of Cairo, containing a fierce attack on *al-Ahrām*'s influential editor, Muḥammad Ḥasanayn Haykal, President Nasser's long-time mouthpiece and close friend. Haykal had written an article the previous Friday warning that the Middle East conflict was threatening to develop into a major world conflagration. This, on the face of it, was innocuous enough. Not for Dr. Anīs. For him, the emphasis Haykal placed on the international ramifications of the conflict meant that he was casting aspersions on the Arab War of Liberation. Moreover, Anīs believes that such pronouncements, in addition to sowing doubts about the heroic struggle of the "Palestinian freedom fighters," imply that the Arabs are called upon to endorse any agreement that the Four Powers might reach on the Middle East. The Middle East crisis, Anīs concludes, must be depicted as it really is – an Arab War of National Liberation, not a mere extension of Super Power conflicts.[13] The al-Fataḥ radio broadcasts in Cairo immediately took up the issue, clearly taking Anīs's side though refraining from attacking Haykal by name.

Yet, by directing their criticism against Haykal, the supporters and spokesmen of the Palestinian fidayeen did not choose a good representative of the new Egyptian tendency to withdraw from dynamic pan-Arabism and turn inwards. Even after the defeat, Haykal remained the champion of Nasserism and refrained from attacking it, at least consciously. The debate with him, however, demonstrated another, much more profound aspect of the weakness of Nasserist ideology in the post-1967 Arab world: the fact that its predominance no longer goes unchallenged.

A good example of this kind of debate is an article by Jalāl as-Sayyid, contributor of a regular feature on the fidayeen in *al-Kātib*, the ideological organ of the Arab Socialist Union. Sayyid sharply criticizes the proliferation of slogans among the Palestinian organizations and their resorting to what he termed "ideological auction sales." He argues that these slogans, far from promoting the cause of "the Palestinian Revolution," serve only to spread confusion and lead to unseemly debates. The issues raised in these debates, he adds, "are as remote from reality as they could possibly be; they are also far from the minds of the masses and totally irrelevant, except for those ideologists and journalists who have turned 'the Palestinian Revolution' into an arena for their intellectual adventures and political auction sales." Moreover, "certain Arab political parties and movements have been using 'the Palestinian Revolution' as a vehicle for spreading their own ideas, forgetting that in over two decades of their existence they had utterly failed to make the Palestine problem advance one step on the right path."

Following this undisguised condemnation of the Ba'thists and the communists, Sayyid writes: "Some of the [fidayeen] organizations compete in proclaiming their Leftism; one has announced its adherence to Marxism-Leninism, and there has been a lot of talk about the class struggle and about revolutionary cadres and about the *petite bourgeoisie.* 'The Palestinian Revolution' has been split into Left and Right, Extreme Left and Reactionary Right, while slogans have been coined calling for the elimination of imperialists and reactionary interests in the Arab region." All these Sayyid considers irrelevant, if not worse. To start with, "it is not easy to delineate class distinctions among the Palestinians, as they have lost their land and are now dispersed." Moreover, the present phase of "the Palestinian Revolution" is one of a Struggle for National Liberation, one that calls for mobilizing all the national forces in the service of the revolution. "The issue today is not one between Left and Right; it is a national issue first and foremost. Those who raise Leftist slogans speak unrealistically and divorce themselves from reality; they simply cannot put their slogans into effect, and will always fall into contradictions." [14]

But Sayyid's severest criticism is directed against those of the Palestinians who, not content with slogan mongering and political auctioneering, seek to accuse others of ideological and political shortcomings. This is a clear reference to what appears to be a widening circle of Arab radical intellectuals – mainly non-Egyptians – who have sought to present "the Palestinian Revolution" as an alternative ideology to that of Nasserism. This would certainly sound like a fairly wild assertion, were it not for the frustrations and the utter intellectual confusion produced by the Arabs' defeat in June 1967. For the fact is that, with practically no military achievement to boast of, and with even less ideological coherence, the Palestinian fidayeen organizations were nevertheless fast becoming the focal point of radical Arab thought and sentiment. It is hardly suprising, therefore, that "the Palestinian Revolution" (which is how the fidayeen movement is called by its protagonists and supporters) was being openly contrasted – mostly favourably – with "the Nasserist Revolution." As a guiding light and an example to emulate – it was now being argued by some radical thinkers – the Nasserist experiment has been a failure, and the Arab revolution of the future must therefore be modelled on the Palestinian pattern.

Is Nasserism, then, becoming outdated as the definite Arab brand of socialism and radical nationalism? At this juncture it is premature to speak of a "post-Nasserist" phase in radical Arab thought; but in the Arab world today there are signs of a far-reaching reappraisal of the Nasserist experiment, and the call for an overall, radical, and far-reaching intellectual revision is overwhelming. Suhayl Idrīs, editor of the Beirut monthly *al-Ādāb,* foremost political-cultural review in Arabic, has called for "continuous self-examination and critical reappraisal," [15] and in May 1970 brought out a specially thick issue with the general heading: "Toward an Arab Cultural Revolution." One of his Iraqi contributors, Fāḍil al-'Azzāwī, gives the new trend fuller expression when he calls for "revolutionary thought with cultural dimensions," and for abandoning "frozen intellectual frameworks." Speaking of "the new Arab generation," 'Azzāwī suggests that yesterday's Modernists and revolutionaries have become obsolete, and asserts that the new generation must supplant them in the same way as they themselves had supplanted an older, intellectually more stagnant generation of writers and thinkers. One of the shortcomings of this "middle" generation, 'Azzāwī writes, is that its members spoke with those of the older generation in the latter's own terms, implying acceptance of their approach and basic premises. What is now needed, however, is a *total* reformulation of concepts. This has to be done, "not in order to win one or two battles in this war, but in order to build a new Arab human being." [16]

The call implicit here is one for an overall, total revision of accepted values and concepts – a call for what amounts to a re-creation of "the Arab man." This call has been widespread in Arab intellectual circles since the 1967 war, and is often accompanied by a great deal of bitterness. Dr. Louis 'Awaḍ, a former Professor of English Literature at the University of Cairo and now literary editor of *al-Ahrām*, has described a trip he made to Europe in the summer of 1969 as "a journey of convalescence" – convalescence not from any physical ailment but from the terrible shock of the events of June 1967, events "which turned our hours into days, our days into years and our years into generations and generations."

The shock, he continues, had "shattered the nerves, broken the heart with shame and darkened the soul with despair." Dr. 'Awaḍ then tries to define the nature of his country's present predicament. "Briefly," he writes, "I believe that our predicament is neither military, nor political, nor economic, nor social, nor moral nor yet spiritual; it is all of these – it is a 'cultural' predicament." 'Awaḍ continues:

> Egypt is like an iceberg, of which only an eighth is seen on the sea's surface, while seven-eighths remain in the deep. Our life is like an iceberg – an eighth of it is out in the light of the twentieth century, seven-eighths in the darkness of the Middle Ages. We are in the same stage as Europe was during her age of transition from medieval times to the Renaissance; we were in travail in the nineteenth century . . . but the baby was stillborn – and when the embryo again took shape at the turn of the century it was again mercilessly aborted. *Our real battle is one between the old and the new, between reaction and progress; even democracy and socialism seem impossible to attain in the absence of a movement towards humanism, religious reform and a cultural revolution.* [17]

The mood is militant and uncompromising, the will to change is evidently extremely strong. Will anything come out of it on the practical plane? In one of his more memorable poems, T.S. Eliot wrote:

> Between the idea
> And the reality
> Between the motion
> And the act
> Falls the shadow.

It is a very heavy shadow indeed that has always fallen between Arab aspirations and realities – and the prospect now is that the yawning gulf may this time, too, lead to more disillusionments and more frustrations.

## NOTES

1 Erik H. Erikson, "Ideology" *The Encyclopedia of the Social Sciences* (New York, 1968), Vol. VII, p. 63.

2 Sāmī Khashaba, *"thaqāfat as-sittīnāt: al-qawmiyya w'al-ḥurriyya"* ["The Culture of the Sixties: Nationalism and Liberty"], *al-Ādāb,* January 1970, pp. 90–92.

3 Shukrī 'Ayyād, *"al-adab al-'arabī ba'd al-khāmis min yūniū"* ["Arabic Literature after the Fifth of June"], text of his address at the Congress. Reprinted in *al-adab fī 'ālam mutaghayyir* ["Literature in a Changing World"] (Cairo, 1971), pp. 136–148.

4 Amīr Iskandar, *"tanāquḍāt fī al-fikr al-miṣrī al-mu'āṣir"* ["Contradictions in Contemporary Egyptian Thought"], *al-Fikr al-Mu'āṣir* (Cairo), August 1970, pp. 18–25.

5 *Ibid.*, pp. 18–21.

6 *Ibid.*, pp. 21–23.

7 Ṣādiq Jalāl al-'Aẓm, *an-naqd adh-dhātī ba'd al-hazīmā* ["Self-Criticism after the Defeat"] (Beirut, 1968), pp. 132–133.

8 *Ibid.*, pp. 92–93.

9 *Ibid.*, pp. 165–166.

10 See 'Iṣmat Sayf ad-Dawla, *"al-muqāwama fī wajhat naẓar qawmiyya"* ["The Resistance from a Nationalist Point of View"], *al-Ādāb,* January 1970, pp. 2–10, 54–64.

11 Sādiq Jalāl al-'Aẓm, *"khams mulāḥaẓāt ḥawla thawrat thalātha wa-'ishrīn yūliū"* ["Five Remarks on the July 23 Revolution"], *Mawāqif* (Beirut), November-December 1969. Reprinted in his *dirāsāt yasariyya ḥawl al-qaḍiyya al-filasṭīniyya* ["Left Studies on the Palestinian Problem"] (Beirut, 1970), pp. 179–191.

12 Ṣādiq Jalāl al-'Aẓm, *op. cit.,* pp. 126–127.

13 Muḥammad Anīs, *al-Jumḥūriyya* (Cairo), 2 April 1970.

14 Jalāl as-Sayyid, *"ath-thawra al-filasṭīniyya"* ["The Palestinian Revolution"], *al-Kātib,* February 1970, pp. 61–63.

15 Suhayl Idrīs, editorial, *al-Ādāb,* December 1969, p. 2.

16 Fādil al-'Azzāwī, *"kara'tu al-'adad al-mādī min al-ādāb: al-abḥāth"* ["I Read the Previous Issue of al-Ādāb: Articles"], *al-Ādāb,* January 1970, p. 14.

17 Louis 'Awaḍ, *al-funūn w'al-junūn fī awrupa 1969* [Art and Lunacy in Europe 1969"] (Cairo, 1970), pp. 7–10. [Italics in the original.]

# APPENDIX

## THE CHARTER OF NATIONAL ACTION
*(MĪTHĀQ AL-'AMAL AL-WAṬANĪ)*

# THE CHARTER OF NATIONAL ACTION



## 1. GENERAL VIEW: AN INTRODUCTION

The 23rd of July, 1952, marked the beginning of a new and glorious phase in the history of the constant struggle of the Arab people in Egypt. On that important day, the people embarked on a pioneer revolutionary experience in all domains amidst extremely difficult, dark and dangerous circumstances. Through their sincerity to the Revolution and their unshakable revolutionary will the people succeeded in bringing a basic and deep change in their life for the realisation of their great human hopes.

The devotion of the Egyptian people to the cause of the Revolution, the clarity of their vision and their undying struggle against all challenges, have enabled them to produce a wonderful example of the national Revolution which is the contemporary phase of the free man's struggle throughout history for a better life, free of the chains of exploitation and underdevelopment in all their material and moral forms.

The day they began their glorious Revolution on 23rd of July 1952, the Egyptian people turned their back for good on the outworn considerations which shattered their positive efforts. The people trod on the effects remaining from centuries of despotism and injustice. They dropped indefinitely all the negative factors which suppressed their will to reshape their life anew.

The potential of the revolutionary change which the Egyptian people unleashed on the 23rd of July would appear in its full power if we should recall the forces of evil and darkness which were lurking to nip in the bud any hope in the great Nile Valley.

The foreign invaders occupied their land; close by were the military bases, fully armed to terrify the Egyptian motherland and destroy its resistance. The alien Royal Family ruled according to its own interests and whims and imposed humility and submission. The feudalists owned the estates which they monopolised, leaving nothing to the toiling farmers except the remaining straw following the harvest. Capitalists exploited Egyptian wealth in several ways after they succeeded in dominating the Government and made it serve their own interests.

What increased the danger of the revolutionary stand to those forces clustered together against the people was the fact that political leaderships which organised the people's struggle had surrendered one after the other; they were lured by class privileges and were drained of every power or resistance. They were even used after that to deceive the masses under the guise of a forged democracy. The same happened with the army, which the dominating powers, operating against the interests of the people, tried to weaken on the one hand, and to divert from supporting the national struggle on the other. Those powers were on the verge of using that army to threaten and suppress the struggle.

Facing all those probabilities in the morning of 23 July 1952, the Egyptian people raised their heads with faith and pride. They marched along the path of the Revolution, determined to face difficulties, dangers and darkness and strongly resolved to triumph and confirm their right to life, whatever the burden and sacrifices.

The Egyptian people's revolutionary will appears in its great and proper perspective if we recall that those valiant people began their revolutionary march with no political organisation to face the problems of the battle. Moreover, this revolutionary march started without a complete theory for the revolutionary change. In those eventful circumstances, the sole basis of work was the famous six principles carved out of the demands and needs of the people's struggle. The mere declaration of those principles amid the difficulties, dangers and darkness was proof of the strength and unshakable basis of the will for revolutionary change.

(1) Facing the lurking British occupation troops in the Suez Canal zone, the first principle was: Destruction of imperialism and its stooges among Egyptian traitors.

(2) Facing the despotism of feudalism which dominated the land and those on it, the second principle was: Ending feudalism.

(3) Facing the exploitation of wealth resources to serve the interests of a group of capitalists, the third principle was: Ending monopoly and the domination of capital over the Government.

(4) Facing the exploitation and despotism which were an inevitable consequence to all that, the fourth principle was: Establishment of social justice.

(5) Facing conspiracies to weaken the army and use the remaining part of its strength to threaten the internal front eager for revolution, the fifth aim was: Building a powerful national army.

(6) Facing political forgery which tried to veil the landmarks of true nationalism, the sixth aim was: Establishment of a sound democratic system.

* * *

These six principles which the popular struggle passed on to the revolutionary vanguard mobilised from within the army to serve that struggle, and the revolutionary forerunners outside the army who brought their instant and natural support to those principles, were not a complete theory of a revolutionary task. In the circumstances, those principles were a guide to work, showing the depth of that revolutionary will, providing it with its needs and underlining its resolution to reach the end. The great people who inscribed the six principles in their martyrs' blood and inspired by the hope for which they sacrificed their lives, the people who rushed the revolutionary vanguard from within and outside the army to face the responsibilities of the revolutionary task, guided by those six principles passed on to that vanguard through the struggle of generations – those great people endeavoured to deepen their fight and broaden its meaning. Those people were the great instructor who, in the wake of the revolutionary task on the 23 July 1952, undertook two historic operations with far-reaching effects.

(1) First, those people developed and activated the six principles through trial, and correlated them with national history. This progress was leading to a detailed programme paving the way before the infinite aims of the Revolution.

(2) Second, those people prompted the revolutionary vanguard with the secrets of their great hopes, widening the scope of that vanguard by feeding it with new elements every day capable of contributing to the shaping of their future.

Those great people did not stop at the role of instructor to the revolutionary vanguard, but made use of their consciousness to safeguard it against the evils of others as well as personal evils. The people did not stop at the defeat of enemy attempts to harm the revolutionary vanguard, but resisted all deviations that might occur through oversight or conceit, and continued to guide their revolutionary vanguard to the course of its duties.

This will of the Revolution animating the people of Egypt and its sincerity brought new criteria for national action. This will and its concomitant sincerity have ensured that no obstacle or restriction can check the process of change except the just needs and demands of the masses. In the circumstances faced by the struggle of the people of Egypt, conventional logic could have tempted it through bargaining, compromise and reform ideas inspired by charity and donation. According to conventional logic, that was the only possible means to face external aggressive domination and internal exploiting control, in the absence of a political working system and complete theory for action.

But the will of the Revolution animating the people of Egypt and its sincerity defied this conventional logic and faced it with unleashed energies, full of potentialities for creative and pioneering action. The 23rd of July, 1952 was the date for that revolutionary explosion. On that day, the Egyptian people rediscovered themselves and opened their eyes to their enormous latent potentialities. These enormous potentialities have added a new experience to the history of revolutions; and the years that have passed since the 23 July 1952 will prove to be of great value to the struggle of many people. This experience has proved that the subdued peoples can revolt, and can even stage an overall revolution.

During this experience the Egyptian people went through many revolutions with intermingled battles and interconnected stages. In a short period of time, the people defeated all the enemies of their numerous revolutions and emerged with an increasing power and impetus leading to the drive for progress. In its struggle against imperialism, the Egyptian people were able to paralyse the power of certain classes of the old regime that were capable of deceiving them, under the false pretence of sharing with them the fight against imperialism, with which they, in fact, had common interests.

The war of liberation which – according to the conventional conception – required the unity of all classes in the motherland has in fact won victory when it safeguarded itself against any treacherous blow from the rear. The Egyptian people went through the battle of liberation against imperialism, undeceived by pretence. Throughout the battle they were cautious to isolate from their ranks all those whose common interests with imperialism called for the pursuit of exploitation.

In the meantime, the Egyptian people who faced the revolution for the sake of progress and attempted to pool, encourage and direct the savings towards development, have never forgotten that the big local capitalism was, throughout many national revolutions, able to convert the results of these revolutions into profits for capitalists. For, by possessing those savings which can be invested in development, capitalism can secure monopoly, enabling it to reap all the profits of development. In their deep-rooted revolutionism, the Egyptian people directed a blow to all local monopolies which, at the time, imagined that the people were in dire need of them, owing to the pressing needs of development. This deep-rooted revolutionism enabled the Egyptian people, as they pooled all efforts for production, to ensure, in the first place, complete control of the production machinery.

In the meantime, the Egyptian people revealed their struggle against imperialism and against the attempts of capitalism to exploit national independence for its own interests, under pressure of development requirements. Simultaneously the Egyptian people refused the dictatorship of any class and decided that the dissolution of differences among classes should be the means to real democracy for the entire people's working forces.

Again, the Egyptian people insisted, under the circumstances of those intermingled battles, to establish for the new society they looked forward to, new social relations, based on new values to be given expression by a new national culture. The Egyptian people went through the stages of development with vigour, sweeping aside the effects left behind by a feudal society, in which capitalism underwent the socialist change without bloodshed.

Those phases of the overall revolution form, in fact, a series of revolutions. According to the conventional logic of revolutionary movements in history, this series of revolutions must have been achieved in independent, successive stages. After each phase national efforts are pooled to be ready for the following stage. Yet, what the Egyptian people achieved through the overall revolution with its manifold trends reveals a new revolutionary experiment, even judged by the standards of world revolutions. Such an achievement was accomplished thanks to a number of guarantees provided by the national struggle.

**First.** – A will for revolutionary change which rejects all restrictions and limitations on the rights and needs of the masses.

**Second.** – A revolutionary vanguard which the will for revolutionary change has enabled to seize power in the state and channel this power from the service of existing interests to the service of those who are legitimately entitled to it – namely, the masses.

**Third.** – A deep consciousness of history and its effect on contemporary man on the one hand, and of the ability of man in turn to influence history on the other.

**Fourth.** – A mind open to all human experiences, from which it benefits and to which it contributes with no fanaticism or complex.

**Fifth.** – Unshakable faith in God, His Prophets and His sacred messages which He passed on to man as a guide to justice and righteousness.

* * *

The main weight of the struggle of the Arab people of Egypt and of their pioneering experiment is reflected in its impact on the life of the Arab Nation. It went beyond the borders of the small nation and embraced the whole of the Arab homeland. The experiment of the Egyptian people had far-reaching repercussions on the struggle of the Arab Nation. The Revolution of the Egyptian people awakened the possibilities of revolution in the entire Arab world. There is no doubt that this awakening was one of the main factors leading to the success of the Revolution in Egypt. The strong repercussions of the Revolution of the Egyptian people on the whole Arab world turned into a strong driving force providing them with energy and renewed vigour.

This interaction in itself confirms the unity of the peoples of the Arab world. While the comprehensive revolutionary experiment laid its initial responsibilities on the Arab people of Egypt, the response of the other Arab peoples to this experiment was one of the main factors leading to the Egyptian people's triumph. There is no doubt that today the Egyptian people are called upon to place the benefits of their victory at the service of the overall revolution in the rest of the Arab world.

The repercussions of victory achieved by the Arab people in Egypt are not confined to the borders of the Arab world. The new pioneering experiment has had far-reaching effects on the liberation movement in

Africa, Asia and Latin America. The Battle of Suez, which was one of the major landmarks in the Egyptian revolutionary experiment, was not merely a moment in which the Egyptian people discovered themselves or the Arab Nation discovered its potentialities, but was a moment of international significance and helped all oppressed peoples discover infinite latent powers in themselves and find out that they can revolt and that revolution is the only course to take.

## 2. THE NECESSITY OF THE REVOLUTION

Experience has shown and ever confirms the fact that revolution is the only course which the Arab struggle can take to head for a better future. Revolution is the only means by which the Arab Nation can free itself of its shackles, and rid itself of the dark heritage which burdened it. For the elements of suppression and exploitation which long dominated the Arab Nation and seized its wealth will never willingly submit. The national forces must crush them and win a decisive victory over them.

Revolution is the only way to overcome under-development, forced on the Arab Nation through suppression and exploitation. For the conventional methods of work are no longer capable of bridging the gap of under-development which has long existed between the Arab Nation and advanced countries. It is therefore imperative to deal radically with matters and ensure the mobilisation of all the nation's material and spiritual potentialities to undertake this responsibility.

Moreover, revolution is the only way to face the big challenge awaiting the Arab and other underdeveloped countries, namely, the challenge offered by the astounding scientific discoveries, which help widen the gap of development between one country and another. With the knowledge they reveal, those discoveries add to the progress of advanced countries and, in so doing, widen the gap further between them and others, despite all the good efforts the latter may exert to narrow it. The revolutionary path is the only bridge which the Arab Nation can cross to reach the future it aspires to.

The Arab Revolution which, at present, is both the implement and reflection of the Arab struggle, needs to equip itself with three powers, by means of which it can face and win the battle of destiny it is now fighting. Thus the Arab Revolution would realise its objectives and destroy all its enemies. These powers are:

**First.** – Consciousness based on scientific conviction arising from enlightened thought and free discussion, unaffected by the forces of fanaticism and terrorism.

**Second.** – Free movement that adapts itself to the changing circumstances of the Arab struggle, provided that this movement observes the objectives and the moral ideals of the struggle.

**Third.** – Clarity of perception of the objectives, which never loses sight of them, and which avoids being swept away by emotion and diverted from the high road of the national struggle wasting a considerable part of its energy.

The great need for these three powers arises from the particular circumstances of the Arab revolutionary experiment, circumstances under the influence of which it assumes its role in directing the course of Arab history. Today, the Arab Revolution is called upon to strike a new path before the objectives of the Arab struggle. Ages of suffering and hope finally gave shape to the objectives of the Arab struggle. These objectives, which are a true expression of Arab national conscience, are:

Freedom

Socialism

Unity

The long suffering for the achievement of these objectives helped the nation to define and analyse them. Today, freedom has come to mean: freedom of the country and freedom of the citizen. Socialism has become both a means and an end, namely sufficiency and justice. The road to unity has come to be the popular call for the restoration of the natural order of a nation, torn apart by its enemies against its own will and interests, and the peaceful endeavour to promote this unity and finally its unanimous acceptance as a crowning achievement.

These objectives have always been the slogans of the Arab struggle; but the Arab Revolution now faces the responsibility of striking a new path before these objectives. The need for a new road is not prompted by a mere desire for innovation or mere considerations of national dignity, but arises from the fact that the Arab Revolution is now facing new circumstances, therefore, demanding more suitable solutions.

The Arab revolutionary experiment, therefore, cannot afford to copy what others have achieved. Though the characteristics of peoples and the ingredients forming the national character of each impose the adoption of different methods for the solution of their problems, the greatest difference in method is that imposed by the changing circumstances, prevailing in and governing the whole world, particularly those far-reaching changes which occurred in the world after the Second World War (1939–1945).

These circumstances bring about radical changes in the atmosphere of national struggle in the world. This, however, does not mean that the national struggle of peoples and nations is today required to create new conceptions for its great objectives, but rather to find the methods suited to the trend of general evolution and the changing nature of the world.

The outstanding changes that took place in the world after the Second World War may be summed up as follows:

**First.** – The spectacular strengthening of the forces of nationalist movements in Asia, Africa and Latin America to the extent that they were able to lead many a victorious battle against the forces of imperialism. Such nationalist movements, therefore, have now become an internationally effective force.

**Second.** – The emergence of the communist camp as an enormous force, with steadily increasing material and moral weight and effectiveness in facing the capitalist camp.

**Third.** – The great scientific and technological advance suddenly achieved in methods of production, opening up unlimited horizons before efforts for development. The same advance was also achieved in the development of arms which are now potentially so destructive to all parties involved that they themselves have become a deterrent against war. This, apart from the outstanding and radical change brought about by the same scientific and technological progress in means of transport, as a result of which distances and barriers both physical and intellectual between one country and another have now virtually disappeared.

**Fourth.** – The results of all this in the field of international relations, the most notable of which being the increasing weight of moral forces in the world, such as those provided by the United Nations Organisation, the Non-Aligned States and world opinion.

Side by side with these, however, is the need of imperialism under these circumstances to resort to indirect methods such as the conquest and domination of people from within, the formation of economic blocks and monopolies, the waging of cold wars which include among their methods the attempt to undermine the confidence of the smaller nations in their capacity to develop themselves and to provide an equal and positive contribution to the service of human society.

Such far-reaching changes in the world are accompanied by new circumstances which have an indisputable effect on the struggles of all nations, including the Arab Nation, and on their endeavour to attain their national aims. While the aims of the Arab national struggle remain freedom, socialism, and unity, world changes have influenced the means of achievement. As a result of the interaction between world changes and the will of the national revolution, it was no longer believed that freedom could be attained by placating the imperialists or bargaining with them. In 1956 the Arab people in Egypt were able to take up arms and defend their freedom, achieving a decisive victory in Port Said, not to be forgotten. In the same way in their determination to secure freedom, the Arab people were able to carry on a war in Algeria, lasting more than seven years.

Moreover, socialist action is no longer compelled to observe literally laws formulated in the 19th century. The progress in means of production; the development of nationalist and labour movements in the face of domination by imperialism and monopolies; the increasing changes of world peace as a result of the influence of moral forces and, at the same time, of the effect of the balance of atomic terror – all these factors combined of necessity created, and should create, a new situation for socialist experiments, entirely different from what existed in the past.

The same can be said of the experiments to achieve unity in the 19th century, most notable of which are those made by Germany and Italy and which can no longer be repeated. The need for a peaceful appeal and for the unanimous approval of the whole people is not merely an expression of the desire to cling to an idealistic method in nationalist action, but it is also, and above all, an absolute necessity at present if the national unity of all Arabs is to be safeguarded. In our present endeavour to achieve the national unity of the entire Arab Nation, we are struggling against enemies who still retain bases on the Arab soil itself, whether in the form of reactionary palaces collaborating with imperialism to protect their own interests or in the form of "colonies" belonging to the racial Zionist movement used by imperialism as focal points of military threat.

In facing this world the Arab Revolution must have a new approach that does not shut itself up within the confines of theories, which are at once limited and limiting, although it must by no means deny itself access to the rich storehouse of experience gained by other striving peoples in their similar struggles. Social experiences cannot live in isolation from one another. As part of human civilization, they only remain alive through enriching movement and creative interaction. The torch of civilization has passed from one hand to another, but in each land it crossed, it acquired a fresh supply of oil to make its flame brighter across the ages. Such are social experiences. They are capable of passing from one place to another but not of being blindly copied; they are capable of useful study and examination, but not of being learnt by heart parrot-fashion by mere repetition.

This then is the first duty of the popular revolutionary leadership in the Arab Nation. It means that the great part of the responsibility for this pioneer revolutionary action devolves upon the popular revolutionary leadership in the United Arab Republic, since natural and historical factors have laid upon the United Arab Republic the responsibility of being the nucleus state in this endeavour to secure liberty, socialism and unity for the Arab Nation. Such popular leaderships are now called upon to study their own history, to examine their present reality and then proceed to build their future while standing on firmer grounds.

## 3. THE ROOTS OF THE EGYPTIAN STRUGGLE

A very long time ago there were no barriers among the countries of the area where the Arab Nation exists now. It was exposed to the same currents of history, and its positive participation in affecting that history was one. Egypt in particular did not live in isolation from the surrounding area. It consciously – and sometimes even unconsciously – influenced it and was in turn influenced by it in the way the part interacts with the whole. This is an established fact borne out by the study of Pharaonic history, the maker of Egyptian civilisation and the first civilisation of man, and subsequently confirmed by the events which took place during the ages of Greek and Roman domination.

The Islamic conquest shed light on this fact and placed it in a new context of spiritual thought and feelings. In the history of Islam, the Egyptian people, guided by the message of Mohamed, assumed the main role in defence of civilization and mankind. Before the whole area was swept by the darkness of the Ottoman invasion, the Egyptian people had assumed – with unequalled courage – grave responsibilities in the interest of the whole region.

The Egyptian people had borne the material and military responsibility of stemming the first wave of European colonialism, taking cover behind the Cross of Jesus, while in fact colonialism and the message of that great teacher are poles apart. The Egyptian people had assumed as well the material and military responsibility of repelling the attacks of the Tartars who swept over the plains of the East and crossed its mountains bringing destruction and ruin. The Egyptian people had also borne the literary responsibility of preserving the heritage and wealth of Arab civilisation. They made of their noble university, Al-Azhar, a stronghold of resistance against the colonialist and reactionary factors of weakness and disintegration imposed by the Ottoman Caliphate in the name of religion, while in fact religion is incompatible with such factors.

It was not the French campaign against Egypt that led to the Egyptian awakening by the beginning of the 19th century, as some historians claim. For when the French campaign came to Egypt, it found Al-Azhar simmering with new trends which had their impact on life throughout Egypt. The French campaign also found the Egyptian people resenting Ottoman colonialism disguised in the form of the Caliphate, which imposed on the Egyptian people a false conflict between genuine religious faith and the will to live which rejects tyranny.

That campaign found fierce and constant resistance against the rule of the Mamelukes and their attempts to oppress the Egyptian people. The high price this resistance cost the Egyptian people in national wealth and vitality did not shake their determination and faith.

The French campaign, however, brought in a new supply of revolutionary energy for the Egyptian people at that time. It brought in glimpses of modern science developed by Europe out of sciences taken over from other civilisations, foremost among which is the Pharaonic Arab civilisation. Furthermore, it brought outstanding professors who studied the affairs of Egypt and revealed the secrets of its ancient history. This supply of revolutionary energy inspired self-confidence and opened up new horizons that incited the eager imagination of the Egyptian people.

This popular awakening was the driving force behind the reign of Mohamed Aly. It is almost unanimously assumed that Mohamed Aly laid the foundation of modern Egypt. Yet the tragedy of that age was that Mohamed Aly believed in the popular movement that paved the way for him to govern Egypt only as a springboard for him to reach his ambitions. Thus, Mohamed Aly drove Egypt to futile adventures which sought individual interest and ignored the interests of the people.

Modern Japan headed for progress at the same time as that of the Egyptian awakening. While Japanese progress managed to proceed steadily, individual adventures impeded the movement of Egyptian awakening and brought a setback with grievous damage. This setback widely opened the gate to foreign interference in Egypt, while the people had previously foiled continuous attempts at invasion, the latest at that time being Frazer's campaign against Rosetta.

Unfortunately, the setback occurred at an important stage in the development of colonialism. For colonialism at the time had developed from mere occupation of the colonies and draining their resources to a stage of financial monopolies aimed at the investment of the capital seized from those colonies. The setback in Egypt opened the gates to the domination of world powers. International financial monopolies started to play their grave role in Egypt. They channelled their activities to two distinct directions, namely the digging of the Suez Canal and the transformation of Egypt's land into a vast field for cotton growing. The aim was to provide British industry with the cotton which America then rarely exported to Britain following the end of British domination in America. Later, American cotton was withheld entirely from Britain as a result of the American Civil War.

During that period, Egypt lived through a dreadful experience. All the potentialities of national wealth were exhausted to serve the interests of foreign powers and a number of foreign adventurers who managed through the disastrous setback of the Egyptian awakening movement to place the Emirs of the Mohamed Aly dynasty under their power. Yet, the spirit of these people was never broken; the great disasters of the period prompted them to store up energy which they discharged at the appropriate moment.

That energy lay in the education which thousands of Egyptian youths attained when they were sent to Europe to master modern science in the flourishing days of the reign of Mohamed Aly prior to the setback. Returning home, those youths brought good seeds which the fertile revolutionary soil of Egypt welcomed and nursed to produce a flourishing new culture on the banks of the Nile.

It was not a coincidence that those seeds represented the flashes which attracted the attention in the area of those elements who were looking hopefully to Egypt. They made of Egypt in the second half of the 19th century a platform for thought in the Arab world, a stage for its arts and a rallying ground for all Arab revolutionaries crossing artificial and illusory boundaries.

The imperialist monopolies which coveted the area felt the rising new hope. Britain, because of her concern about the route to India in particular, never lost sight of Egypt. Those monopolies, therefore, threw the whole of their weight in the revolutionary battle which began to take shape between the popular powers and the adventurous alien Mohamed Aly dynasty.

The Orabi revolution marked the peak of the revolutionary reaction against the setback. The British military occupation of Egypt in 1882 was an expression of the determination of colonialism to ensure the continuity of the setback and to maintain suppression and exploitation of the people of Egypt, to guarantee the interests of foreign financial monopolies, and to support the authority of the Khedive against the people. The power of the British military occupation, the plots of the imperialist monopolist interests, the feudal system established by the Mohamed Aly dynasty through its monopoly of the land sharing part of it with its friends or with the associates of exploiting foreigners, all these could not put out the torch of the revolution in Egypt.

The sound of revolutionary cries in the Nile Valley was always heard in the face of ruling terror, supported by the forces of foreign occupation and international imperialist interests. Hardly had the din of the guns which bombed Alexandria, and the noise of the battle fought by the valiant Egyptians who were betrayed at Tal-el-Kebir faded when new voices were heard, voices expressing the brave people's eternal will to live and the awakening which neither difficulties nor disasters could put out. Ahmed Orabi's voice stopped but that of Mustafa Kamel began to ring loudly on Egypt.

It is surprising that this period, which imperialism and those who collaborated with it thought to be a period of stagnation, was one of the richest periods in the history of Egypt, in its searching into the depths of its soul, and its mustering anew of its revolutionary impulses. During this period, Mohamed Abdu's call for religious reform was heard. Lutfi El Sayed stressed that Egypt should belong to the Egyptians. Qasim Amin called for the emancipation of woman.

These calls heralded a new revolutionary wave which was soon to rise in 1919 following the First World War and after the failure of the Allies to fulfill the attractive promises they made during the war. Most outstanding among those promises was that made by Wilson, who himself soon denied it and recognised the British protectorate in Egypt.

Saad Zaghloul led the new revolutionary wave, guiding popular unflinching struggle, which, though the target of successive blows during more than a century, continued unabated.

The 1919 Revolution of the Egyptian people is worthy of deep study. For the factors that led to its failure were the very factors that motivated the 1952 Revolution. There are obvious reasons for the failure of that revolution. These should now be weighed in all fairness and honesty:

**First.** – The revolutionary leaderships almost completely overlooked the needs for social change. The explanation of this was obvious, considering the nature of the times which made of the class of landowners the basis of the political parties responsible for leading the revolution. Although the popular rush towards the revolution was clear in its social context, the revolutionary leaderships could not see that. So much so, that a wrong analysis by some historians prevailed at the time, alleging that the Egyptian people are unique among the nations of the world in that they never revolt except in conditions of prosperity. To prove this, they stated that the revolution took place in an atmosphere of prosperity, accompanied by the rise in cotton prices at the end of the First World War. But this reasoning is superficial. For that prosperity was confined to the classes of landlords, merchants and foreign exporters who benefited from the rise in prices. Consequently, the gap widened between them and the toiling peasants who with their sweat and blood irrigated the cotton fields, and whose conditions remained unaffected by the rise in prices. The deprivation suffered by the masses that formed the base was in flagrant contradiction with prosperity enjoyed by those at the top. This deprivation was one of the causes of friction that lit the spark of the revolution.

The deprived were the fodder of the revolution and its victims. Yet in overlooking the social aspects of the revolutionary motives, the leaderships that formed the vanguard of the 1919 revolution could not clearly see that a revolution cannot achieve its aims for the people, unless its drive goes beyond the apparent political façade reflected in the demand for independence and tackles the core of the economic and social problems. The demand to Egyptianise some financial activities was the most that could be done at the time, although the call for a radical redistribution of national wealth was the vital and pressing demand of the time.

**Second.** – The revolutionary leaderships at the time failed to extend their vision beyond Sinai with the result that they could not arrive at a definition of the Egyptian character. They were incapable of deducing from history the fact that there is no conflict whatsoever between Egyptian patriotism and Arab nationalism. The leaderships failed to learn from history. They also failed to learn from the enemy they fought, and who treated the entire Arab Nation, with all its peoples, according to a common plan. Thus these revolutionary leaderships were unaware of the danger of the Balfour Declaration which set up Israel as a dividing line tearing the Arab territory apart, and acting as a base of threat. By this oversight, the Arab struggle was deprived of the Egyptian revolutionary energy at one of the gravest moments of the crisis. Consequently, the imperialist forces managed to deal with an Arab Nation torn and exhausted.

The British administration of India was responsible for dealing with the Arab Peninsula and Iraq. Syria and the Lebanon were left to France. At the time, the Arab Nation suffered such humiliation that even imperialist agents were able to take over the helm of Arab revolutionary movements. According to those agents' advice and direction, thrones were set up for those who betrayed the Arab struggle and deviated from its aims. In the meantime the national revolutionary movement in Egypt imagined that those serious developments did not concern it, and that in no way was its fate related to them.

**Third.** – The revolutionary leaderships could not adapt their methods of struggle to the methods adopted by imperialism to face the revolutions of the peoples at the time. Imperialism discovered that military force could only fan the flames of popular revolution; and so the sword was replaced by deceit. Formal and superficial concessions were rendered to the revolutionary leaderships which failed to distinguish between appearance and reality. The logic of class distinctions tempted them to accept this confusion. At that time, imperialism gave independence only in form, withholding its content. It gave the slogan of freedom while keeping back its reality. Thus, the revolution ended by declaring an independence of no content and a crippled freedom under the guns of the occupation.

Complications increased dangerously, due to the self-government granted by imperialism. It also led, in the name of the constitution, to unsettled disputes over the booty. Consequently, party conflict in Egypt became a force, which kept the people busy and fretted away the revolutionary energy. The 1936 treaty, concluded between Egypt and Britain, and signed by a national front that comprised all the political parties active at the time, was like a document of surrender to the great bluff by which the 1919 Revolution was taken in. The preamble of the treaty stipulated that Egypt was independent, while its articles in every clause deprived this independence of every value or significance.

## 4. THE MORAL OF THE SETBACK

The truly dangerous period in the long struggle of the Egyptian people was a period full of deceit, namely from the setback in 1919 until the popular forces became aware of the danger threatening them and arising from the logic of bargaining and surrender. It was then that the psychological preparation for the July 1952 Revolution began. This period, had it not been for the adamant will and true mettle of the people, could have led the country to a state of despair, stifling or paralysing every incentive for change.

This period, which we can now regard as that of the great crisis, was full of misleading façades concealing the shaky remnants of the 1919 Revolution. The leadership remnants of the revolution were still in the forefront, but they had lost all their revolutionary energy. They had surrendered all the slogans raised by the people in 1919 to the big landlords who formed the supporters of the existing party organisations, that included a number of opportunists attracted by the distribution of the booty following the setback of the revolution. At the time a group of parasites emerged. The deviation attracted groups of intellectuals to the corrupt party atmosphere. These could have been able to safeguard the aspirations of the genuine revolution, but the temptation was stronger than their resistance. This deviation also paved the way for a batch of capitalists who in fact inherited the role of 19th century foreign adventurers with all its superficiality and disregard for the development of the land. It only cared for the exploitation of the greater parts of the country's wealth and the sapping of this wealth in the shortest time possible.

Sometimes these parties all fell into the arms of the palace, sometimes into the arms of imperialism; they had one and the same interest and therefore stood in one camp. Superficial differences may have emerged between them at times, but the major fact was that they stood in the camp opposing the people's interests and opposing the trend of progress. The power of the people constituted a menace to their alien position. The tendency for progress was sure to drift both of them together towards the same fate.

At the same time there was a deceitful democratic façade which the defeated remnants of the 1919 Revolution exploited to divert the people from their true demands. Democracy as it was exercised in Egypt during this period was a shameful farce. The people no longer had any power; they became a tool in the hands of authority, or more accurately victims of this authority. The voices of the people no longer decided the direction of the national path. The voices of the people were steered according to the will of the ruling powers and their collaborators. That was the natural outcome of neglecting the social aspect of the causes of the 1919 popular Revolution. For those who monopolised and dominated the means of livehood of the peasants and workers could consequently monopolise their votes and dictate their will. The freedom to earn a living is a necessary guarantee to the freedom of voting.

This violent crisis unleashed the prerogatives of the royal family which the people struggled hard to oppose. But the setback of the revolution encouraged the royal family to exceed all limits. In the atmosphere of the crisis, the constitution accepted by the revolutionary leaderships was no more a gift from the intruder, but a mere scrap of paper bearing but a trace of pseudo rights flung to the people for their diversion. Because of their increasing weakness, the revolutionary leaderships which had championed the popular struggle surrendered before the mounting power of the palace. They all knelt down seeking the favours that would lead to the seats of power. They therefore abandoned the people and lost all respect for their dignity, forgetting that they were thereby willingly giving up their only source of power. They finally sold their souls to the devil, reaching a point where a change of cabinets could be effected at a certain price to be paid to the palace and its intermediaries. When national leaderships uproot themselves from the people's soul they condemn themselves to death.

The Motherland will feel for a long time the bitter humiliation it experienced at that critical period as a result of the imperialists making light of its struggle, a derogation that was beyond human endurance. To revolt against imperialism is the natural right of all colonised peoples. But the bitter hatred felt by our people towards imperialism, which they still experience despite the lapse of time, emanates from this period. Imperialism, at that time, did not only intimidate all the peoples of the Arab Nation but also made light of their struggle and right to life.

Imperialism denied all the pledges it made during the First World War. The Arab Nation was then under the impression that the day of independence and unity was near. The aspiration for independence received severe blows. The Arab States were divided among the imperialist states to satisfy their ambitions. Moreover, the imperialist statesmen coined humiliating words such as "Mandate" and "Trusteeship" to cover up their crimes.

Part of the Arab territory of Palestine was handed to an aggressive racial movement with neither historical nor natural justification, to be used by the imperialists as a whip in their hands to fight the struggling Arabs if one day they were able to overcome their humiliation and survive the crises. The imperialists intended this territory to be a barrier dividing the Arab East from the Arab West, and a constant drain on the energy of the Arab Nation diverting it from positive construction. All this was carried out in a provocative manner disregarding the existence of the Arab Nation and its dignity.

It was the irony of fate that armies of the Arab Nation who entered Palestine to safeguard Arab rights, should be under the supreme command of one of the cheaply bought hirelings of imperialism. The military operations were placed in the hands of a British officer who received his orders from the very statesman who gave the Zionist movement the Balfour Declaration on which the Jewish State in Palestine was based. Long years will elapse before the Arab Nation can forget the bitterness of the experience it underwent during that period, trapped between terrorism and humiliation. The Arab Nation emerged from that experience with an adamant determination to hate and defeat imperialism. It emerged with a most useful lesson on the true nature of imperialism. For imperialism is not merely a looting of the people's sources, but an aggression on its dignity and pride.

The Egyptian people were ready to resume their historic role even before the end of the Second World War and before the spectre of the occupation tanks was removed from their main cities. The Egyptian people expressed themselves through obstinate refusal to take part in the war which to them was but a strife over the colonies and markets between racialism and Anglo-French imperialism, which involved mankind in tremendous tragedies through mass killings and destruction. The Egyptian people rejected all the slogans advertised by the belligerents to deceive the peoples. The entire Egyptian people withdrew the remaining little support of those who collaborated with the occupying power, seeking black market profits imposed by the war and its dark shadows. A wave of anger and indignation swept over Egyptian youth against all those who extended their hands to occupation and accepted it. In Egypt in those days could be heard the echo of bullets and bomb explosions; secret organisations with different aims and methods increased in number.

This was not the Revolution, but rather a preparatory stage. That was the period of indignation which paved the way to the possibilities of the Revolution. Anger is a passive phase. The revolution is a positive task aiming at the establishment of new systems. The anger of the Egyptian people which paved the way to change was no longer confined to few individuals: it spread among the entire people. The peasants' rebellions against the tyranny of feudalism reached the stage of armed contests between those who rose against serfdom and the despotic landlords who controlled the fates of those whose lives had been connected with the land from times immemorial, even though they had for so long been deprived of its possession.

The burning of Cairo, irrespective of how far it had been engineered by intriguers, could have been stopped if it had not been for the outburst of anger in the people which only led to further conflagration. The dominant ruling class in the capital was not aware of the needs of the people; so deeply were they immersed in their luxuries that they were insensitive to the sufferings and misery of the masses. The spark of anger caused more fires in Cairo than those caused by the hidden intriguers who put the city to the torch.

By the beginning of the year 1952, a crucial year in the history of Egypt, the masses both in town and in country had already given adequate expression to their real will. The greatest thing about the Revolution of 23 July 1952 is that the armed forces who set out to stage it were not the makers of the Revolution but its popular tool. The greatest task accomplished by the revolutionary vanguard in the army on that immortal night was that they took control of everything in the army and they chose for it the only right place, namely the side of the popular struggle. They accomplished a task of first-rate importance and involving great dangers. They set things right defying the power of all the ruling authorities of the time, which tried to isolate the army from the popular struggle.

On that great night the Revolution broke out as a result of the army occupying its natural place in the country, by putting itself under the leadership of the people to serve its ends and realize its aspirations. The army on that night declared its loyalty to the people's struggle, thereby paving the way for the will to change. By taking the side of the popular struggle the army then achieved two great things. It deprived the internal forces of exploitation of their tool with which they threatened the people's Revolution. It also provided the popular struggle with necessary arms to enable it to face the foreign forces of occupation and to repel the blows of treachery and treason.

The Revolution itself did not break out on the eve of July 23rd. But on that glorious night the gate was flung open for it. The revolutionary consciousness in Egypt proved its ability to bear the great responsibilities laid upon it by changing conditions. From its pure patriotic sense, it acquired the capacity for clear vision and far-sightedness, which enabled it to surmount the obstacles that might have stood in the way of any revolutionary change under circumstances similar to those Egypt lived in those days.

The great event which occurred on the eve of July 23rd could have ended in a mere change of cabinet or of the system of government. On the other hand, it could have turned into a military dictatorship to add one more experiment to the list of fascist experiments that had failed. But the genuineness and strength of the revolutionary consciousness controlled the direction of events and gave all nationalist elements a realisation of their role in directing the national struggle.

The genuineness and strength of this consciousness necessitated that the great event of the eve of 23 July should be a step along the road towards a radical and all-embracing change which would bring back national aspirations to their proper revolutionary channel, from which they had been diverted as a result of the setback suffered in the 1919 Revolution. Furthermore, the genuineness and strength of this consciousness made it impossible to accept the possibility of a military dictatorship, but placed the popular forces, with the forces of the peasants and workers at the head, in the position of actual leadership.

Similarly, in that critical stage genuine revolutionary consciousness rebelled against the reasoning of those who called for reform and, instead, chose total revolution. The needs of our country were such that it was not enough to patch up the old and decaying building, try to keep it from falling by means of supports and give the exterior a fresh coat of paint. What was needed was a new and strong building resting on firm foundations and towering high in the sky.

The most powerful argument against the reasoning of those who called for more reform was that the old building did actually crumble and fall to pieces in the face of the new experiment. The sudden and complete collapse of the system that existed before the Revolution was a sure sign of the futility of any attempt to patch it up. Yet the fall of the old regime was not the objective of the revolutionary outlook, which in its ideals and aspirations was more concerned with the setting up of a new building than with the ruins in shape.

The gate which was flung open on the eve of 23 July remained open for a considerable period of time before the inevitable and long awaited change was admitted. In the first place, the ruins of the old regime lay cluttered in the way; there were still the decayed remains of its worn-out and defeated cupidity. At the same time all political leaderships in public life collapsed under the ruins of the old regime, which they themselves helped to create by their deviation from the principles that should have been followed in the 1919 Revolution. They all participated in the policy of "bargain and give in", which accompanied that period of crisis and stamped it with its shameful character.

Class distinctions had removed from the rank of the popular forces, which looked forward to and called for the revolution, useful elements fit to occupy a position of intellectual leadership. Also, the revolutionary vanguard that was responsible for the events of the eve of 23 July was still not ready to assume the responsibility of the revolutionary change which it had prepared for.

It opened the gate before the Revolution under the banner of the famous six principles, but these principles were only banners for the Revolution and not a technique for revolutionary action or a method to follow for the radical change.

Things were exceedingly difficult, especially in the context of the vast and far-reaching changes in the world. But in its role as instructor the Egyptian people, the creator of civilization, taught their vanguard the secrets of their great hopes and aspirations. They set in motion the six principles by means of trial and error towards a clearer vision and understanding, by which the planning of the new and aspired-to society could be made. The toiling people proceeded to amass their building material and rally all their revolutionary forces from the vast mass of the people's forces capable of participating in that great venture. To their national army they assigned the task of safeguarding the building operation. Then they watched vigilantly, and efficiently supervised the pioneer and constructive change in the direction of a cooperative, democratic socialism.

## 5. ON SOUND DEMOCRACY

A revolution is in its very nature a popular and progressive action. It is the action of a whole people mustering their strength in a determined attempt to remove all obstacles and barriers standing in the way of life they conceive as desirable. It is also a jump across a gulf of economic and social underdevelopment, with the intention of making up for what was lost and of realising the great aspirations which form part of what the people ideally want for future generations. True revolutionary action, therefore, would not be possible unless it possessed these two attributes: popularity and progressiveness.

A revolution is not the work of one individual, otherwise it would be merely a subjective and desperate reaction against a whole society. Nor is a revolution the work of one group, otherwise it would be a mere clash between this group and the majority of the population. The value of a true revolution lies in its degree of popularity, in the extent to which it is an expression of the vast masses, in the extent to which it mobilises their forces to rebuild the future, and also in the extent to which it enables these masses to impose their will on life.

A revolution, also, by its very nature signifies progress. The masses do not call for change or endeavour to realise or impose it merely for its own sake, *i.e.*, from sheer boredom. They only do so in order to attain a better life and in an attempt to raise the level of their reality to that of their aspirations. The aim of a revolution is progress; material and social underdevelopment are the real driving force behind the will to change and the forceful and determined movement from what actually is to what should or is hoped to be.

Democracy is the true sign showing that a revolution is a popular action. Democracy means the assertion of sovereignty of the people, the placing of all authority in their hands and the consecration of all powers to serve their ends.

Similarly, socialism is the true sign of the progressive nature of a revolution. Socialism means the setting up of a society on a basis of sufficiency and justice, of work and equal opportunity for all, and of production and services.

Seen in this light, both democracy and socialism appear as one and the same extension of the revolutionary act. Democracy is political freedom while socialism is social freedom. The two cannot be separated since both are indispensable to true freedom. They are, so to speak, its two wings without both of which it cannot soar to the horizons of the awaited morrow.

The depth of the revolutionary consciousness of the Egyptian people and the clarity of their vision, through being true to themselves, enabled them to form a correct judgment of their position after their great victory at the battle of Suez. In the midst of their victory celebrations the Egyptian people did not fail to realise that it was not their freedom that they had won from the battle of Suez, but rather the release of their will to shape their freedom in accordance with the principles of the Revolution. The glorious battle enabled them to discover their abilities and potentialities with the result that it became possible to direct them according to the principles of the Revolution, in order to achieve freedom.

According to the great Egyptian people, victory over the imperialists was not the end but the beginning of real action. It was only a rather convenient half-way station from which to resume the war for the cause of true freedom and ensure its continued flourishing on their soil. The question which arose quite naturally in the aftermath of the great victory at Suez was the following: To whom does this liberated will, which the

Egyptian people managed to extricate from the heart of the terrible battle, really belong? The sole historical answer that could be found to this question was this: This will can only belong to the people, and it can serve no other cause but theirs. Peoples do not wrench their will from the clutches of usurpers to lay it aside in the museums of history. They wrench their will, which they strengthen with all their national abilities, to make it a power capable of meeting their needs.

Such a stage in the struggle is the most dangerous in the experiences of nations. It is the point after which many popular movements suffered a setback, movements which although they first seemed full of glorious hopes and expectations subsequently, after their first victory over external pressure, forgot themselves. They wrongly assumed that their revolutionary aims had all been realised, with the result that they left things unchanged, forgetting that internal elements of exploitation were closely related to forces of external pressure, the close collaboration between them being a fact pressed by conditions of mutual benefits and interests at the expense of the people. Later, such popular movements gave themselves up to deceptive constitutional façades while imagining they truly attained complete freedom. But these movements always discover, often too late, that in their failure to bring about a revolutionary change, in the economic sense, they have robbed political freedom of its true guarantee. Of true political freedom they have only kept the contradiction between it and national reality.

Similarly, at this critical stage in the national struggle other popular movements suffer a setback when in their internal changes they follow theories which do not arise out of national experience. To recognise the presence of natural laws governing social action does not mean to accept ready-made theories and take them as an adequate substitute for national experience. The real solutions to the problems of one people cannot be imported from the experiences of another. In its attempts to grapple with the responsibility of social action no popular movement can afford to dispense with experience.

National experience does not assume *a priori* the falsehood of all previous theories, nor does it categorically reject all the solutions reached by others. This would be fanaticism, the full consequences of which national experiences cannot afford to bear, especially since the will for social change, when it first assumes its responsibility, passes through a stage akin to intellectual adolescence during which it needs all the intellectual sustenance it can get hold of. But it also needs to digest its food and mix with it all the secretions produced by its living cells.

It is true that it needs to know all that goes on around it. Yet what it primarily needs is to live its life on its own soil. In the life of a nation, as in the life of an individual, the way to maturity and clarity of vision is through trial and error.

Political freedom, namely democracy, is therefore not the copying of formal constitutional façades.

Similarly, social freedom, namely socialism, does not mean observing rigid theories which have not arisen out of the nature of national experience. After the 1919 popular revolutionary movement, Egypt fell under the great deceit of a sham democracy. After the first recognition of Egypt's independence by imperialism, the revolutionary leaderships surrendered to a pseudo-democracy with a constitutional façade that did not embody any economic content. This was not only a strong blow to freedom in the social aspect. The blow soon attained the external political façade, for imperialism gave no weight to the word "independence" written on paper, and did not hesitate to tear it up at any time to suit its interests.

That was indeed natural. The façade of sham democracy only represented the democracy of reactionaries; reaction is not prepared to break off its relations with imperialism or stop collaborating with it. Therefore, it was logical, regardless of the external sham façades, to find that the cabinets under the democracy of reaction and under the so-called national independence could only function at the incentive of the official representative of imperialism in Egypt. At times, these governments were formed according to his instructions, or orders. At one stage a government was brought into power by imperialist tanks. All this tears away the mask of the sham façade, reveals the great deceit of the democracy of reaction and confirms that political democracy, or freedom in its political aspects, is of no value without economic democracy, or freedom in its social aspect.

It is an indisputable fact that the political system in any state is but a direct reflection of the prevailing economic state of affairs and an accurate expression of the interests controlling this economic state. If feudalism is the economic power prevailing in a certain state, undoubtedly political freedom in this state could only be the freedom of feudalism. It controls economic interests and dictates the political shape of the state, imposing on it to serve its own interest. The same applies when the economic power is in the hands of exploiting capital.

Before the Revolution, the economic power in Egypt was in the hands of an alliance between feudalism and exploiting capital. It was thus inevitable that the political set-up, including the parties, should represent that power and that alliance between feudalism and exploiting capital. It will be recalled that certain parties, under these circumstances, dared to raise a slogan to the effect that the power should be in the hands of the interested parties. Since feudalism and exploiting capital were in control of all interests in the country, that slogan was more than a tacit recognition of the farce imposed by the dominating powers on the Egyptian people in the name of democracy. At any rate, that slogan, however painful it might be, was a frank admission of the bitter truth.

* * *

The domination of feudalism in collusion with the exploiting capital over the economy of the land naturally and inevitably enabled them to dominate political activities in all their forms, guaranteed their direction to serve their alliance at the expense of the people and to subjugate the masses by deceit or terrorism until they either acquiesced or surrendered.

Democracy on this basis was merely the dictatorship of reaction. The peoples' loss of their social freedom led to the robbing of political freedom – bestowed by the ruling reaction – of every significance. Therefore, the 1923 constitution was a gift graciously donated by the king. The parliament established by that constitution did not safeguard the interests of the people but naturally protected the interests of those who bestowed the constitution.

Undoubtedly, several voices were raised within parliament calling for the rights of the people. But these appeals were wasted away and had no serious effect. Actually it was not harmful for reaction to give an outlet to popular indignation as long as it was in possession of all controlling valves and since under all circumstances it had its majority which enabled it to maintain its class dictatorship and safeguard its privileges. The freedom of voting, without the freedom of earning a living and a guarantee to this freedom, lost all its value and became a deceit, misleading the people. Under these circumstances the right to vote presented only three alternatives:

1. In the villages, voting was compulsory for the peasant and could bear no argument. He had no alternative but to cast his vote in favour of, or according to the wishes of, the feudalist lord, the owner of the land. Otherwise he had to bear the consequences of rebellion and be expelled from the land where he worked and earned what was barely enough for his subsistence.
2. In the villages and cities, the "buying" of votes enabled the exploit-

ing capital to guarantee the election of its lackeys or of those whose allegiance was ensured.

3. In the villages and towns, the ruling elements did not hesitate, on several occasions, to resort to open forgery if they felt the existing currents opposed their will and conflicted with their interests.

The conditions governing the polling system, mainly the conditions of an inordinate financial deposit, discouraged the working masses even from approaching the game of polling, for it was only a game at the time. At the same time, the ignorance imposed on the vast majority of the people, under the pressure of poverty, made the secrecy of polling which is the primary guarantee to its freedom, impossible or virtually impossible.

The freedom of popular organisation, the backbone of the freedom of popular representation, under these circumstances also lost its effectiveness and failed to influence in a positive way the state of affairs imposed within the Motherland. Millions of peasants, even the small landowners, were crushed by the feudalist landlords and were not able to organise themselves successfully in cooperatives to enable them to protect the output of their land and consequently give them the power to put up a resistance and make their voices heard by the local machinery. In addition there was the inefficient ruling power in the capital.

Millions of agricultural labourers also lived in conditions akin to forced labour, with a level of wages nearest to starvation. They carried out their work with no guarantee for the future. They could only spend their life in misery and suffering. Hundreds of thousands of workers employed in industry and trade were also not able to challenge the will of the ruling capitalism allied with feudalism and controlling the state machinery and the legislative authority. Work became a commodity in the production process to be bought by the exploiting capital on the terms serving its interests best. The trade union movement, which led that striving class of workers, encountered great difficulties standing in its way and seeking to corrupt it.

* * *

During that period freedom of criticism was lost with the loss of freedom of the press. It was not only a question of the strict laws curtailing freedom of the press, laws restricting the scope of criticism to the extent that almost complete darkness reigned. The effect of technical progress in the press profession was itself no less harmful than that exercised by restrictive and oppressive legislations. The technical progress in the press profession, and its increasing requirement for modern machinery and a collossal amount of paper converted that great profession from an expression of opinion to a complicated capitalist operation.

During this period and in view of this progress the press was only able to survive if it was supported by the ruling parties representing the interests of feudalism or if it completely relied on exploiting capital which had the power to advertise through its ownership of industry and trade. In the first place, the authority of the State and legislation through the unjust laws of publication and censorship which checked truth, was used to make the press subservient to the ruling interests. Secondly, the little freedom left to the press was exposed to an even greater danger as a result of the increasing need of the profession of the press itself for advanced technology. It soon became subservient to the will of the exploiting capital from which it was to receive its inspiration, rather than from the mass of the people and their political and social trends.

The freedom of education, which might otherwise have released new energies of hope, was itself subjected to the same abuse under the rule of reactionary democracy. The reactionary rulers had to make sure that only those concepts which expressed their own interests reigned supreme. The consequences of all that were reflected in the systems and methods of education, which only recognized defeatist and subversive slogans.

Successive generations of Egyptian youth were taught that their country was neither fit for nor capable of industrialization. In their textbooks, they read their national history in distorted versions. Their national heroes were described as lost in a mist of doubt and uncertainty while those who betrayed the national cause were glorified and venerated.

Successive generations of Egyptian youth attended schools and universities whose educational programmes aimed at nothing more than to turn out civil servants to work for the existing systems and under their laws and regulations which disregarded the interests of the people, completely unaware of the need to destroy them or change them radically.

The alliance between feudalism and the reactionary rulers was not even satisfied with that; but by exercising pressure on large groups of intellectuals who were able to be among the revolutionary vanguard it managed to destroy their resistance by facing them with an impossible choice: either to yield to the temptation of the crumbs of class privileges thrown to them, or else to end up in obscurity and oblivion.

The depth of the revolutionary consciousness, together with the genuineness of the revolutionary will of the Egyptian people, exposed the appalling falsehood which ruled the country in the name of the alliance between feudalism and the exploiting capital. This consciousness and that will succeeded in including among the six principles the principle of true democracy. Guided by experience and reality and impelled by great hope, they outlined the form of the democracy of the people – the whole of the working people.

**First.** – Political democracy cannot be separated from social democracy. No citizen can be regarded as free to vote unless he is given the following three guarantees:

He should be free from exploitation in all its forms.

He should enjoy an equal opportunity to have a fair share of the national wealth.

His mind should be free from all anxiety likely to undermine the security of his life in the future.

Only when a citizen possesses these three guarantees can he be said to have political freedom, and can he take part, by means of his vote, in shaping the state authority he aspires to have.

**Second.** – Political democracy cannot exist under the domination of any one class. Democracy means, even in the literal sense, the domination and sovereignty of the people – the entire people. The inevitable and natural class struggles cannot be ignored or denied, but their resolution must be arrived at peacefully and within the framework of national unity and by means of dissolving class distinctions.

The experiment started with the beginning of the organized revolutionary action has proved that it is indispensable that the Revolution should undertake to liquidate the force of reaction, deprive it of all its weapons and prevent it from making any attempt to come back to power and subject the state machinery to the service of its own interests. The bitterness and sanguinary nature of class strife, as well as the grave dangers likely to ensue, are in fact the creation of the force of reaction which does not wish to give up its monopolies or its privileged position from which it continues to exploit the people. The force of reaction possesses the means of resistance; it possesses the power of the state, and if this is taken away from it it turns to the power of capital. If, however, this is taken away from it, then it turns to its natural ally, imperialism.

Because of their monopoly of wealth, reactionary interests are bound to clash with the interest of the whole people. Consequently, the peaceful resolution of class struggle cannot be achieved unless the power of reaction is first and foremost deprived of all its weapons. The removal of such a clash will pave the way to peaceful solutions to class struggles. It does not remove the contradictions in the rest of the social classes, but it creates a chance for the possibility of resolving them peacefully, namely by means of democratic action. If, on the other hand, this clash of interests is allowed to remain, then it will not be resolved except by a civil war which will cause great damage to the country at a time of great international conflict and bitter cold war.

The collaboration between the force of reaction and the exploiting capital must therefore collapse. The road must then be paved for democratic interaction between the various working powers of the people, namely the farmers, workers, soldiers, intellectuals and national capital. The cooperation between the powers representing the working people is the legitimate substitute for the collaboration between feudalism and the exploiting capital. It alone is capable of replacing reactionary democracy by true democracy.

**Third.** – It is the national unity created by cooperation between those representative powers of the people that will be able to set up the Arab Socialist Union. This union will constitute the authority representing the people, the driving force behind the possibilities of the Revolution, and the guardian of the values of true democracy. These enormous popular forces forming the Arab Socialist Union and responsible for the unleashing of its energy and effectiveness make it necessary that when dealing with the form of the political organisation of the state the new constitution of the United Arab Republic must introduce a set of necessary guarantees:

(1) The popular and political organisations based on free and direct election must truly and fairly represent the forces forming the majority of the population, the forces that have for long been exploited and which have a deep interest in the Revolution through their experience of deprivation. These forces are also naturally the storehouse of revolutionary energy, which is both dynamic and forceful. This is only just and fair, since it means that the majority will be represented. It also provides a sure guarantee to the strength of the revolutionary impetus, because it will then be springing from its genuine and natural sources. It follows then that the new constitution must ensure that farmers and workmen will get half the seats in political and popular organisations at all levels, including the House of Representatives, since they form the majority of the people. Moreover they are the majority who have been longest deprived of their inalienable right to shape and direct their future.

(2) The authority of the elected popular councils must always be consolidated and raised above the authority of the executive machinery of the State; that is the natural order regulating the sovereignty of the people, and ensuring that the people will always be the leader of national action. This would be the guarantee which guards the revolutionary drive against stagnation through the complications of the administrative or executive machinery, as a result of negligence or deviation. Again, local government should gradually but resolutely transfer the authority of the State to the people for they are in a better position to feel their own problems and find the proper solutions.

(3) There is a dire need to create a new political organisation, within the framework of the Arab Socialist Union, recruiting the elements fit for leadership, organising their efforts, clarifying the revolutionary motives of the masses, sounding their needs and endeavouring to satisfy them.

(4) Collective leaderships are imperative in the period of the revolutionary drive. Collective leaderships do not only guard against the individual running loose, but also confirm and ensure the reign of democracy in its sublime form.

**Fourth.** – Popular organisations, especially cooperatives and trade unions, can play an effective and influential role in promoting sound democracy. These organisations should form a vanguard force in the various fields of national democratic action. The development of the cooperative and trade union movements provides an endless source to the conscious leadership that directly feels the reactions and responses of the masses. The pressure that stifled these organisations and paralysed their movements has vanished. Besides their productive role the farmers' cooperatives are democratic organisations capable of spotting and solving the problems of the farmers.

It is also high time that agricultural labour unions were established. Industrial, commercial and services trade unions were able, thanks to the July laws, to reach a position of leadership in the national struggle. The workers are no longer commodities in production processes. The labour forces have become masters of the production process. They also share in its administration and profits under the best terms of wages and working hours.

**Fifth.** – Criticism and self-criticism are among the most important guarantees to freedom. The most dangerous obstacle in the way of free criticism and self-criticism in political organisations is the infiltration of reactionary elements. As a result of their control of economic interests the reactionary forces controlled the press. Freedom of opinion was thus deprived of its most valuable instrument. The elimination of reaction puts an end to the dictatorship of one class and paves the way for democracy for all the national forces of the people. It provides the surest guarantees for the freedom of assembly and freedom of discussion.

The ownership of the press by the people was achieved thanks to the law of press organisation which, at the same time, ensured its independence of the administrative government machinery. This law wrenched for the people the most valuable instrument of freedom of opinion and provided the surest guarantee for criticism. The ownership of the press by the Arab Socialist Union which represents all the working forces of the people saved it from the influence of the one ruling class. It also liberated it from the domination of capital and the invisible censorship imposed on it by capital which controlled the resources of the press. The decisive guarantee for freedom of the press lies in its belonging to the people, so that freedom of the press would in turn be an extension to the freedom of the people.

**Sixth.** – The new revolutionary concepts of true democracy must impose themselves on the factors influencing the formation of the citizen – foremost among which are education and the administrative laws and regulations. The object of education is no longer to turn out employees who work at government offices. The educational curricula in all subjects must therefore be reconsidered according to the principles of the Revolution. The curricula should aim at enabling the individual human being to reshape his life.

Laws must also be redrafted to serve the new social relations brought in by political democracy reflecting social democracy. Moreover, justice, which is the sacred right of every individual, should never be an expensive commodity beyond the reach of the citizen. Justice should be accessible to every individual without material obstacles or administrative complications. The government statutes should be radically changed. They were all, or at least most of them, drawn up under the rule of one class. They should be transformed, without delay, to uphold the democratic principles of all the people.

Democratic action in these fields will provide the opportunity for developing a new culture with new values. Such a culture would be profoundly aware of man and sincere in expressing him. It would then throw light on the facts of his thought and feeling. It would move the creative energies latent in him, the efforts of which would in turn be reflected in his experience of democracy, his conception of its principles, and his discovery of its essence.

## 6. ON THE INEVITABILITY OF THE SOCIALIST SOLUTION

Socialism is the way to social freedom. Social freedom cannot be realised except through equal opportunity for every citizen to obtain a fair share of the national wealth.

This is not confined to the mere re-distribution of the national wealth among the citizens but foremost and above all it requires expanding the base of this national wealth, so as to accede to the lawful rights of the working masses. This means that socialism, with its two supports, sufficiency and justice, is the way to social freedom.

The socialist solution to the problem of economic and social underdevelopment in Egypt – with a view to achieving progress in a revolutionary way – was never a question of free choice. The socialist solution was a historical inevitability imposed by reality, the broad aspirations of the masses and the changing nature of the world in the second part of the 20th century.

The capitalist experiments to achieve progress correlated closely with imperialism. The countries of the capitalist world reached the period of economic take-off on the basis of investments they made in their colonies. The wealth of India, of which British imperialism seized the largest share, was the beginning of the formation of the British savings which were used in the development of agriculture and industry in Britain. If Britain has reached its take-off stage thanks to the Lancashire textile industry, the transformation of Egypt into a large field for cotton growing pumped the blood through the artery of British economy leaving the Egyptian peasant starved. Gone are the ages of imperialist piracy, when the peoples' wealth was looted to serve the interests of others with neither legal nor moral control. We should stamp out the remaining traces of those ages, especially in Africa.

Other experiments of progress realised their objectives at the expense of increasing the misery of the working people, either to serve the interests of capital or under pressure of ideological application which went to the extent of sacrificing whole living generations for the sake of others still unborn. The nature of the age no longer allows such things. Progress through looting or through the corvée system is no longer tolerable under the new human values. These human values put an end to colonialism and an end to the corvée system. Not only did they achieve this but they also expressed positively the spirit and the ideals of the age when, through science, those values introduced other methods of work for the sake of progress.

* * *

Scientific socialism is the suitable style for finding the right method leading to progress. No other method can definitely achieve the desired progress. Those who call for freedom of capital, imagining that to be the road to progress, are gravely mistaken.

In the countries forced to remain underdeveloped, capital in its natural development is no longer able to lead the economic drive at a time when the great capitalist monopolies in the advanced countries grew thanks to the exploitation of the sources of wealth in the colonies.

The huge development of world monopolies leaves only two ways for local capitalism in the countries aspiring to progress:

**First.** – Local capitalism is no longer capable of competition without the customs protection paid for by the masses.

**Second.** – The only hope left for local capitalism to develop is to relate itself to the movements of world monopolies, following in their footsteps, thus turning into a mere appendage and dragging the country to doom.

Moreover, the wide gap of underdevelopment which separates the advanced states and those trying to catch up no longer allows the method of progress to be left to desultory individual efforts motivated by mere selfish profit. These individual efforts are no longer capable of facing the challenge. Facing the challenge calls for three conditions:

(1) Assembling the national savings.

(2) Putting all the experiences of modern science at the disposal of the exploitation of national savings.

(3) Drafting a complete plan for production.

These are concerned with increasing the product. On the other hand, fair distribution calls for planning programmes for social action, programmes that enable the working masses to reap the benefits of economic action and create the welfare society to which they aspire and struggle to promote. Work aiming at expanding the base of national wealth can never be left to the haphazard ways of the exploiting private capital with its unruly tendencies. The redistribution of the surplus national work on the basis of justice can never be accomplished through voluntary efforts based on good intentions, however sincere they may be.

This places a definite conclusion before the will of the National Revolution, without the acceptance of which it cannot realise its objectives. This conclusion is the necessity for the people's control over all the tools of production and over directing the surplus according to a definite plan. This socialist solution is the only way out to economic and social progress. It is the way to democracy in all its social and political forms.

The people's control over all the tools of production does not necessitate the nationalisation of all means of production or the abolition of private ownership – nor does it affect the legitimate right of inheritance based on it. Such control can be achieved in two ways:

**First.** – The creation of a capable public sector that would lead progress in all domains and bear the main responsibility of the development plan.

**Second.** – The existence of a private sector that would, without exploitation, participate in the development within the framework of the overall plan, provided that the people's control is exercised over both sectors.

This socialist solution is the only path where all elements participating in the process of production can meet, according to scientific rules capable of supplying society with all the energies enabling it to rebuild its life on the basis of a carefully studied and comprehensive plan.

* * *

Efficient socialist planning is the sole method which guarantees the use of all national resources, be they material, natural or human, in a practical, scientific and humane way aimed at realising the common good of the masses, and ensuring a life of prosperity for them. Efficient socialist planning is the guarantee for the sound exploitation of actually existing resources, or those which are latent or potential. At the same time, it is a guarantee for the continued distribution of fundamental services. It is also a guarantee for raising the standard of the services now offered. It is a guarantee for extending those services to the areas which had fallen victim to negligence and inefficiency which were the outcome of long deprivation imposed by the selfishness of the ruling classes who looked down upon the struggling people.

It follows, then, that planning must be a scientifically organised creative process that would meet the challenges facing our society. It is not a mere process of working out the possible; it is a process of achieving hope. Hence planning in our society is required to find out a solution to the difficult formula. In the solution of that difficult formula lies the material and human success of national action: How can we increase production and, at the same time, increase the consumption of goods and use of services? And this besides the constant increase of saving for the sake of new investments?

This difficult formula with its three vital branches requires the existence of a highly efficient organisation capable of mobilising forces of production, raising their material and intellectual efficiency, and relating them to the production process. Such an organisation is required to be aware that the aim of production is to widen the scope of services and that services – in turn – are a driving force turning the wheels of production. The relation between services and production and their rapid, smooth running movement creates a sound national blood cycle vital to the life of the people wholly and individually. This organisation must depend on centralisation in planning and decentralisation in implementation, which ensures placing the plan's programmes in the hands of all the people.

Consequently, the major part of the plan should be shouldered by the public sector owned by the people as a whole. This does not only ensure the sound development of the production process along the set path of productivity, but is also just, since the public sector belongs to the people as a whole.

It was the national struggle of the masses that provided the nucleus of the public sector, through the people's determination to retrieve and nationalise the foreign monopolies, and restore them to their natural and legitimate place, namely to their ownership by the whole people. Even during the military fight against imperialism, that same national struggle added to the public sector all the British and French capital in Egypt – capital which was seized from the people at the time of foreign privileges and at a time when national wealth was subjected to the looting of foreign adventurers.

Moreover, in seeking social freedom and penetrating into the strongholds of class exploitation that national struggle was able to add to the public sector the major part of production equipment through the July 1961 laws and their deep revolutionary impact reflecting the will for overall change in Egypt.

Those gigantic steps which allowed the public sector to undertake the role of vanguard in the march towards progress drew clearcut lines imposed by national reality and a thorough study of the nation's circumstances, potentialities and aims.

Those lines and principles can be summed up as follows:

**First.** – In the field of production in general: The major skeleton of the production operation such as the railways, roads, ports, airports, the sources of energy, the dams, means of sea, land and air transportation and other public services should be within the framework of public ownership.

**Second.** – In the field of industry: The majority of the heavy, medium and mining industries should be part of public ownership. Although it is possible to allow private ownership in this domain, such private ownership should be controlled by the public sector owned by the people. Light industries must always be beyond monopoly. Though this field is open to private ownership, the public sector must have a role enabling it to guide that industry to the people's interests.

**Third.** – In the field of trade: Foreign trade must be under the people's full control. Thus all import trade must be within the framework of the public sector. Though it is incumbent upon private capital to participate in export trade, the public sector must have the main share in that field to preclude all possible fraudulency. In so far as a percentage could be set in that field, the public sector must be in charge of three quarters of exports, while encouraging the private sector to shoulder the responsibility of the remaining share.

The public sector must have a role in internal trade. The public sector should, within the coming eight years – remaining period of the first overall development plan for doubling national income in ten years – be in charge of at least one quarter of the internal trade to prevent monopoly and expand the range of internal trade for private and cooperative activities. It should be understood, of course, that internal trade means service and distribution against reasonable profit which under no circumstances should reach the extent of exploitation.

**Fourth.** – In the field of finance: Banks should be within the framework of public ownership. The role of capital is a national one and should not be left to speculation and adventure. In addition, insurance companies should be within the same framework of public ownership for the protection of a major part of national saving and to ensure its sound orientation.

**Fifth.** – In the domain of land: There should be a clear distinction between two kinds of private ownership – that which opens the gates to exploitation, and non-exploiting ownership which does its share in the service of the national economy while serving the interests of the owners themselves.

In the field of ownership of rural land, the Agrarian Reform laws have limited individual ownership to one hundred feddans. Yet the spirit of the law implies that this limitation should cover the whole family, namely father, mother and children out of age, to avoid clustering together maximum ownerships allowing some form of feudalism. This spirit can be made to rule within the coming eight years provided the families affected by that law sell the land in excess of those limits in cash to the Agricultural Cooperative Societies or to others.

As regards ownership of buildings, the laws of progressive taxation of buildings, the laws reducing rents and those defining levies, place ownership of buildings beyond exploitation. Yet constant supervision is imperative, although the increase in public and cooperative housing will contribute in a practical manner to combating all attempts at exploitation in this field.

* * *

Through the accomplishment of their great socialist achievement, the July 1961 laws are the biggest triumph of the revolutionary drive in the economic field. These laws, an extension to other preliminaries, formed a bridge that led to the change to socialism with unprecedented success. That decisive revolutionary phase would not have been completed with such efficiency and in such a peaceful spirit had it not been for the deep faith and consciousness of the people, the pooling of their efforts to make a firm stand against the reactionary elements, invading their strongholds and asserting the people's mastery over the country's wealth. The glorious laws of July and the decisive way of their implementation, as well as the successful and brave efforts of hundreds of thousands of citizens working at the organisations whose ownership passed on to the people under those laws, in the delicate period following have insured the preservation and consolidation of productivity in those firms.

All this, while asserting the people's determination to own their resources, shows the people's ability to direct those resources and their readiness, through sincere elements, to shoulder the most difficult and delicate responsibilities. Undoubtedly, the measures adopted in the wake of the July socialist laws have successfully realised a liquidation that was both inevitable and imperative.

Following a reactionary attempt to attack the social revolution, a drastic move to wipe out the vestiges of the era of feudalism, reaction and domination was effected. This move cut short all attempts at infiltration or betrayal of the people's aspirations with the object of serving the personal interests of the ruling and dominating privileged classes. These measures asserted that the people are unflinchingly determined to reject every form of exploitation whether it be the consequence of class inheritance or of parasitic opportunism.

However, we should bear in mind that reaction has not been eliminated forever. Reaction is still in possession of material and intellectual influences that may tempt it to stand in the way of the sweeping revolutionary current, particularly when it relies on the remnants of reaction in the Arab world backed by the forces of imperialism. The revolutionary vigilance is under all circumstances capable of crushing every reactionary infiltration whatever its methods and whatever the supporting powers.

It is of prime importance that our outlook towards nationalisation be freed from the stigmas that private interests have tried to attach to it. Nationalisation is but the transfer of one of the means of production from the sphere of private ownership to that of public ownership. This is not a blow to individual initiative as alleged by the enemies of socialism but rather a guarantee to and an expansion of the range of general interest in cases urged by the socialist change effected for the benefit of the people.

Nationalisation does not lead to a decrease in production. Experience has proved the ability of the public sector to shoulder the greatest responsibilities with maximum efficiency, whether in the achievement of the production targets or in raising the standard of its quality. Although some mistakes may occur during this great evolution we must keep in mind that the new hands that have assumed the responsibility are in need of training to undertake such responsibility. At any rate it was inevitable that the major national interests should be handed over to the people even at the cost of facing temporary difficulties.

Nationalisation is not, as alleged by some opportunist elements, a punishment inflicted upon private capital when it deviates and consequently should not be applied except for punishment. The transfer of a means of production from the sphere of private ownership to that of public ownership is more significant than mere punishment.

The great importance attached to the role of the public sector, however, cannot do away with the existence of the private sector. The private sector has its effective role in the development plan. It must be protected to fulfill that part. The private sector is now required to renovate itself and strike a new path of creative effort not dependent, as in the past, on parasitic exploitation.

The crisis which befell private capital before the Revolution actually stemmed from the fact that it had inherited the era of the foreign adventurers who, in the 19th century, helped transfer abroad the wealth of Egypt. Private capital was accustomed to live under a protective trade policy which gave it benefits at the expense of the people. It was also accustomed to dominate the Government with the aim of pursuing a policy of exploitation.

It was futile for the people to bear the cost of the protective trade policy to enhance the profits of a group of capitalists who mostly were no more than local façades to foreign interests wishing to carry on their exploitation from behind the scenes. Therefore, the people could not forever remain indifferent to the manoeuvres to direct the Government in favour of the minority controlling the wealth, and to guarantee the maintenance of their privileged position at the expense of the people's interests.

Progress through socialism is a consolidation of the bases of sound democracy, the democracy of all the people. Progress in the political domain under capitalism – even if we imagined it possible in the present international conditions – can only mean a confirmation of the rule of the class, possessing and monopolising all interests. In this event, the returns would go to a small minority of the people who have so much money in excess that they squander it on various forms of wasteful luxury defying the deprivation of the majority. This sharpens the edge of the class strife and wipes out every hope for democratic evolution.

But the socialist path, providing opportunities for a peaceful settlement of the class strife and affording possibilities for dissolving class distinctions, leads to the distribution of the returns among all the people according to the principle of equality of opportunity for all. The socialist path thereby paves the way for an inevitable political development leading to liberation from the rule of the feudalist dictatorship allied with capitalism and the establishment of the rule of democracy representing the rights and aspirations of the working people.

The political liberation of man cannot be achieved unless an end is put to every shackle of exploitation limiting his freedom. Socialism and democracy form the wings of freedom with which socialism can soar to the distant horizons aspired to by the masses.

## 7. PRODUCTION AND SOCIETY

Gone is the time when the fate of the Arab Nation, its peoples and individuals was determined in foreign capitals, at the tables of international conferences and in palaces of the forces of reaction, allied with imperialism.

The Arab man has retrieved his right to fashion his life through revolution. The Arab man shall determine by himself the destiny of his nation on the fertile fields, in the huge factories, from the top of the high dams and with the enormous energies of the driving force.

The battle of production is the true challenge in which the Arab man will justify his worthy position under the sun. Production is the true criterion of the dynamic Arab force. By production we can end our underdevelopment, rush towards progress, face and overcome difficulties and intrigues, finally achieve victory over all our enemies, and rout their defeated ranks.

* * *

The objective set by the Egyptian people, through the Revolution, to double their national income at least once every ten years, was not a mere slogan. It was the result of calculating the amount of the drive required to face underdevelopment and rush for progress, keeping in mind the increasing rise of the population. This increase constitutes the most dangerous obstacle that faces the Egyptian people in their drive towards raising the standard of production in their country in an effective and efficient way. While attempts at family planning aimed at facing the problem of the increasing population deserve the most sincere efforts backed by modern scientific methods, the need for the most rapid and efficient drive towards the increase of production necessitates that this problem should be taken into consideration in the process of production, regardless of the effects which may result from the experiment of family planning.

The doubling of the national income every ten years allows for a rate of economic growth which greatly exceeds the rate of increase in the population. It also provides a real opportunity for raising the standard of living in spite of this complex problem. The ability of the Egyptian people should be put to the test positively, by their adhering to that aim which should never be lost sight of by the national struggle. In fact, it is the true measure of the national will, and it is directly related to the attempts to shorten the period of doubling the national income to less than ten years, by as much as the national effort can bear. The attainment of this goal is possible through economic and social planning, without sacrificing the living generations of citizens for the sake of those still unborn.

To attain this goal it is not necessary to exhaust their energies under the pressure of responsibility, but all that it requires from them is honest and systematic work, within the framework of the productive aims of the plan, and inspired by the social thought which outlines for it the way to set up the new society, as well as by what that thought can evolve by way of new moral values and broad and vital human ideas. This requires colossal efforts in the fields of developing agriculture, industry and the chief skeletons of production necessary for this development, particularly the energies of driving force and means of transport.

The Arab application of socialism in the domain of agriculture does not believe in nationalizing the land and transforming it into the domain of public ownership. But from experience and study it believes in individual ownership of land, within limits that would not allow for feudalism. This conclusion is not just an outcome of responding to the sentimental longing of farmers for the ownership of land, but the fact is that this conclusion is derived from the real circumstances of the agricultural problem in Egypt. These circumstances have confirmed the ability of the Egyptian farmer for creative work, given favourable conditions.

The efficiency of the Egyptian farmer, throughout a long history full of experience, has reached a capacity of exploiting land to an advanced level, especially when the opportunity is provided for benefiting from the results of scientific agricultural progress. Moreover, long ago Egyptian agriculture arrived at sound socialist solutions to its most complicated problems. Foremost among these are irrigation and drainage, which are now, and have been for a long time, within the framework of public services. Thus, the right solutions to the problem of agriculture do not lie in transferring land into public ownership, but they necessitate the existence of individual ownership of land, and the expansion of ownership by providing the right to own it to the largest number of wage-earners together with supporting this ownership by means of agricultural co-operation, along all the stages of the process of agricultural production.

Agricultural co-operation is much more than mere simple credit to which it was confined till recently. It starts by the process of pooling agricultural exploitation, which proved to be very successful. It goes parallel with the financial process which protects the farmer and liberates him from usurers and middlemen who take the largest part of the fruit of his labour. Co-operation also enables the farmer to use the most modern machines and scientific means to raise production. It helps the farmer in marketing, which enables him to obtain the highest returns for his continuous labour and toil.

The revolutionary solution to the problem of land in Egypt is by increasing the number of land-owners. Such was the aim of the laws of land reform issued in 1952 and 1961. This aim – besides the other aims of raising production – was one of the motive powers behind the great irrigation projects, whose powerful symbol is the Aswan High Dam, for the sake of which the people of Egypt have suffered all sorts of armed, economic and psychological wars. This Dam has become the symbol of the will and determination of the people to fashion its life. It is also a symbol of its will to provide the right of land ownership for large multitudes of farmers, for whom this opportunity was never provided throughout centuries of continuous feudal rule.

The success of this revolutionary attempt at solving the agricultural problem, based on increasing the number of landowners, cannot be consolidated except by agricultural co-operation, and by the expansion of its scope to the extent of providing a strong and vital economy for the small land holdings. Besides, there are three areas, in which the great battle of production must take place for the sake of the development of the countryside. These are:

**First.** – The horizontal extension of agriculture, by reclaiming the desert and the waste land. The process of land reclamation should never cease for a second. The area of green fields must become larger every day in the Nile Valley. We should reach a stage at which every drop of the Nile water could be transformed on its banks into creative life that would not be wasted. Today many are waiting for their turn to own land in their country. The future brings forth with every new generation masses of those who look forward to owning land.

**Second.** – The vertical extension in agriculture through raising the productivity of cultivated land. Modern chemistry has touched in a revolutionary way the methods of cultivation. This is done through fertilisers and developing new kinds of seeds. Moreover, wonderful possibilities – through organised science – enable us to develop the animal wealth and thus definitely strengthen the agricultural economy of the farmer. There are also big possibilities behind re-studying the economics of agricultural crops in the Egyptian land. Variation of agricultural crops could be based on the results of that study.

**Third.** – The industrialisation of the countryside which is based on agriculture opens vast ranges for the chances of work in the country. We should always remember that industry due to mechanic progress cannot use the whole surplus of working hands on the cultivated land. We should remember this at a time when we believe – beyond all doubt – that the right for work in itself is the right for life, in so far as it is the actual confirmation for the existence and the value of the human being.

Therefore, the labour problem should find part of its solution in the countryside. The industrialisation of the countryside, besides its ability to raise the value of agricultural production, supplies the working elements in the fields with new powers of technical workers who serve the agricultural production in all its stages. The revolution of the production process in the countryside will help at the same time in finding organised human powers capable of changing the face of life in the villages in a revolutionary and decisive way.

Co-operation will create co-operative organisations that are able to drive human efforts in the countryside to face its problems. In the same way the syndicates of agricultural workers shall mobilise the efforts of millions who have been wasted by unemployment.

These are the cells that could breathe life anew in the countryside, and set up a civilisation bringing the village nearer to the level of the town. That the village should reach a civilised level is not only a necessity imposed by justice, it is one of the fundamental necessities of development.

The town has a moral responsibility towards the village. It has to undertake and accomplish serious work in the village without any feeling of superiority. When the village reaches the civilised standard of the town, particularly in the field of culture, the individual's awareness for planning will start. This awareness will be able to confront the most difficult problem which faces and threatens planning, namely the problem of the continuous increase of population. Deep awareness of the necessity of planning in the individual's life is the decisive solution to the problem of the continuous increase of the population. This awareness will change the individual's feeling of submission to Fate as regards the problem, and replace it with a feeling of responsibility that drives the individual to plan the family economy.

Industry is the strong support of the National build-up. Industry is capable of realising the greatest hopes in the field of social and economic evolution. Industry is a creative energy that could respond to well-studied planning and carry out its programmes. In so doing industry overcomes unforeseen difficulties, and so it is capable of enlarging the production base in a revolutionary and decisive manner, and in a very short time.

Our approach to industry must be deliberate, and must take into consideration all social and economic issues in the great battle of evolution.

**From the Economic Point of View:**

* Our approach must aspire to the latest scientific achievements. If we obtain the advanced tools of work, we do not only make a sound start but we also make up for our underdevelopment.
* By means of new equipment, Egyptian industry will have a distinguished position that compensates for the industrial progress which started in other countries at a time when the production instruments were not as advanced as they are now.
* We must put aside the assumption which says that using modern instruments does not give a full chance of work, on the grounds that modern machines do not need large labour power. This conception may prove sound at the beginning, but it is not valid in the long run. For modern instruments are capable of enlarging the base of production quickly. This opens new horizons of industrialisation, and so gives wider chances of labour as a result.

The fields of industrial work in Egypt are unlimited. Egyptian industry could extend creative work all over the Egyptian land. The sources of natural and mineral wealth still keep many of their secrets. Large areas of land have been neglected for long. Efforts aimed hitherto at exploiting these large areas of land were but scratches on its surface.

Only industrial scientific work can explore the wealth of the Egyptian land and exploit its natural and mineral riches to serve progress. These sources can be the backbone of industry that would create new tools of production. Special care should be devoted to heavy industries, for these only are the bases for modern industry. Raw materials, whether agricultural or mineral, need local industrialisation which adds extra value to them in the markets. Thus it consolidates the capacity for industrial production and opens wide fields for labour.

Moreover, great concern should also be devoted to consumer industries. Apart from offering numerous possibilities of work, those industries meet an important share of consumer demands and save important sources of foreign currency. In addition, those industries afford the possibility of expanding the volume of exports to markets which are close to us and where we still have not reached an internationally competitive position with regard to heavy industry. The food industries – which are part of the consumer industries – can, more than any other, consolidate rural economy and afford unlimited possibilities for markets in developed countries where consumer demands increase with the raising of the standard of living.

In a general way, industrial planning must include the partial or total industrialisation possible of raw materials, for this achieves the biggest development targets.

It leads to an increase in production and meets consumer demands, apart from affording opportunities to those capable of work and demand it as a sacred human right. Such industrialisation would also be a source of foreign currency that would help meet the ever increasing demands of development.

**In the Social Domain:**

Industry is responsible for establishing the essential human equilibrium between development demands and consumer needs. The philosophy on which the industrialisation policy in Egypt was based has realised that aim, through the balance established between the heavy industry trend and that of consumer industries. Heavy industry, no doubt, provides the solid foundation to the gigantic industrial set up. Yet, despite the definite priority that should be given to heavy industry, it must not hamper the progress of consumer industries.

The masses of our people have long been deprived; to mobilize them completely for the building of the heavy industry and overlook their consumer needs is incompatible with their established right to make up for their long deprivation, and at the same time it delays – with no sound reason – the possibilities of responding to the people's wide hopes. On the other hand, industry develops the shape of activity in Egypt in a far-reaching manner. The great success achieved by industry since the beginning of its organised programmes was the practical support to the revolutionary rights obtained by the working class as part of the July 1961 laws.

Those revolutionary rights made machinery the property of work and not work the property of machinery. The workman became master of the machine and not a cog in a wheel in the production set-up. Those revolutionary rights which ensured a minimum wage, positive participation in management coupled with a true share in production profit shall, within the framework of working conditions, ensure the dignity of the working man.

As a result, the working day has become seven hours. This revolutionary change in labour rights must be met with a revolutionary change in labour duties. Labour responsibility for the production equipment placed at its disposal by society as a whole should be complete. The production responsibility of labour through the equipment it safeguards and operates with honesty and efficiency, and through participation in management and profits, is complete.

The new system does not abolish the role of labour organisations, but rather adds to its importance. The new system expands this role. Those organisations no longer remain a mere counterpart of management in the production operation, but become the leading vanguard in development. Labour unions can exercise their leading responsibilities through serious contribution to intellectual and scientific efficiency and thus increase productivity among labour. Those unions can also assume their functions by safeguarding labour rights and interests and by raising the workmen's material and cultural standards. This covers plans of co-operative housing, and cooperative consumption as well as the organisation of leave and free periods to bring health, psychological and intellectual benefits for the welfare of labour masses. The position of labour in the new society can only be measured through the success of industrial development and the working potentialities and efficiency to achieve that aim.

* * *

Expansion in the driving force potential and in establishing the main production skeletons is the basis of the drive towards the new production objectives in both agriculture and industry. The penetration of the driving force into every part of Egypt supplies the revolutionary spark capable of operating the potentials of the comprehensive economic and social change from underdevelopment to the progress to which the national struggle aspires.

Efficient networks of railways, roads and airports should cover the whole country, since easy transportation can perform miracles in the field of unity of production in the country and leads to common prosperity with no isolated part of the land.

* * *

The various aspects of industrial production requirements afford great possibilities for non-exploiting national capital to perform, together with the public sector, an important and responsible role in the entire process of production. Moreover, the maintenance of the role of the private sector beside that of the public sector, renders control over public ownership more effective.

By encouraging competition within the framework of the general economic planning, the private sector is also an invigorating element in the public sector. The July 1961 revolutionary laws did not aim at destroying the private sector, but had two basic objectives:

The first is the creation of some form of economic equality among the citizens which ensures legitimate rights and removes the effects of a minority monopolising all opportunities at the expense of the majority, and at the same time contributes to the dissolution of class distinctions in a way that enhances the possibilities of a peaceful struggle between them and paves the way for democratic solutions to the major problems confronting the process of development.

The second objective is to step up the efficiency of the public sector owned by the people, to consolidate its capacity to shoulder the responsibility of planning and to enable it to play its leading role in industrial development on a socialist basis.

These two objectives have been crowned with sweeping success confirming the power of the revolutionary drive and the depth of national unity. The realisation of these two objectives wipes out the residue of the complexes created by exploitation that cast a shadow of doubt on the role of the private sector. Consequently, the path open to this sector today, to promote the process of development, is only restricted by the socialist laws now in force, or by the steps deemed necessary by the popular authorities elected in future.

The socialist framework carefully set up by the July laws wiped out the vestiges of exploitation and left the door open to individual investment that would serve the general interest in the field of development. It would equally serve its owners by providing them with a reasonable profit without exploitation. Those who claim that the July laws restricted individual initiative are committing a grave error. Individual initiative must be based on work and risk. In the past, everything was based on opportunism rather than work, and on the protection of monopoly, which excluded every possibility of risk. This is the pretext individual capital used to justify its share of profits.

On the other hand, individual initiative as it existed was incapable of shouldering the responsibility of nationalist aspiration. The new investments now directed towards industry are a hundred times as much as the amount invested in the year preceding the Revolution.

The redistribution of wealth does not impede development; it actually invigorates it, since it increases the number of people able to invest.

Just like public capital, private capital, in its new role, must realise that it is subject to the directive of the popular authority. It is this authority that makes its laws and directs it according to the people's needs. It is able to check its activity if it attempts to exploit or deviate. It is ready to protect it. Yet protection of the people is its first duty.

* * *

Foreign capital and its role in local investment is a question we should deal with at this stage. Foreign capital is regarded with dark doubts in underdeveloped countries particularly those which were colonised. The sovereignty of the people over their land and their restoration to the helm, allow them to set the conditions under which foreign capital may be invested in the country.

The matter calls for setting up a system drawn from the essence of the national experience. It also takes into account the nature of world capital always striving after unexploited raw materials in areas not yet ready for any economic or social revival, where it could obtain the highest share of profits.

In the first place, in the process of national evolution, all foreign aid with no strings attached is accepted to help attain the national objectives. The aid is accepted with sincere gratitude for those who offer it regardless of the colour of their flags.

In the second place, in the process of national evolution all unconditional loans are accepted provided they could be refunded without difficulty or strain. Experience shows that loans are a clear operation; their problem completely ends with their amortisation and the reimbursement of their interests.

In the third place, in the process of national evolution, the participation of foreign capital as an investment is accepted in indispensable operations, especially those requiring new experience, difficult to find in the national domain.

Acceptance of foreign investment implies that a foreigner would participate in the administration. It also implies that a share of the annual profits would be transferred to the investors indefinitely. This matter should not be left without limitation. First priority goes to unconditional aid. The second place is reserved to unconditional loans. There follows the acceptance of foreign investment in unavoidable circumstances, in aspects of modern evolution requiring international experience.

In their conscious revolutionary outlook, our people consider it the duty of the advanced states to offer aid to those still struggling for development. In their conception of history our people believe the states with a colonialist past are, more than others, compelled to offer to the nations aspiring to development part of the national wealth they sapped when that wealth was a booty for all looters. Offering aid is the optional duty of the advanced states. It is a form of a tax that must be paid by the states with a colonialist past to compensate those they exploited for so long.

Production is all to the people. It is at their service to realise their happiness and ensure the well-being of every individual. Society is not an abstract conception. Society is formed of every person living on the soil of the homeland, whose aspirations are bound by the aspirations of other citizens for a morrow cherished by them and for coming generations. The true object of production is to provide the greatest amount of services which would be the banners of prosperity flying over society.

In proportion to the expansion of the base of production, and the new national investments that could be increased daily through national effort, new scopes are opened affording equal opportunities for all citizens.

Equality of opportunity, which is the expression of social freedom, can be defined in basic rights for every citizen. Efforts must be devoted for their realisation.

**First.** – The right of each citizen to medical care, whether treatment or medicine, would not become a commodity for sale and purchase. It would become a guaranteed right not dependent on a certain price. This care should be within the reach of every citizen, in every part of the country, and in easy circumstances rendering service possible. Health insurance must be expanded to embrace all citizens.

**Second.** – The right of each citizen to receive education which suits his abilities and talents. Education is the means of consolidating and honouring human freedom; it is also the energy which can rejuvenate national action and daily adds new ideas to it and bring in leading and serious elements in its various fields.

**Third.** – The right of each citizen to secure the job which accords with his abilities and interests and the type of education he has received. Beside being of economic importance in a man's life, work is an assertion of human existence itself. In this respect it is indispensable that there should be a legally sanctioned minimum of wages. Similarly, justice rules that there should be a maximum of income fixed by the taxation system.

**Fourth.** – Insurance against old age and sickness must be provided on a much larger scale so that protection is afforded to those who have taken their share in the national struggle and for whom the time has come to be sure of their right to security and rest.

Since the children of today are the makers of our future, it is the duty of working generations to provide them with all the chances that will enable them later to assume successfully the responsibility of leadership.

Woman must be regarded as equal to man and must therefore shed the remaining shackles that impede her free movement so that she might take a constructive and profound part in shaping life.

The family is the first cell in a society and it must therefore be afforded all means of protection so that it might be better able to preserve the national tradition, to rejuvenate its texture, and to carry along the whole of society in the direction of the goals set by the national struggle.

* * *

The welfare society is able to formulate new moral values, not subject to the influence of the remaining pressures left over from ailments, from which our society had suffered so long. In their turn these new values must be reflected in a free national culture which awakens the sense of beauty in the life of the free individual.

The freedom of religious belief must be regarded as sacred in our new free life. The eternal spiritual values derived from religions are capable of guiding man, of lighting the candle of faith in his life and of bestowing on him unlimited capacities for serving truth, good and love. In their essence all divine messages constituted human revolutions which aimed at the reinstatement of man's dignity and his happiness. It is the prime duty of religious thinkers, then, to preserve for each religion the essence of its divine message.

The essence of religious messages does not conflict with the facts of our life; the conflict arises only in certain situations as a result of attempts made by reactionary elements to exploit religion – against its nature and spirit – with a view to impeding progress. These elements fabricate false interpretations of religion in flagrant contradiction with its noble and divine wisdom. All religions contain a message of progress. But the forces of reaction, desiring to monopolise all the goods of the earth and use them to serve their own selfish interests alone, committed the crime of attaching their greed and cupidity to religion and of reading into it something that contradicts its very spirit with the object of stemming the current of progress.

The essence of all religions is to assert man's right to life and to freedom. In fact, the basis of reward and punishment in religion is equality of opportunity for every man. Every individual starts his religious life before his Maker with a blank sheet, so to speak, on which are recorded his deeds accomplished by his own free will. No religion can accept a system of class distinction, by which the majority inherit the punishment of poverty, ignorance and disease while a small minority monopolise the reward of all prosperity. God in His great wisdom has made equality of opportunity the basis of His judgement of all people.

We must always bear in mind that, for an individual, freedom is the greatest stimulus to struggle. Slaves can carry loads of stone, but only free men are able to soar high among the stars. Free conviction is the firm basis of all faith. Without freedom, faith would turn into fanaticism which is a barrier that shuts out all new thought and keeps those who suffer from it untouched by the current of evolution enhanced by the efforts of all people everywhere.

Freedom alone is capable of impelling man to move forward and to catch up with those who are ahead of him. Free man is the basis of a free society which he alone can set up. The freedom of an individual to shape his destiny, to define his position in society, to express his opinion, and by means of his thought and experience and hopes to take an active part in leading and directing the evolution of his society is inalienable human right which must be protected by law.

We must clearly realise that in a free society law is subservient to freedom and is not a sword drawn in its face.

Similarly we must clearly realise that no individual can be free unless he is first liberated from the shackles of exploitation. It is this fact that makes social freedom a way, to achieve political freedom. Our immediate aim is to do away with exploitation, and to make possible the exercise of the natural right to have an equal opportunity, to dissolve class distinctions and to end the domination of one class and hence remove the clash between classes which constitutes a threat to the freedom of the individual citizen, and even to the freedom of the whole of the country by violating the rights of the people, thus creating the chance of exposing the country to the lurking dangers of foreign forces vigilantly on the look out to drag it to the arena of cold war and make of it its battlefield and of its people fodder for their guns. The removal of the clash between classes which arises out of interests that can never be reconciled, between those who exercise exploitation and those crushed by exploitation in the past society, cannot overnight lead to the dissolution of all class distinctions or lead to social freedom and true democracy.

Yet the removal of the clash between classes makes it possible, by eliminating the exploiting class, to dissolve peacefully class distinctions, and to open the gates for democratic exchange which brings the whole society nearer the era of true freedom. That was one of the great social objectives of the July laws which directed a deadly blow at the centers of exploitation and monopolies. That great revolutionary action made it possible to have a sound democracy for the first time in Egypt.

* * *

While the free world acts like a torchlight for sound democracy, a free judicial system is equally an ultimate guarantee of its limits.

Freedom of speech is the first premise of sound democracy.

The rule of law is its final guarantee.

Freedom of speech is the expression of freedom of thought in all its manifestations. All guarantees should be provided for freedom of the press, which is the most outstanding form of freedom of speech. True democracy, in its profound sense, eliminates the contradiction between the people and the government, when it transforms the press into a popular means. But like representative councils the free press should be an honest censor of the means of the popular will.

The supremacy of law requires a conscious development of its articles and texts, so as to express the new values in our society. Again law, which in itself is one of the forms of freedom, must accompany it in its drive towards progress. Its articles should not be restrictions keeping new values out of our life. The new society, which the Arab people of Egypt are building on the basis of sufficiency and justice, needs a strong shield in a world whose moral standards have not risen to the level of its intellectual progress.

The role of the United Arab Republic Armed Forces is to defend the process of social construction against external dangers. The Armed Forces must be ready to crush any imperialist reactionary attempt at preventing the people from realizing their great aspirations. That is why the people offer their Armed Forces what makes them always ready and places them in a position of power to enable them always to serve their aspirations with absolute loyalty and dedication.

The Armed Forces of the United Arab Republic should enjoy a decisive superiority on land, sea and air. They should be capable of quick movement within the Arab area, whose security is primarily the responsibility of the United Arab Republic Armed Forces. Moreover these forces must be armed in a way in keeping with modern scientific progress, and must possess sufficient deterring weapons to stem the greed of ambitious powers and defeat them should they start any aggression.

There is no doubt that self-advancement is the best way of defence against lurking dangers. But we must realize that we live in an area exposed to aggressive ambitions. The prime aim of our enemies is to prevent us from reaching the stage of strength which achieves development, so that we may always remain at the mercy of threats. The United Arab Republic which is, in particular, the vanguard, base and fighting fortress of the Arab progressive struggle, is the natural target of all the enemies of the Arab nation and of its progress.

The world imperialist forces and monopolies aim at a fixed target, namely to put the Arab territory extending from the Ocean to the Gulf under its military control, in order to be able to continue its exploitation and loot its wealth. Imperialist intrigues went to the extent of seizing a part of the Arab territory of Palestine, in the heart of the Arab Motherland, and usurping it without any justification of right or law, the aim being to establish a military Fascist regime, which cannot live except by military threats.

The real danger of this threat emanates from the fact that Israel is the tool of imperialism. At present the United Arab Republic is, both historically and actually, the only Arab Nation which can assume the responsibility of building a national army capable of deterring imperialist, Zionist aggressive plans.

The continued popular march towards economic and social progress makes the national army a true shield to protect the struggle, rather than a mere superficial crust that covers the border lines. The effectiveness of national armies lies in the nation's economic and social power. For progress is the huge store that supplies the means of fighting with its material and human needs, which can repel any challenge and win and maintain victory.

We must always bear in mind that the needs of defence should never have the upper hand over the needs of development. If defence is not supported by development it will not be able to stand for long the strain of the continuous battle. Economic and social development is the heart that provides the striking force of the nation with power and steadfastness, and enables it to deal fatal blows to the enemy, however long the battle may last.

Our society believes that freedom for the Motherland and the citizen can be provided, after all, by peace based on justice. But until the time comes when its great principles are stabilized and prevalent all over the world, our society has to be always ready to back peace by power, for the sake of the freedom of the homeland and the citizen.

## 8. THE SOCIALIST APPLICATION AND ITS PROBLEMS

Creative human labour is the only means for society to achieve its aims. Labour is an honour. It is also a right, a duty and a sign of life. Human labour is the only key to progress. The nature of our times can never accept any means for the realization of aspirations other than human labour.

In centuries past some societies were able to realize their drive by providing the investments of national development through looting the wealth of colonies, exploiting the riches of peoples and forcing them to slave labour, for the sake of others. In other societies, this drive became possible under circumstances of exploiting the working class in an inhuman way, to serve interests of national and foreign capitalism.

This drive was realized, in other experiments under extremely cruel pressure exercised on living generations, who were deprived of all the fruit of their labour for the sake of a promised future that they could not see or reach or achieved their drive only after they had been subjected to inhibitions, terror and oppression.

The nature of our times can no longer tolerate all this. Mankind is now aware of the evils of imperialism, and has pledged itself to wipe it out. The working class cannot be driven through forced labour to realize the objectives of production. The creative energies of peoples can shape the morrow without being driven towards it through mass bloodshed. Scientific progress makes it possible and practical for peoples to achieve their drive without resorting to such absolute means. Besides, the nature and the ideals of the age render the use of such absolute means impossible. Organised national action based on scientific planning is the path leading to the desired future.

National action based on planning must be clear to the machinery of production at all levels. The responsibility of each individual in this action must be clear to him, so that he may, at any time, know his exact position in the national action. This demands that the overall plan – as regards its economic and social objectives – should be translated into detailed programmes to be put within the reach of the machinery of production.

This also demands the imposition of time limits on production as regards quantity and quality. The productive powers should adhere to these time limits, provided that the whole process is accomplished within the framework of the allotted investments. Quantity and quality in the production process cannot be separated from the working out of time and cost. Otherwise, we lose the vital balance of the production process and, thus, expose it to danger.

The same applies to the programmes of services. Every citizen should be aware of his defined responsibility in the whole plan, and should be fully conscious of the definite rights he will enjoy in the event of the success of the plan. This consciousness leads to a distribution of responsibility on the scale of the whole nation, in a way that expands the possibilities of realising objectives. It is at the same time a revolutionary process carrying the meaning of national action from the sphere of vague generalities to the clarity of experience. This clarity of experience relates the individual human being, in his daily struggle, to the whole movement of society and moves him in the direction of history. At the same time, it enables the individual human being to direct the movement of history.

The philosophy of national action should be conveyed to all working forces in the various fields. It should be conveyed to each of them in the way that suits him best. That will be a constant guarantee to the existence of a relation between thought and experience, between theoretic doctrine and practical application.

Mental clarity is the greatest help for the success of experience. Similarly experience, in its turn, adds to the clarity of thought, strengthens and enriches it and enables it to act and react upon reality. From this creative exchange national action acquires greater potentialities for the achievement of success. In this respect it is most necessary to encourage the written word so that it may be a link among all, a link that can be easily preserved for the future. Moreover, it forms an important link in the relation between thought and experience.

It is necessary to encourage those who are responsible for the policy of national action, to record their thoughts to be put before those responsible for the execution of this national action. Similarly, it is necessary to encourage all those in charge of execution to record their remarks to be put before those responsible for guidance. This issue cannot be left to mere chance. It should be organised. Its organisation will supply the national action with unlimited horizons of thought combined with details of practical application, which will increase the store of national efficiency and widen the range of profit.

Great periods of change are naturally full of dangers which are themselves part of the nature of such periods. The greatest means of insurance against these dangers, however, lies in the exercise of freedom particularly through elected popular councils. The whole of the national action, at all its levels, can never safely achieve its objectives except through democracy.

To apply democracy we should see that it is maintained in all production centres and so enable all working in them to devote their national and technical efforts towards the perfection of the task. Certainly, this will be accomplished in accordance with a hierarchical system of responsibility. To apply democracy, the authority of popular councils should have authority over all production centres and over the machinery of local or central administration.

This is a constant guarantee for the authority of determining the objectives of production remaining in the hands of the people. At the same time, it is a guarantee for the people to have the authority of censorship over the execution of these objectives.

Exercising criticism and self-criticism always gives national action an opportunity to correct and adjust itself to its great objectives. The peoples' struggle and their effort to achieve progress always pay the price for any attempt to hide or ignore truth. If popular leaderships allow truth to be hidden or ignored, they not only fail to fulfil their duties towards the people who placed leadership in their hands, but they also isolate themselves from their masses, and admit their inability to solve the problems of these masses. Accordingly it becomes inevitable for such leaderships to give up their office or for the people to overthrow them and withdraw from them their responsibilities granted to them by the people.

Freedom of constructive criticism and brave self-criticism are necessary guarantees for setting up the national structure on a sound basis. Moreover, these guarantees are more inevitable during periods of successive change in the history of revolutionary action. Exercising freedom in this way is not only necessary for safeguarding national action, but it is also necessary for enlarging its base and for providing guarantee for those who are involved in it. Exercising freedom in this way is the effective method for mobilising many elements who may hesitate to participate in national action.

Freedom is the sole means that would put an end to the passivity of these elements and induce them to work willingly for the objectives of the struggle. Exercising freedom following the great revolutionary operation redistributing the national wealth in July 1961 does not form a danger to the security of the national struggle. It is, rather, a safety-valve for it. For exercising freedom creates the popular force capable of pounding on every attempt for conspiracy aimed at robbing the people of the fruits of its struggle.

Furthermore, exercising freedom creates renewed leaderships of revolutionary action and enlarges these leaderships. It also pushes them forward and creates a leadership of collective thought capable of checking the arbitrary tendencies of individuals and thus providing long-term guarantees for national action.

Freedom of leaderships must derive its right from the freedom of the popular base. Leaderships cannot undertake their tasks through force and fanaticism. Real leadership consists in being sensitive to the demands of the people, in expressing these demands, and in finding means to answer them and in mobilising the people's powers to back the efforts designed to meet these demands.

The new constitution must organise the operation of popular leadership referring to their bases to confirm their responsibility before the original sources of their power. We must always remember that the popular bases are charged with spontaneous revolutionary impulses. The revolutionary impulses of the bases and their constant insistence on progress will form a driving force for the revolutionary quality of the leadership.

To set in motion the people's energies towards action must not be attempted through immersing the masses into hope. The great change by nature, is accompanied by looking forward to the objectives of the struggle on a long-term basis. Yet, it is most necessary in this period to make it clear before the people that achieving the aspired objectives is difficult. The mere revolutionary change in the structure of the society of the past does not realise the dreams of the masses. Continuous efforts alone are capable of converting dreams into realities.

No one has the right, at this stage, to deceive the masses with hopes. Revolutionary honesty necessitates that the masses should have a full picture of their responsibilities so that they may achieve their hopes. That should constantly be taken into consideration. It should be accompanied, however, with a due consideration of the grand aspirations of the masses, and at the same time due consideration of the morale of those responsible for directing the work designed to realise these aspirations.

* * *

Intellectual adolescence poses a danger that we should face and crush. Those who try to shape the national struggle into forms, or interpret it in terms that would check its drive, and those who spread hesitation minimize the strength of society in proportion to their own weakness and incapacity for creative thought that springs from the national reality.

National progress cannot be achieved through high sounding slogans. Liberating the creative energies of any people is a task closely related to history, nature, and the common and effective developments in the world where that people lives. No people can start progress from a vacuum, for a vacuum leads people nowhere. The danger of intellectual adolescence during this stage creates a sort of intimidation which hinders the process of trial and error.

The new leaderships undertaking to set in motion national development constitute an enormous force which must be protected if they are to carry out their task with the required degree of success. The wealth which this country, the maker of civilization, possesses in the way of experts and technicians in all spheres, is very great and must be vigilantly guarded, protected and developed.

Yet, on certain occasions these leaderships are in need of being protected against themselves. Such leaderships may wrongly assume that the great problems of national development can be solved by the complicated procedures of bureaucracy and administration. But, such procedures only add fresh burdens to the national action without in any way helping it. If allowed to persevere in their wrong assumption, these leaderships would become an insulating class that would stop the flow of the revolutionary action and prevent its results from reaching the masses which are in need of them. Administration commits a grievous error if it imagines its huge machinery to be an end in itself. Such machinery is only a means to service and ensure that it is properly rendered to the people.

The struggle for power equally leads to a paralysis of leaderships working for national development, since each of them will in this case stand as an obstacle in the way of the other's efforts, impede its work and cancel its effect. Similarly, the accumulation of great powers in few hands indisputably leads to the passage of real power to those who are not in fact responsible before the people. It was this consideration that was the real cause of the enactment of the revolutionary law that stipulated that there should only be one job for one man, which was not only a just procedure, but constituted also an attempt to bring the country to the point where each man holds the job which suits his particular abilities and experiences.

The new leaderships must be aware of their social role. The gravest danger to which they can possibly be exposed at this stage is for them to deviate from their right path and imagine themselves to represent a new class that has replaced the old and has taken over its privileges.

In this process of national development those in charge of great projects need to believe that over-expenditure, even when no private profit is involved, is a kind of deviation; it is a squandering of the wealth of the people which constitutes the necessary fuel in this battle of development. Over-expenditure includes unjustified excess in production costs, and at the same time failure to study new projects in a responsible manner and it extends to negligence in execution and lack of the vigilance necessary for the correct procedure of work.

All these are dangers typical of the period of great changes. But, given freedom, it is possible to overcome and limit their effect.

Revolutionary action should be scientific. The revolution is not an action to wipe out the ruins of the past but rather to build up the future. If the revolution were to relinquish science it would become a mere emotional outburst enabling the nation to let off steam, but it would not change its state. Science is the true weapon of the revolutionary will. Here emerges the great role to be undertaken by the universities and educational centres on various levels.

The people are the leaders of the revolution.

Science is the weapon with which revolutionary triumph can be achieved. Science alone can guarantee that trial and error in the national action would lead to a development with guaranteed consequences. Without science, trial and error become haphazard tendencies that may succeed once but fail scores of times.

The responsibility of the universities and scientific research centres in shaping the future is not less important than responsibility of the various popular authorities. Without science, popular authorities may inflame the enthusiasm of the people, but it is only with science that they can hope to realise the demands of the people. Therefore, the universities are not ivory towers but rather forerunners discovering a mode of life for the people.

Our ability to master the various branches of science is the only way left us to compensate for underdevelopment. If the national struggle relies on advanced science it would have a greater opportunity for progress; it would make the former underdevelopment seem an advantage, for then by comparison the new achievement would appear spectacular. If the nations on whom underdevelopment was imposed could now make a start supported by advanced science, they would be at a starting point, superior to that from which other advanced nations began. They would thus have a strong impetus to catch up with those advanced nations and surpass them.

The major economic and social problems confronting our people at present must be resolved on a scientific basis. The scientific research centres are required at this stage of the struggle to develop themselves so that science would be in the service of society. At this stage, science for its own sake is a responsibility which our national potentiality cannot shoulder. Therefore, science for society should be the motto of the cultural revolution at the present stage. The achievement of the objectives of the national struggle will enable us, at a further stage of our development, to make a positive contribution to the world in the domain of science for its own sake.

Science for society is not an obstacle that binds the scientists to deal with problems of everyday life; this would be a limited interpretation of the loaf of bread we are seeking to obtain. We cannot waste a moment before entering the atomic age. We lagged behind in the age of steam and the age of electricity. This underdevelopment, although arbitrarily imposed by imperialism, has and still is costing us a great deal. We are now required, at the dawn of the atomic age, to join those who have embarked on this age.

Atomic energy for war is not our objective. Atomic energy for prosperity is able to perform miracles in the struggle of national development. We should always remember that spiritual energies which people derive from their ideals of divine religions and cultural heritage can perform miracles.

These spiritual energies of the people can provide a dynamic power for the realisation of the popular aspirations. They also arm the people with patience and courage with which to confront every possibility and overcome all difficulties and obstacles.

While the organisation of development requires, of necessity, material foundations, spiritual and moral incentives alone are able to furnish this development with the noblest ideals and most sublime objectives.

## 9. ARAB UNITY

The responsibility of the United Arab Republic in effecting, consolidating and safeguarding progress embraces the Arab Nation as a whole. The Arab Nation is no more in need of giving evidence of the unity binding its peoples. Unity has passed this stage and is identified with the Arab existence itself. Suffice it that the Arab Nation has a unity of language, forming the unity of mind and thought.

Suffice it that the Arab Nation is characterised by the unity of history creating unity of conscience and sentiments.

Suffice it that the Arab Nation enjoys a unity of hope, the basis of the unity of future and fate.

Those who are attempting to undermine the concept of Arab unity in its foundation, giving as proof differences among Arab governments, are looking at the matter in a superficial way. The mere existence of those differences is in itself an indication of the existence of this unity. These differences stem from the struggle in the Arab world. The rallying of the popular, progressive elements in every part of the Arab Nation, and the rallying of the elements of reaction and opportunism in the Arab world, are indications that the same social currents are sweeping over in the Arab Nation, guiding and coordinating its steps across the artificial barriers. The rallying of the popular, progressive elements, having one and the same hope in every part of the Arab territory, and the rallying of the forces of reaction, having interests in every part of the Arab world, are actually more indicative of unity than dissension.

The concept of Arab unity no longer requires a meeting of the rulers of the Arab Nation in order to depict solidarity among the governments. The phase of the social revolution has developed that superficial concept of Arab unity and brought it to a stage where unity of objective has become a symbol of unity. The unity of objective is an accomplished fact for the popular bases in the entire Arab Nation.

The disparity in the objectives of the rulers is an aspect of the inevitable revolutionary progress and the diversity of the stages of development attained by the Arab peoples. Yet the unity of objectives of the popular bases will be capable of bridging the gap between various stages of development. The unity of the Arab Nation has attained a stage of solidarity enabling it to cope with the stage of social revolution.

The methods of military coups d'état, the methods of individual opportunism and the methods adopted by the ruling reaction can only indicate that the old regime in the Arab world is madly in despair and is gradually losing its nerve, while hearing at a distance from its isolated palaces the steps of the masses advancing towards their objectives.

The unity of objective must be a slogan of Arab unity in its progress from the phase of political revolution to that of social revolution. The slogan that was useful at earlier stages of the national struggle, namely that of the political revolution against imperialism, must be abandoned. Imperialism has now changed its attitude and has become incapable of directly confronting the people. Its natural hideout was within the palaces of reaction.

Imperialism itself has unwittingly helped advance the date of the social revolution, when it took cover behind the exploiting elements which it directs. As a matter of fact, genuine revolutions have benefited from the actions of their adversaries, thereby obtaining a new impetus. Imperialism has unmasked itself and so has reaction by being too eager to co-operate with it. It therefore became incumbent upon the people to strike at them and defeat them at one and the same time to assert the triumph of the political revolution in the remaining parts of the Arab Nation, and to consolidate the Arab man's right to a better social life that he could not attain except by revolutionary means.

* * *

At this stage, the Arab task is in need of all the experience achieved by the Arab Nation in its long and glorious history. It is also in need of its profound wisdom as much as it is in need of its revolutionary spirit and will to effect a drastic change.

Unity cannot be nor should it be imposed. Actually the nation's main objectives should be equally honourable in their ends and means. Therefore, coercion of any kind is contrary to unity. Not only is it an immoral act but it also constitutes a menace to the national unity of each Arab people, and therefore it is a threat to the concept of the unity of the Arab Nation as a whole.

Arab unity is not a uniform constitutional form that must inevitably be applied. It is rather a long path with several stages leading to the ultimate aim. In the Arab world any nationalist government representing the will and struggle of the people within a framework of national independence is a step towards unity, in the sense that it eliminates every contradiction between that government and the ultimate goals of unity.

Any partial unity in the Arab World expressing a popular will of two or more of the Arab peoples is an advanced step towards unity, drawing near the day of total unity, paving the way for it and extending its roots in the Arab soil. Such circumstances pave the way before the call for total Arab unity. If the United Arab Republic considers it her message to strive for complete Arab unity, attainment of this objective would be promoted by the clear-cut methods that must, at this stage of the Arab struggle, be defined in a decisive and binding manner.

The peaceful call is the first step. The scientific application of all the progressive concepts of unity contained in this call is the second step towards achievement of a positive result. Hastening the various stages of development towards unity would create – as experience has shown – economic and social loopholes that could be exploited by the elements opposed to unity to undermine it.

The development of the action for unity towards its ultimate and comprehensive objective must be accompanied by practical efforts to fill the economic and social gaps stemming from the difference in the stages of development of the various peoples of the Arab Nation. This difference was imposed by the isolationist elements of reaction and imperialism.

Great and conscious efforts must be channelled to pave the way for new intellectual trends so that they could face destructive attempts, overcome the remnants of intellectual disintegration caused by the pressure of the circumstances of the 19th century and first half of the 20th century, and wipe out the traces of the intrigues and manoeuvres, often blocking a clear vision.

The United Arab Republic, firmly convinced that she is an integral part of the Arab Nation, must propagate her call for unity and the principles it embodies, so that it would be at the disposal of every Arab citizen, without hesitating for one minute before the outworn argument that this would be considered an interference in the affairs of others.

In this sphere, the United Arab Republic should take care not to become involved in the local party disputes in any Arab state. This would place the call for unity and its principles beneath its level.

If the United Arab Republic feels that it is her bounden duty to support every popular, national movement, this support must remain within the framework of the basic principles, leaving the manoeuvres of the struggle to the local elements to rally the national potentialities and drive the struggle towards its end in conformity with the local process of development and potentialities.

The United Arab Republic is, therefore, required to open new vistas for cooperation between all the nationalist progressive movements in the Arab World. She is required to reciprocate intellectually with them for the benefit of the common experience. However, she cannot impose on them a precise form for revolution.

The establishment of a union between the nationalist popular progressive movements in the Arab World will impose itself on the coming stages of the struggle.

This does not and should not affect the existence of the Arab League. If the Arab League is not able to lead the Arab cause towards its noble and ultimate objective, it can at least lead it a few steps forward.

The peoples want the complete fulfillment of their aspirations. The Arab League – being a league of governments – cannot go beyond what is possible. What is possible is a step forward towards the ultimate aim. Achievement of the part helps to bring nearer the day when the whole can be attained. Therefore, the Arab League deserves every support, taking into consideration its actual capacity limited by the circumstances of its foundation and by its own nature.

The Arab League is able to coordinate certain aspects of Arab activity at the present stage. At the same time, it should not under any pretext and while refuting any allegation become a means to freeze the present, thereby undermining the future.

## 10. FOREIGN POLICY

The foreign policy of the people of the United Arab Republic is a true and faithful reflection on its national action. If the foreign policy of a people ceases to be such a reflection it becomes a sham pretence that exposes itself and sheer hypocrisy and a mere trading in slogans.

Such is the farce in which reactionary governments find themselves involved when they try in a misleading way to borrow a glittering foreign policy which does not echo or truly express national reality. Such governments are unmasked by conscious peoples who avenge themselves on them and exact from their governments the price of their attempted deception.

As a true and faithful reflection of its national action the foreign policy of the people of the United Arab Republic runs in three channels, dug deep and straight by means of the struggle of a brave people that stood against, and triumphed over, all kinds of pressure. The three deep channels in which the foreign policy of the United Arab Republic runs and which express all her national principles are the following:

War on imperialism and domination. Fighting against imperialism with all the country's potentialities and in every possible way, exposing it in all its shapes and masks and waging a battle on it in all its dens.

Labouring to consolidate peace, since the atmosphere and possibilities of peace present the only favourable chance for the protection of national progress.

Lastly, international cooperation for the sake of prosperity, since the common prosperity of all peoples is no longer divisible and to achieve it collective cooperation has now become imperative.

In its fight against imperialism, the people of the U.A.R. have set a living and almost legendary example in the history of the struggles of peoples. Our people were able to expose Ottoman imperialism which they resisted in spite of its subtle attempts to hide itself behind the mask of the Islamic Caliphate. Our people too resisted the French invasion with the result that the adventurer who shook the whole of Europe was obliged to sail forth by night back to France across the Mediterranean. Later, they withstood the plots of world imperialism and international monopolies which used as their tool the Mohamed Aly Dynasty.

The waves of revolution then surged, one following upon the other and, after many years of noble sacrifice, they swept all the barriers put up by imperialism on our soil to defend its existence. Our people stood against three Empires, the Ottoman, the French and the British, resisted their invasion of their soil and emerged triumphant in the end.

For decades, even for centuries, our people paid a high price for the victories they achieved over imperialism. But eventually they achieved the victory which in the opinion of history justified all their sacrifices and made their value appear even greater.

After the great revolutionary victory achieved in the morning of July 23, and on the people's road of revolutionary progress, the victorious masses trod upon the remains of the alien royal era, stormed the strongholds of feudalism, and pulled out the roots of the forces of reaction. They were the mainstay of imperialism in our country. After our people had attacked and destroyed them, imperialism lost its link with our pure Motherland and the remaining step was therefore to force its forces to bring down their flags, swallow their pride and depart across the sea.

After decades of imperialism, our people managed to make the forces of aggression evacuate twice in one year. That was in 1956, a decisive year in our national struggle. Imperialism, which evacuated our country according to an agreement put into effect in June 1956, was soon to come back in October of the same year, thinking that it was able to subjugate the will of our people, to humiliate them and oblige them to submit to the will of the imperialists.

Our people, who were determined to protect their independence, to reject all the imperialist tricks designed to drag them into spheres of influence, led a stupendous resistance in the whole of the Middle East against the Baghdad Pact until it collapsed, and did not hesitate to oppose the armed tripartite aggression in which two of the world's great powers took part. These powers launched their attack from Israel, the base of imperialism, which was brought into existence by means of plots with the object of intimidating the Arab Nation and tearing it apart.

In the battle of Suez, imperialism revealed itself, its bases and its accomplices. Armed imperialism pounced upon the people of Egypt because those people were trying to realise their independence and achieve progress by making use of one of their own national resources which had for long been exploited by imperialism, and the value and profits of which had been monopolised by it.

By regaining the Suez Canal, the Egyptian people dealt a fatal blow to imperialism and monopolies. They proved their strong mettle in their resolute acceptance of all the consequences of their determination to the extent of consenting to enter into armed conflict with overwhelming forces.

By their admirable steadfastness and their bitter fighting against the invaders, the Egyptian people managed to shake the world's conscience and move it in a manner unprecedented in the course of international events. The admirable turn the battle took constituted a turning point in the history of liberation movements. The striving people who had been facing the mighty tyrants alone, became no longer alone.

As a result of the brave national resistance, the situation was completely reversed. Those who rallied against our people in an attempt to isolate them found themselves isolated from the whole world while all the peoples of the world stood by our people, and waved to them to express their greetings and support.

The bitter defeat of imperialism in the Suez War had put an end to the age of armed imperialistic adventures. Thanks to the struggle of our people, the end of that loathsome age came for all the peoples of the world.

Imperialism, which still retained its aims, soon changed its method. Yet our people were on the alert, vigilantly looking out for any imperialist attempts at disguise which they continued to trace and against which they rallied the powers of other peoples.

In insisting on combating all military pacts aiming at dragging the peoples, against their own will, into the orbit of imperialism our people raised the voice of truth, loudly cautioning and warning on all occasions.

The insistence of our people on liquidating the Israeli aggression on a part of the Palestine land is a determination to liquidate one of the most dangerous pockets of imperialist resistance against the struggle of peoples. Our pursuit of the Israeli policy of infiltration in Africa is only an attempt to limit the spread of a destructive imperialist cancer.

The insistence of our people on resisting racial discrimination expresses a clear understanding of the real meaning of the policy of racial discrimination. In its real nature, imperialism is the foreign domination to which peoples are exposed, aimed at enabling the foreigner to exploit their wealth and efforts. Racial discrimination is only a type of exploiting the wealth and efforts of peoples. Discrimination between people on the basis of colour paves the way for a discrimination between the value of their efforts. Slavery was the first form of imperialism and those who still pursue the methods of imperialism commit a crime the effects of which are not confined to their victims. They cause damage to the human conscience as a whole and impair its attainments.

Our people have spared no effort in their pursuit of peace. Our people's pursuit of peace has guided their steps to international centres which have now become radiating enough to illuminate the path to peace.

Our people who played a sincere role at the Bandung Conference and helped make a success of it, and who, by means of their participation in the work of the United Nations Organization and their endeavours to remove the dangers to peace, proved their deep faith in peace. In Bandung, our people spoke with those of the other states of Asia and Africa the same language it spoke before the great powers in the U.N.

In their call for peace, in their action to support its possibilities, our people worked with all others and faced them by the force of free expression.

Our people, who took part in all the great human efforts devoted to the ban of nuclear tests, and who participated positively in the efforts for disarmament, did all that as a result of their absolute faith in peace, since they have an absolute faith in life.

Our people know the value of life, because they attempt to make it in their own country. The sincerity of their call for peace arises from their dire need for it. Peace is the sure guarantee for their ability to pursue their sacred struggle, for the sake of development. It is their efforts for peace which have armed our people with the slogan of non-alignment and positive neutrality.

Today, the prevalence of this slogan in many continents of the world is a great tribute to the faith of our people in serving peace. The first call for convening the first conference of non-aligned states came from Cairo and met with wonderful approval by many peoples. It was, at the same time, a human tribute to the route we have followed in the service of peace, in which we firmly believe.

Even those who try, now, to exploit the slogan of non-alignment and positive neutrality in order to conceal from their people their alignment to war camps and imperialism give indirect praise to our people. Our people were the pioneers in raising this slogan. Their sincere belief in it and their struggle for it, issues from a real need for it, in order to progress.

International co-operation for the common prosperity of the peoples of the world is a natural continuation of the war against imperialism and exploitation. It is a logical continuation of the work for peace, in order to provide the ideal atmosphere for development.

International co-operation for prosperity brings the foreign policy of the U.A.R. to attain its ultimate aim, which is a reflection of its national struggle. Our people offer their hand to all the peoples and nations working for international peace and human prosperity.

The international struggle of our people was a struggle in defence of their lawful rights, as well as the rights of the Arab Nation, to which they feel they belong, as the part belongs to the whole. Our people raised – even in the darkest circumstances of the bitter struggle that they were forced to enter into – the eternal slogan: "peace, not surrender". It was an obvious gesture that they accept international co-operation, but resist domination.

Our people believe that prosperity is indivisible, and that international co-operation for prosperity is the strongest guarantee for international peace. Peace cannot be stabilized in a world where the standards of the people vary enormously. Peace cannot be stable on the brink of the deep abyss that separates the advanced nations from those upon which underdevelopment was imposed.

The clash that is sure to break out between developed and underdeveloped countries is the second danger that threatens international peace. It comes next to the first danger which lies in a surprising nuclear war.

International co-operation for prosperity is the only hope for peaceful development, which narrows the gap between the standards of nations and sows the seeds of love among them, instead of sowing the seeds of hatred. International co-operation for prosperity on the part of the developed countries constitutes the human atonement for the age of imperialism, the atonement made by those responsible for that age as well as those who were not.

International co-operation covers a wide field, in which the U.A.R. tries to move. It includes the revelation of scientific secrets to all, because the monopoly of science threatens humanity with a new form of imperialist domination. It also includes the call for the peaceful use of atomic energy, in order to serve the cause of development and bring light to the dark facts of underdevelopment.

Again, it comprises the propagation of the idea of diverting the huge funds spent on the manufacture of nuclear weapons to the service of life, instead of menacing and jeopardizing it. It comprises also the call for facing international economic blocs, so that they might not be used by the strong to destroy the attempts made by others for the sake of progress. Our people extend their intentions, coupled with actions, for international co-operation beyond all oceans and to all countries.

While our people believe in Arab unity, they also believe in a Pan-African movement and in Afro-Asian solidarity. They believe in a rally for peace that pools the efforts of those whose interests are associated with it. They believe in a close spiritual bond that ties them to the Islamic world. They believe in belonging to the U.N., and in their loyalty to the U.N. Charter, which is the outcome of the suffering of peoples in two world wars, separated only by a period of an armed truce.

There is no contradiction or clash between all these ideals in which our people believe. In fact all these ideals form links of one chain.

Ours is an Arab people and its destiny is tied to the destiny of the unity of the Arab Nation.

Our people live at the north-eastern gate of struggling Africa and cannot be isolated from its political, social and economic development.

Our people belong to the two continents where the greatest battles of national liberation rage. These battles of national liberation are the most outstanding feature of the 20th century.

Our people have faith in peace as a principle. They believe in it as a vital necessity. Consequently, they spare no effort in working for it with all those who share the same conviction.

Our people believe in the message of religions, and they live in the area where those divine messages were received.

Our people live and struggle for the sake of the sublime human principles which the peoples inscribed with their blood in the U.N.

Charter. Many clauses of this Charter were inscribed with the blood of our people, as well as that of others.

* * *

Our people are determined to shape their life anew in their own land, by means of freedom, truth, efficiency, justice, love and peace.

Our people have a sufficiently strong faith in God and in themselves to enable them to impose their will on life, in order to re-model it according to their aspirations.

## Proclamation of the Charter by the National Congress of Popular Forces

On 30 June 1962, the National Congress for Popular Forces, out of which the Arab Socialist Union was to emerge, approved the text of "The Charter of National Action." The following announcement was read by the Secretary-General of the Congress:

Our people, having taken the firm resolve to adopt a new way of life, marked by liberty, equity, efficiency, amity and peace, they are endowed, through their faith in God and confidence in themselves, with the faculty to impose their will upon life in a bid to mould it anew in conformity with their aspirations.

We, the members of the National Congress of Popular Forces, representing all the sectors in the United Arab Republic, and reflecting a popular will marked by unity and solidarity, declare full faith in God and in the creed of right, well-being and peace, while considering human rights to be sacred in the bid to ensure prestige, dignity, justice and liberation.

In reaffirmation of our right to take firm steps along the path of our human, social and political Revolution; in the bid to ensure solidarity, dissolve all differences among classes, stressing the sublime implications of virtue and of self-abnegation in the individual's conduct and in relations among groups of people; in emphasising our pattern of life within a framework of our spiritual and moral values; in priding ourselves upon our past heritage and our present struggle as well as our action for the future, we proclaim our people to be an integral part of the Arab nation.

In performing our historical duty and our immortal mission for the preservation of world peace based upon equity, we hereby adopt this Charter, proclaiming it as the path leading to the full achievement of the objectives of our Revolution at present and our guide for the future.

We, therefore, thus proclaim our Charter, calling on God to witness our resolve to make it the law of our lives and the rule of our conduct, taking advantage of our utmost capacity to put all its lofty principles into effect.

# INDEX

(All page numbers in italics refer to the Appendix.)